D0875548

THE CISTERCIAN FATHERS SERIES: NUMBER TWENTY-FIVE

BERNARD OF CLAIRVAUX

SERMONS ON CONVERSION

Bernard of Clairvaux

SERMONS ON CONVERSION

ON CONVERSION,
A SERMON TO CLERICS
and
LENTEN SERMONS ON THE PSALM
'HE WHO DWELLS'

Translated with an introduction by
MARIE-BERNARD SAÏD OSB

CISTERCIAN PUBLICATIONS
KALAMAZOO, MICHIGAN
1981

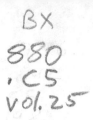

© Cistercian Publications, Inc., 1981

The translations herein presented have been made from the critical edition of Jean Leclercq and H. M. Rochais, *Sancti Bernardi Opera*, volume IV, published at Rome in 1966 by Editiones Cistercienses.

On Conversion, A Sermon to Clerics is a translation of *Ad clericos de conversione; Sancti Bernardi Opera* IV: 69-116.

Lenten Sermons on the Psalm 'He Who Dwells' is a translation of *Sermones in quadragesima de psalmo 'Qui habitat'; Sancti Bernardi Opera* IV: 383-492.

Bernard of Clairvaux 1090-1153
Bernardus Claravallensis

Library of Congress Cataloguing in Publication Data:

Bernard de Clairvaux, Saint, 1091?-1153.
    Sermons.

    (Cistercian Fathers series; 25-   )
    "The translations herein presented have been made from the critical edition of Jean Leclercq and H. M. Rochais, Sancti Bernardi opera, volume IV, published at Rome in 1966 by Editiones Cistercienses."
    Includes index.
    CONTENTS: 1. On conversion, a sermon to clerics and Lenten sermons on the psalm He who dwells.
    1. Catholic Church — Sermons. 2. Sermons, English — Translations from Latin. 3. Sermons, Latin — Translations into English. I. Saïd, Marie Bernard.
    BX 1756.B42S45   1981   252'.02   80-25325

Linotyped at Galesburg, Michigan by Francis Edgecombe   *Printed in the United States of America*

TABLE OF CONTENTS

ON CONVERSION, A SERMON TO CLERICS

Introduction 11

Text 31

LENTEN SERMONS ON THE PSALM 'HE WHO DWELLS'

Introduction 83

The Psalm 113

Text 115

Table of Abbreviations 262

Selected Bibliography 263

Index 264

Scriptural Index 270

FORETHOUGHTS

MY INTRODUCTORY NOTES aim at remaining within the scope of the ordinary reader of the Cistercian Fathers series and at the same time I hope they will open up vistas of research. The bibliographical references are authoritative but not exhaustive.

The english rendering is as faithful as human frailty can make it. However, as the Douai version of the Prologue to Sirach says: 'Words do not have the same fire in them when translated into another tongue. I entreat you therefore to come with benevolence, and to read with attention, and to pardon us for those things wherein we may seem, while we follow the image of wisdom, to come short in the composition of words'.

I am grateful to Father Jean Leclercq OSB for his kindness in reading through these notes and for the help he has given me on more than one occasion.

M. B. SAÏD OSB

ON CONVERSION,
A SERMON TO CLERICS

INTRODUCTION

T HE AUTHOR of the *Sermon on Conversion to the
Clergy*, St Bernard, the great abbot of Clairvaux, was
among the monks of his time one of those exceptions
which prove the rule. As Steven Runciman has written, 'It is
difficult now to look back across the centuries and appreciate
the tremendous impact of his personality on all who knew him.
The fire of his eloquence has been quenched in the written
words that survive. As a theologian and a controversialist he
now appears rigid and a little crude and unkind. But from the
day in 1115 when, at the age of twenty-five, he was appointed
Abbot of Clairvaux, till his death nearly forty years later he
was the dominant influence in the religious and political life of
western Europe. It was he who gave the Cistercian Order its
impetus; it was he who, almost single-handed, had rescued the
Papacy from the slough of the schism of Anacletus. The fer-
vour and sincerity of his preaching combined with his courage,
his vigour and the blamelessness of his life to bring victory to
any cause that he supported, save only against the embittered
Cathar heretics of Languedoc.'[1] He was a figurehead of his
times to such an extent that his 'disapproval meant the disapproval of French public opinion.'[2] We know that he was the
councillor of popes, princes, and kings and that he loved his
brother-monks with an altogether motherly tenderness. He
was the ambassador of Jesus Crucified, the Saviour of the
world. It is not astonishing then that, himself entirely aflame
with the love of God, his greatest desire was to save souls, to
urge them to conversion, and to win them over to Christ in the
monastic life.[3]

Thus, when Bernard stopped at Paris sometime between Lent 1139 and the early part of 1140,[4] on his way back from one of his many business trips, he, according to custom, addressed the students. There seems to be some hesitation as to the actual date of this lecture. Watkin Williams[5] thought that it was delivered between Easter 1140 and the convening of the Council of Sens in June of the same year. But, working through the text with an eye to the present translation, I was able to recognize and verify certain allusions and reminiscences to the liturgical texts of Christmastide. In particular the following:

> *a little child . . . he was born for that and given us* (¶1),[6] from Is 9:6, used in the first reading at Vigils for Christmas as well as in the antiphon of Lauds and the introit of the third Mass on Christmas Day;
>
> *Spoken by the Lord's own mouth* (¶1), from Is 40:5 in the third reading at Vigils for Christmas;
>
> *Seeking light by the light, like some eager imitator of the Wise Men* (¶24), recalls the hymn *Hostis Herodes* of the feast of the Epiphany;
>
> *This word . . . came from the royal throne* (¶26) depends on Wis 18:15 used in the antiphon *Omnipotens* of the office for the fourth Sunday of Advent and in the office of the Sunday within the octave of Christmas, as well as in the introit of the mass *Dum medium silentium* of the same day.

These texts are fairly significant when we remember how receptive St Bernard was to his cultural background and how his mental categories and language were stamped with the Bible and with the prevailing liturgical season and readings. Much of what has been said[7] about the influence of the Bible on the psychology of Bernard the author could also be said of the liturgy's impact. It seems reasonable then to accept the date proposed by Jean Leclercq — that is to say, a date sometime between Lent 1139 and the early part of 1140. Father Leclercq, having noted these same texts, adds this remark: 'These allusions are not found in the shorter version of the sermon. It appears then that the longer text was drafted during Christmastide, perhaps on the occasion of a sermon delivered to the clerics at Paris, on the basis of a first short text written primarily for All Saints Day.[8]

The sermon seems to have been quite an event. It is reported by the early biographers of Bernard, notably by Geoffrey of Auxerre, who writes in the *Vita prima*:

> One day our holy Abbot was going through the region of Paris. The bishop of this city, Stephen, and many others begged him to make a halt in the city, but in vain. Bernard was in fact always careful to avoid any public gathering unless there was some very serious reason for his being present. Thus, when evening came he planned to journey by another route. At dawn, however, the first thing he said to the brothers was: 'Go and tell the bishop that we will go to Paris as he asked us to do.' So a great number of the clerics gathered together because they had been (*solebant*) asking him to preach the word of God to them. Suddenly, three of them, moved by compunction and being converted (*conversi*) from vain studies to the worship of true wisdom[9] renounced the world and became disciples of the servant of God.[10]

Geoffrey refers to this sermon in his commentary *Super Apocalypsim*.[11] The passage is interesting because it reports a fragment which we do not find in the editions made by Dom Jean Mabillon and Jean Leclercq.

The account Geoffrey gives of his conversion in the *Vita prima* does not entirely agree with that given in the *Exordium magnum*, or even with another given by Geoffrey himself.[12] But the relevance of this incident as related in each account has to do with the significance and impact of Bernard's sermon. 'Conversion' must be taken in its traditional sense of 'becoming a monk.' To be 'converted' meant going into a monastery. 'They renounced the world', writes Geoffrey. And this is just what Bernard was inciting them to do when he said: 'Let your profession of perfection cease to be a mockery and now appear in the form of religion.[13] Let the outward appearance of the life of celibacy cease to be a vain thing void of truth. How can chastity remain unscathed amidst delights. . . . Flee and save your souls.[14] Flock to the city of refuge[15] where you can do penance for the past.'[16] We know that in the Middle Ages the monastery was considered an asylum, a refuge[17] and the monastic life the only true wisdom, the only true philosophy and love of wisdom.[18] When St Bernard speaks of the *caelibis vitae forma* (¶37) he was indeed referring to the life of celibacy, the celestial life, the angelic life, to use an ancient synonym for the monastic life in both Western and Eastern monastic tradition. It is obvious to anyone who has an iota of common sense and any working knowledge of monks and monasticism that to speak of the 'angelic' life is not to pretend that monks are angels. They are very human. But in ancient tradition to live without sexual intercourse was to live the angelic life, being in the body but not—to some extent—of the body.[19] And as Bernard himself says in another of his sermons: 'Who would hesitate to qualify as heavenly and angelic a life given up to celibacy?'[20]

Another indication that Bernard is using 'conversion' as a synonym for personal 'monastification'—the process of becoming a monk—is seen in paragraph 24 where he speaks of a 'paradise of pleasure . . . a flowering and lovely garden'; further on in the same passage he suggests that the reason should persuade the still recalcitrant will to enter 'a most beautiful garden.' This is the theme of the paradise of the cloister, *paradisus claustri*, where the soul finds contemplative rest.[21]

There is nothing astonishing in the fact of Bernard wanting to 'convert' souls for, as his great friend William of St Thierry tells us, he was God's fisherman and had a way of winning souls over for God:

> The force of his preaching began to shine out especially in the way in which he softened to conversion (*ad conver-*

sionem emolliret) even the hard hearts of his hearers, and he rarely came home without a catch. Later on, by his happy progress and growing familiarity with the word and the example of his own monastic life (*exempli conversationis*), the net of God's word[22] in the hands of God's fisherman soon began to take in such large shoals of rational fish that it seemed that he was going to fill the boat of his house at each catch.[23]

The context proves that the word 'house' refers to Bernard's abbey of Clairvaux.

THE MANUSCRIPT TRADITION

Having established the date and purpose of the sermon on conversion, let us now go into the story behind the text.[24]

The manuscripts which have come down to us show that this sermon exists in two forms, one shorter than the other but with no trace of its being an abridgement. Sixty manuscripts were examined by the editor of the contemporary critical edition;[25] twenty-five of them gave the shorter version. In the Engelberg manuscript[26] the work is presented as a sermon for All Saints Day, and it does in fact develop the theme of the beatitudes read in the gospel for the day. A comparative reading of this sermon and Bernard's first sermon for All Saints Day[27] reveals certain similarities. One might wonder whether the shorter version were not, after all, an abridgement of the longer sermon *On Conversion*. But then, as Jean Leclercq asks,[28] why alter the text? The state of the question sets

> psychological and literary problems which may not be avoided, even if they cannot be solved. It is clear that we have here two early drafts of a same text. Which is the primitive one? Are both to be attributed to Bernard? Does the first represent a first draft of one or of two discourses delivered by the Abbot of Clairvaux and jotted down from memory by either himself or by Geoffrey of

Auxerre, and the second a written edition? Or is this a summary of the first? In this case it is difficult to explain why it is precisely the more careful formulas which have been omitted.[29]

The answer to these queries — first raised in 1947[30] — now seems to be that we have two successive editions of the same sermon. This was quite in keeping with Bernard's custom.[31] The shorter version would appear to be the text of the sermon as it was actually preached. Perhaps Bernard then revised this edition, enlarging and titivating as he went. It will be noticed that after the commentary on the beatitudes in the edited text Bernard says: 'But I am tiring you with this rambling sermon, and I have detained you longer than I should.'[32] It is at this point that the shorter version comes to a close. It seems a quite natural ending and, furthermore, Bernard has said what he set out to say: he has developed the theme of conversion announced in his opening paragraph. In the revised text Bernard added some fairly lengthy afterthoughts and connected his theme with the morals of the clergy of his time. A few succinct phrases of Jean Leclercq sum up the situation and Bernard's position:[33] 'Bernard was a reformer not only in the monastic sphere but in every sphere of the Church's life because he loved the Church and wanted to see her become ever more worthy of being loved, served with love.'[34] A little earlier in this same article we read: 'This security of the Church as a whole requires the fidelity of all those who live in her, and especially of her ministers. And Bernard, speaking to his contemporaries, constantly denounces the temptations which assail them: ambition and the desire for wealth. He is always harping on the duties of disinterestedness. He speaks in prophetic accents, inspired by Christ's maledictions, of all those who abuse their power, urging God's ministers to constant purification.'[35]

Bernard's invective against ambition and wealth is characteristic of this great cardinal mind of the twelfth century, a period of change and rebirth not only in learning and letters, but also in the social, economic and religious field. Concomitantly with the progress of the Commercial Revolution, people had begun to consider greed rather than pride as the predominant sin. Commenting upon the social impact of the opening passage of chapter seven, on humility, of the Rule of St Benedict, R. W. Southern has written: 'It would be hard to find anywhere outside the Bible so short a passage which has worked its way so powerfully into Christian thought.'[36] This was true as long as the benedictine institution exercised the prevailing influence in the christian world. But with the crisis of cenobitism which took place in the late eleventh and early twelfth century, there sprang up other, more eremitical, forms of religious life which lay reactional stress on poverty and simplicity.[37] This religious fact was the most elevated manifestation of the changing social mind. As Lester K. Little has written, 'What was utterly new in the eleventh century was that a thoroughly Christian society . . . started to become an urban-commercial society. When the guardians of tradition searched the old morality for guidance, they found only strong opposition to the life of commerce.'[38] The result was that: 'If pride was the greatest vice of those who held power in the precommercial society, then avarice held a corresponding place in connection with the rich people of commercial society.'[39]

This distinction between pride and avarice and the shifting emphasis from one social vice to another, described and analyzed by historians though it is, is not the whole story. Avarice is just one of the many forms of pride. It would perhaps be more exact to say that the shift was not so much from one social vice to another as from one social manifestation to another of the same basic, perennial sin of pride. The accession of money to power with the advent of the Commercial Revolution made it an effective arm for the enemy of man. St Bernard, whose spiritual teaching is our main concern here, was well aware of the close alliance between pride and avarice: 'Man now impudently arrogates the dignity of the peacemakers and the rank of the Son of God. . . . He has not yet come to be a man who sees his poverty, but he says "I am rich and need nothing", whereas in fact he is poor, naked, wretched and pitiable. There is nothing in him of the Spirit of gentleness. . . . It is not justice that he looks for, but money. Insatiably he hungers for honours, he thirsts for human glory . . . imagining that godliness is a means to gain.' (¶33) This paragraph (33) opens with the words, 'When we think with sadness about the actual state of the Church . . .'. And it is indeed a fact that things were much worse in Bernard's times than now, however sorely pressed the Church may seem to be. We are comforted if we set the Sermon on Conversion in the context described by a book such as *The Wandering Scholars*.[40]

Bernard knew that among the vagrant student population there were genuine scholars, but there were also those of the 'baser type, the unfrocked or runaway monk or clerk'. This context helps us understand the threat implied by Bernard's words: 'I cannot think what harsher curse I could call down upon a man than that he should get what he is asking for when he runs away from sweet repose out of curiosity which revels in restlessness.' (¶14) Cases of clerical conversion were not infrequent, but the would-be monk often applied unsuccessfully to a monastery for admittance. 'Philip of Ottisberg', notes Helen Waddell, 'canon of Cologne, studying under Rudolf in Paris, was touched by divine grace and left the school, giving all his fine clothes to the poor scholars, and came to the Cistercians at Bonnevaux, asking to be made a novice. But the brethren seeing him in *cappa trita atque vetusta* judged him to be a *scholarem pauperem et vagum* and at first refused him admission.'[41] This wariness on the part of monks was not altogether unfounded for there were cases such as this one: 'Nicholas, a *clericus vagus*, . . . fell sick and thought he was going to die and came to the Cistercians at Heisterbach, and was received with some ado into the order. But when the devil was well, *cum quadem irrisione*, he cast aside the cowl and fled.'[42]

Bernard does not content himself with condemning ambition, avarice, impurity and the many other vices of the clergy, he also sketches the programme of a truly worthy pastor. This seems to suggest that he edited his spoken sermon in order to make it a sort of treatise analogous to his *De moribus et officio episcoporum* and his *De consideratione*.[43]

In the present translation, at the request of the editors of the Cistercian Fathers series, the shorter text has been left to one side. The english rendering given here is that of the longer Sermon to the Clergy,[44] and we must now examine the manuscript tradition of this sermon.

Among the thirty-five manuscripts of *De conversione, ad clericos* in its longer form, eight out of the ten earliest witnesses were followed in the establishment of the text of the critical edition.[45] In almost all of these manuscripts the title expressly states that we are dealing with a sermon and not a treatise. However, several of them are divided into chapters, each having its own heading as though the sermon were in fact a treatise.

The text of the critical edition was established then on the witness offered by eight early manuscripts. Seven of these come from libraries in France, and the eighth from the Biblioteca Apostolica Vaticana. An examination of the eight manuscripts reveals that they are to be divided into two groups, each of which is dependent upon two distinct *exemplaria*.[46] Both groups of texts have certain omissions and morphological errors due to faults of the copyists. The common and complete archetype had to be built up from both groups of witnesses. One has certain more difficult readings: the syntax and grammar are more refined; vocabulary is more precious and precise; words are ordered in a more literary and less colloquial manner; sentences are more elliptic, any redundant words having been eliminated. Certain of these modifications are characteristic of the improvements which Bernard made on re-reading his own texts. It would seem then that this group of manuscripts testifies to the existence of a text revised by Bernard's own hand.[47]

Jean Leclercq selected this group as the basis of the principal text. If we remember that there were two drafts of the shorter version and a first draft of the longer, we shall realize that the revised text represents a fourth edition. Three of the four copies of this come from monasteries situated fairly close to one another: the benedictine abbey of St Omers, the cistercian abbey of Clairmarais and the benedictine abbey of Anchin, which possessed the earliest collection of the complete works of St Bernard.[48] Among these three manuscripts the least faulty is the early thirteenth-century one from Clairmarais, a daughter-house of Clairvaux. It was this text which Jean Leclercq selected as the basic text for the critical edition. The titles of each chapter are those found in this thirteenth-century manuscript, with one exception. In the seventeenth century Dom Jean Mabillon added roman figures to divide the text into chapters. These figures have also been retained.

THE CONTENTS OF THE TEXT: A PSYCHOLOGY

OF CONVERSION

In the text of the Sermon on Conversion we find 'an exposition of what we might call the psychology of that conversion which leads to a garden of spiritual delights which seems to be the *paradisus claustri*.'[49] And we know too that 'another theme St Bernard cherished is that of the departure and return of the prodigal son and in connection with this subject all the stages of sin and conversion are analyzed with much sense of concrete reality and psychological acumen.'[50]

We have already seen that Bernard was a fisher of souls and that he wanted all men to be saved so that the blood of Christ should not have been poured out in vain: 'Spare your souls, brothers; I beg you spare the blood which has been poured out for you . . . flock to the city of refuge.' (¶37) We would be tempted to say, if we did not know better, that for St Bernard there could be no salvation except within monastery walls. He himself had seen the vanity of this passing world and he had despised the great things and the even greater hopes that were offered to young men of his birth, breeding, and intelligence. That was how he came to enter Citeaux.[51] Moveover, he believed it is God's will that men be converted and come back to the heart: there is no true life except in conversion (¶1). He was addressing clerics already set apart in some measure for the service of God, but Bernard wanted this renunciation to be put into full effect and not a mere symbol of outward appearance; he wanted them to live their profession of chastity and charity within the setting of the cloister and thus shielded from the ambient dangers of life in the world (¶37). The only lasting good is the glory of the life to come. Here below all is vanity. No man can retain after death the goods he has stored up for himself in this life (¶16). He will harvest according to his sowing (¶17).

But no one can be converted, no one can receive a vocation to the monastic life unless he hears the divine voice calling out within (¶2). The word of God is offered to all men without distinction, even unwilling souls (¶3) but it must be listened to and received. By the light of this word, for it is also a beaming ray of light (¶3), men will come to see their transgressions and be moved to penance. The word of God is living and active, and when God said 'be converted', the children of men were converted. This is a clear indication that conversion is no human affair but one which is wrought by the workings of divine grace (¶2). St Bernard desires only to be the Lord's faithful instrument and to let down the net at his command: 'If only I too might, at this word, let down the nets of the word today, and experience what has been written, "lo, he sends forth his voice, his mighty voice." ' (¶2) With God there is no discrimination of persons. Grace is offered to all and sundry. The chief obstacle to our hearing this voice is that we stop up our ears, we are deaf to his call, we harden our hearts, we refuse to listen, we refuse to see the light of divine grace illuminating the darkness of our sin. God's voice is indeed a light, a great beam of light enlightening our hearts and revealing our pitiable state. If we are attentive, if we examine our conscience in the light of God's holy word, we see to what extent our past life has been incompatible with the christian state. We come to blush with shame (¶3). No one can do this preliminary spade work for us. We must come to experience our own misery,[52] for we alone can know what is going on within our mind.

All past events are to be censured. The memory stores up in its secret recesses the remembrance of past evil deeds, either our own or those which we know others to have committed (¶28). It is deeply stained and these stains can only be removed by that living and effective word which says 'your sins are forgiven.' Once the soul has realised that there is a great famine in its country (¶15) and in spite of the fact that the belly of the memory is congested with much muck (¶4), if it has any true love for itself, it comes to do penance. Penance must be done in this lifetime; the soul must make reparation with the senses which have been the cause and occasion of sin. After death there will be no sense, for there will be no body: there will be no action and therefore no satisfaction (¶6). Moreover, it is best for us to do penance here below, to enter the monastery and there repent. And if we have discovered the worms eating away at our conscience, then we must pluck up courage and stifle them rather than foster them for eternity (¶7).

God is so kind that at the beginning of conversion we think that we shall be able easily to overcome our faults and failings. The difficulty of our being cured is only seen little by little (¶7). Gradually we come to examine carefully our conduct and way of living in order to perfect ourselves in the conversion of our manners. We realise that we must set to work through the custody of the senses, because investigation has shown that it is through the senses that death, sin, has seeped into our souls (¶8).

But this is not so easy as it at first seemed. The will does not comply with reason; we are still given to doing our own will in spite of the fact that this is entirely forbidden within the monastery. Self-will is one of those more spiritual vices, like pride and jealousy (¶7), that we do not easily detect, being as yet carnal. Endeavoring to flee from the land of sin and shake off the yoke of servitude to vice, we find that we are all the more burdened and goaded by the lust of the flesh (¶22). The members revolt (¶9) and the struggle becomes harder. The soul sets to work to purify the memory, for if the outward circumstances of sin have to a great extent been removed by our entry into the monastery — our coversion —, the memory is so tainted that the source of evil lies within our very soul.[53] Bernard sketches the scene very vividly, and it would be easy to draw up a list for daily examination of conscience (¶10).

When Bernard has finished describing the spiritual adventures of the purgative way, he leads us gently on to the illuminative way. The transition starts with paragraph 12, in which Bernard introduces the gentle breeze of consolation for the soul inclined to discouragement by the obstinacy of his will and the difficulty of living an honest life. Our very wretchedness is going to be the cause of our blessedness, for God is merciful and if we are humbly poor in spirit, finding no rest, displeased with ourselves, then God takes compassion on us. But his mercy needs our misery, just as the doctor needs our sickness to be able to cure us. Bernard becomes more winning, more persuasive. He reviews the vices, but now without invective. Instead, he shows how stupid we are to cling to such things, for the world can only delude us with its vanities. What idiocy it is to prefer the husks of the swine to the father's banquet (¶15). Bernard goes on to show how we must continue to work at the conversion of our manners, either through the fear of hell (¶20) or through the fear of God which is the beginning of wisdom (¶22). He warns us that the struggle will become still harder; the war against the passions must be waged even more furiously as the recalcitrant will counterattacks with greater force and energy, bringing up wiles and strategy. Only repentance and the bitter tears of mourning[54] will clear the eyes so that they do not become dim with straining to pierce the darkness. Tears will wash away the darkness and then we shall begin to perceive that pleasantly serene light which leads to light (¶23).

Entering upon the way of union, we can now peer through the key-hole and catch a glimpse of the Bridegroom in fleeting moments of sweet contemplation (¶24). This leads us to realise something of the bliss of life within the claustral paradise. We see the garden of delight and are encouraged to entice our sick and still rebellious will to share in the joys that our reason has already grasped by dint of careful meditation on the word of God. Little by little our reason gains sway over our will until it too is moved with the desire to enter this paradise and there to make its home (¶24). The four cardinal virtues, springing from wisdom, the river which rejoices this delightful garden, will be fostered by this life of sweet repose and we shall be fortified to taste and see that the Lord is sweet, to experience by foretaste the joys of the life to come which no man has ever heard spoken of (¶25). But this is a locked garden, a secret science. Only the unction of the Spirit can avail to teach us. Books and great learning are useless (¶25).

Then Bernard goes on to reveal that God has a secret sacred plan for souls enamored of him: the charter of heaven is glossed sweetly and at length. Let a man 'endeavor, however little, to experience the taste of righteousness so that he may desire it in greater abundance and thus merit greater abundance' (¶27).

The struggle is not yet over. The last and most serious task remains to be done: the bilge water must be drawn off, the memory must be purified from its stains (¶28). Yet how may we cut our life away from our memory? By that incisive and decisive word of God telling us that our sins are forgiven us. Once they are forgiven we need no longer fear or blush. The reign of trust and confidence has begun. Yet in order to be pardoned by God's mercy, we must ourselves be merciful: merciful to others and towards our own soul. We must repent and lament with the gift of tears. Amidst these very tears God will stoop down in sublime condescension and kiss us with the kiss of his mouth (¶29). Purified by the burning coal of God's kiss,[55] we have that most blessed of visions promised to the pure in heart. We shall see God, dimly it is true, but this vision is nevertheless consummation (¶30).

Moved by divine jealousy on our behalf (¶31) Bernard takes up the theme of conversion, addressing more directly unworthy priests within the Church, the ambitious who 'set themselves up as ministers of grace' (¶32). Bernard considers sadly the state of the Church whose priests have aspired to orders without having 'heard the voice of the Lord first calling them back to the heart' (¶33). Though not all are to be accused, not all are to be excused either. Bernard lays a heavy charge to clerks in sacred orders: ambition, pride, viciousness, luxury, adultery, incest (¶34). There seems to be only one remedy: penance and flight (¶37). The key to all is humility: 'nothing is hard to the meek, nothing arduous for the humble' (¶38). Let us take the lowest place and we shall be exalted to so high a degree that we shall be numbered among those blessed who suffer persecution for the sake of righteousness. Suffering with love is the touchstone of all true holiness and the participation in the glory of the 'Good Shepherd who did not hesitate to lay down his life for his sheep.' Such souls 'leap and dance for joy because they suffer many things for Christ and thus lay up for themselves an even greater reward close to him' (¶40).

What could be sweeter, brothers and sisters, than this voice of the Lord inviting us to return to the heart? See how in his kindness he himself shows us the way. To him be the glory, both now and in the day of eternity.

MARIE-BERNARD SAÏD OSB

Abbaye du Sacre Coeur
Oriocourt

NOTES

1. Steven Runciman, *A History of the Crusades*, 2 (Harmondsworth:Penguin, 1965) 252.
2. Ibid., 251.
3. *Exordium magnum Cisterciense*, II.13; ed. B. Griesser (Rome, 1961) 106-7.
4. See Jean Leclercq, Introduction to the critical edition of Bernard's works, *Sancti Bernardi Opera*, IV (Rome, 1966) p. 61, n. 1. Hereafter cited SBOp.
5. Watkin Williams, *Of Conversion. A Sermon to the Clergy by Saint Bernard of Clairvaux* (London, 1938) p. vii.
6. The figures in parentheses refer to paragraphs of the text On Conversion.
7. See, for example, Jean Leclercq, 'Le cheminement biblique de la pensée de S. Bernard' in *Studi medievali*, 3a serie, VIII, 2 (Spoleto, 1967), and the pages devoted to the Bible in the homilies of St Bernard on *Missus Est*, in *Recueil d'études sur S. Bernard et ses écrits*, 3 (Rome, 1969) 213-62.
8. SPOp 4:62, n. 1.
9. See Conv, 25. On the worship of true wisdom, interesting information is to be gathered from reading Jean Leclercq, *Études sur le vocabulaire monastique au moyen âge, Studia Anselmiana*, 48 (Rome, 1961) 39-79.
10. Geoffrey of Auxerre, *S. Bernardi vita prima*, IV.11.10; PL 183:327.
11. Geoffrey of Auxerre, *Super Apocalypsium, sermo 18*; ed. F. Gastaldelli (Rome, 1970) pp. 218, 350-65: 'I know what is holding you back, what is delaying you. If I should say, leave these visible things as frivolous and harmful and receive those lasting good things, accept heavenly blessedness without delay, none of you, unless he is manifestly mad, were he really believing, would decline to assent to this exchange. But your faces fall, your hearts tremble, your ardent desires grow cold when I coax you to leave behind earthly things and to stand ready for those of heaven. Oh, if only you would fall asleep among clerks and your soul could sing of your beloved, "his left hand is under my head", wherein are riches and glory, "and his right hand embraces me", wherein lies great length of days. Oh, if only instead of falling between two stools, you could — in the words of the psalmist — lie down and sleep, serenely established in hope, or rather, rejoicing in hope, having already attained in hope the salvation which you desire, then you would discover by experience that the expectation of the righteous is joy, and far sweeter than present satisfaction.' [A translation of Geoffrey's sermons on the Apocalypse is forthcoming in the Cistercian Fathers Series — ed.]
11. Ibid.
12. See *Fragmenta de vita et miracula S. Bernardi*, 49; ed. R. Lechat, *Analecta Bollandiana*, 50 (1932) 115, and cited by Leclercq in *Recueil d'études sur S. Bernard et ses écrits*, 2 (Rome, 1966) 187-8.
13. 2 Tm 3:5.
14. Jer 48:6.
15. Jos 21:36.
16. Conv 37.
17. On this subject, see Leclercq, *Otia monastica: Études sur le vocabulaire de la contemplation au moyen âge, Studia Anselmiana*, 51 (Rome, 1963) 137-9.
18. See note 9 above.

19. Among other works and easily accessible is J. Leclercq, *Le vie parfaite, points de vue sur l'essence de l'état religieux* (Paris, 1948) 19-26. In this book it will be noticed that the life of celibacy is only one of the components of the 'angelic' life. A shorter account may be read in a paper delivered by the same author to the ecumenical congress on angels held at Mont-Saint-Michel in September 1966, and published in *The Downside Review*, 85 (1967) 127-37, and in *Aspects of Monasticism* (Cistercian Studies Series 7) 151-62.

20. Div 37.5.

21. Cf. Leclercq, *Otia monastica*, pp. 75, 107, and *Études sur le vocabulaire*, p. 138, n. 46. This last text is worth citing: 'The paradise of the Church has, in fact, three paradises: the paradise of the desert, the paradise of the cloister, the paradise of reclusion. . . . There one is free to attend to reading, meditation, prayer, compunction, contemplation.'

22. Cf. Conv 2.

23. *Vita prima*, I.13.61; PL 185:260 CD.

24. For all the following information concerning the manuscript tradition, I am, of course, dependent on and indebted to Jean Leclercq, *Études sur S. Bernard et le texte de ses écrits, Analecta S.O.C.* 9 (Rome, 1953) 73-6; *Recueil d'études*, 2 (Rome, 1966) 185-91; and the Introduction to the critical edition of the text itself in SBOp 4:61-7.

25. *Études sur S. Bernard*, p. 74, n. 4.

26. This manuscript is described and set in context by Leclercq in *Recueil* 2:185-201.

27. SBOp 5:327-41.

28. *Études sur S. Bernard*, 74.

29. *Recueil* 2:191.

30. The article 'Inédits bernardins dans un manuscrit d'Engelberg', in *Recueil* 2, was first published in *Revue Mabillon*, 37 (1947) 1-16.

31. On St Bernard as a writer and an editor, see in particular several articles in the three *Recueil d'études sur S. Bernard*.

32. Conv, 31.

33. 'St Bernard on the Church', *The Downside Review* (July, 1967) 274-94.

34. Ibid., 291.

35. Ibid.

36. R. W. Southern, *The Making of the Middle Ages* (London, 1959) 232-3.

37. For this chapter in monastic history, see J. Leclercq, *La spiritualité du moyen âge* (Paris, 1961), Chapter VI: *Les ordres nouveaux*. [English translation *The Spirituality of the Middle Ages*, A History of Christian Spirituality, II.]

38. Lester K. Little, 'Pride goes before Avarice: Social Change and the Vices in Latin Christendom', *The American Historical Review*, 76/1 (February 1971) 31.

39. Ibid., 38.

40. Helen Waddell, *The Wandering Scholars* (Collina Fontana, 1968; first published 1927).

41. Ibid., page 309, n. 95, citing Caesarius of Heisterbach, *Dialogus miraculorum* I. 38, II. 15.

42. Ibid., p. 199.

43. SBOp 3:393-493. [English translation by John W. Anderson and Elizabeth T. Kennan, *Five Books on Consideration: Advice to a Pope* (Cistercian Studies Series, 37).]

44. The latin text is in SBOp 4:69-116.
45. Further and more technical details may be found in SBOp 4:61-7.
46. Ibid., 66.
47. The praises of rubber and razor are sung by J. Leclercq in *Recueil* 3:54.
48. *Études sur S. Bernard*, 124-8. See the map below, p. 100)
49. SBOp 4:64.
50. *Recueil* 3:169.
51. *Vita prima*, I.3.8; PL 231:BD.
52. On the theme of experience in the teaching of St. Bernard, see Jean Mouroux, 'Sur les critères de l'experience spirituelle d'après les Sermons sur le Cantique des Cantiques', *Saint Bernard Théologien, Analecta S.O.C.* 9 (1953) 251-67; and J. Leclercq 'Saint Bernard and the Christian Experience', *Worship* 41 (1967) 222-33.
53. Two interesting articles on the structure of the soul and on the conscience are to be found in *Saint Bernard Théologien*: M. E. von Ivanka, 'La structure de l'âme selon S. Bernard', pp. 202-208; and P. Delhaye, 'La conscience morale dans la doctrine de S. Bernard', 209-222.
54. For the theme of the gift of tears and compunction in the monastic tradition, see Leclercq, *L'amour des lettres et le desir de Dieu* (Paris, 1957) 34-36 [English translation: *The Love of Letters and the Desire for God* (New York: Fordham University Press, 1974²) 72-3]. For eastern monastic spirituality, the best introduction might be I. Hausherr, *Penthos, La doctrine de la compunction dans l'Orient chrétien* (Rome, 1944). [An English translation is projected for the Cistercian Studies Series – ed.]
55. For the kiss of God, see Thomas Merton, 'A Life Free From Care', *Cistercian Studies* 5/3 (1970) 217-226.

ON CONVERSION,
A SERMON TO CLERICS

ON CONVERSION,
A SERMON TO CLERICS

I. No one can be converted to the lord unless he is anticipated by the will of the lord and unless his voice cries out interiorly

1. **T**O HEAR THE WORD OF GOD, I believe you have come.* Nor do I see any other reason for you to have flocked here so eagerly. I entirely approve this desire and I congratulate you on your zeal. Blessed are they who hear the Word of God, but only if they observe it.* Blessed are they who are mindful of his commandments, but only if they do them.* For he has the words of eternal life,* and the hour is coming (if only it were already here!) when the dead shall hear his voice,* and those who hear him shall live, for life is in his will.* And if you want to know, his will is our conversion. Listen to him then:* 'Is it my will that the wicked shall die', says the Lord 'and not instead that he should be converted and live?'* From these words we realize that there is no true life* except in conversion and that there is no other means of entering into life, as the Lord likewise says: 'Unless you are converted and become as little children, you shall not enter the kingdom of heaven.'* It is

Ac 13:44; 19:10

Lk 11:28

Ps 103:18
Jn 6:69

Jn 5:25
Ps 30:5
Mt 11:14

Ezk 18:23
1 Tm 6:19

Mt 18:3

quite right that only little children should enter, for it is a little child who leads them. For
this, he was born and given to us.* I seek then
the voice which the dead are to hear,* and by
which, having once heard, they shall live. Perhaps the dead must have the good news preached
to them as well.* In the meanwhile, there occurs
the short but pithy word spoken by the Lord's
own mouth, as the Prophet testified: 'You have
said',—obviously addressing the Lord his God—
'be converted, sons of men'.* Nor is it at all out
of place to view conversion as required of a son
of man, for it is utterly necessary to sinners.
The heavenly spirits* are commanded rather to
praise, as becomes the righteous, as the same
Prophet sings, 'Praise your God, O Sion'.*

2. Moreover, the fact that he said, 'you have
said'* should not, in my opinion, be passed over
lightly or simply heard in passing. For who
would dare to compare human discourse to
what God is said to have spoken? Indeed, the
word of God is living and active* and his voice
is powerful and majestic.* For he spoke and
they were created.* He said 'let there be light'
and there was light.* He said 'be converted'†
and the children of men were converted. Clearly, then, the conversion of souls is the working
of the divine, not the human, voice. Simon, the
son of John,* was called and appointed a fisher
of men by the Lord,* and yet even he toiled all
night in vain and took nothing until, letting
down his nets at the Lord's word, he was able
to enclose a great shoal.* If only I too might at
this word let down the nets of the word today*
and experience what has been written: 'lo, he

Is 9:6
Jn 5:25

1 P 4:6

Is 1:20

Ps 33:1

Ps 147:12

Ps 90:3

Heb 4:12
Ps 29:4
Ps 148:5
*Gen 1:3
†Ps 90:3

Jn 21:15
Mt 4:19

Lk 5:5-6
Cf. *Vita prima*
I. 13.61

sends forth his voice, his mighty voice.* If I lie, Ps 68:33
then clearly I shall be speaking from myself.* Jn 8:44
And if I look after my own interests rather than
those of Jesus Christ,* then you may judge my Ph 2:24
word as coming from me and not from the
Lord. What is more, even if we speak of God's
justice* and seek God's glory,† it is from him *Ps 58:1
alone that we must hope for results. We must †Jn 8:50
ask him for it, so that our own voice may be in
harmony with the voice of majesty. May I suggest then that you prick up the ears of your
heart in order to hear this inner voice and that
you make an effort to hear God speaking within
rather than the man speaking without. For that
is his voice, powerful and full of majesty, which
shakes the wilderness,* pierces all secret things Cf. Ps 29:4, 8
and drives away the sluggishness of souls.

II. The voice of the lord offers and pre-sents itself to all men, proposing itself even to the unwilling soul

3. Nor do we have much difficulty in hearing
this voice; the difficulty is rather in stopping
our ears* from hearing it. For that voice offers Is 33:15
itself, presents itself, and never ceases to knock
at the door* of each one of us. Indeed, it says, Rev 3:20
'For forty years I was close to this generation
and said "They are people who err in their
heart".'* He is still close to us, he is still speak- Ps 95:10
ing and it is not by chance that someone hears
him. He is still saying, 'They are people who
err in their heart';* wisdom is still crying aloud Pr 1:20-21
in the streets, 'Turn back, transgressors, to your
heart.'* For this is the Lord's first word,† and *Is 46:8; †Hos 1:2

we notice that it is this word which seems to
have led the way for all those who convert to

Ps 85:8   their hearts,* not only calling them back, but
leading them back and laying the charge before

Ps 50:21   their very face.* For this voice is not only a
Ps 68:33   mighty voice,* but it is also a beam of light,
Is 58:1   both informing men of their transgressions* and
1 Cor 4:5   bringing to light things hidden in darkness.*
Nor is there any difference between this inward
voice and this light, as the one same Son of God
is both the Word of the Father and the bright-

Heb 1:3   ness of his glory.* Yet the substance of the soul,
spiritual and simple in its nature, seems also devoid of any distinction in its senses, yet is whole
— if we may speak of wholeness — both seeing
and hearing. What other effect does that beam
or that word have than to bring the soul to self
knowledge? It opens the book of the conscience, passes in review the wretched sequence
of life, unfolds the sad events of its history,
enlightens the reason and, the memory having
leafed is set, as it were, before its own eyes.
What is more, these two [memory and reason]
are not so much faculties of the soul as the soul
itself, so that it is both observer and observed: it

Ps 50:21   appears resolved against itself* and is dragged
by these heavy-handed officers before its own
assizes to be judged by its own thoughts. Who
can support this judgement without distress?

Ps 42:6   'My soul is troubled within me,'* says the Lord's
prophet. Why be astonished then that you
cannot stand before your own face without
squirming, without feeling either distress or
shame?

III. THIS ENABLES THE REASON TO READ AS IN A BOOK AND TO GRASP THE EVIL OF ITS SOUL, AND THEN TO CENSURE, CONDEMN, AND REPROVE

4. Do not hope to hear from me what it is within your memory that your reason detects, censures, judges and sentences. Apply your hearing within, roll back the eyes of your heart, and you will learn by your own experience what is going on. For no one knows what is in a man, except the spirit of the man which is in him.* If pride, envy, avarice, ambition, or any other like pest is hidden there, it will scarcely be able to escape* this scrutiny. If it should be guilty of any fornication, theft,* cruelty, any fraud or other fault whatever, the defendant will not remain hidden from this inner judge, nor can he be whitewashed in its presence. Even though all the itching of evil pleasure quickly passes and any charm of sensual satisfaction is short-lived, still it stamps on the memory certain bitter marks, it leaves filthy traces. Into that reservoir, as into a sewer, all these disgusting and dirty thoughts drizzle and run off. Weighty is the book wherein have been inscribed all these acts with the pen* of truth. The stomach now endures bitterness,* yet the wretched palate seemed to have been tickled for a fleeting instant by some frivolous sweetness. Wretched man! my stomach aches, my stomach aches!* How could the stomach of my memory not ache, when it is crammed with so much muck? Which of us, brothers, suddenly notic-

1 Co 2:11

Jb 2:8
Mt 15:19

Jb 19:23
Rev 10:9-10

Jer 4:19

ing that the outer garment he wears is stained with filthy spittings and soiled with all sorts of dirty stains, does not shudder from head to foot and, hastily tearing it off, throw it aside in disgust? Therefore, anyone who discovers that it is not his clothing, but his own inner self under his clothing, that is in such a state should ache all the more and be disturbed in mind because he is putting up with what makes him shudder. The contaminated soul cannot doff itself as easily as it doffs its garments.* Who among us, moreover, is so strong and so patient that if he should happen to see his flesh suddenly becoming white as if sick with leprosy — as Miriam the sister of Moses saw* — could remain calm and give thanks to his Maker? For what is this flesh if not some sort of corruptible garment with which we are clothed? Or, what is this physical leprosy as the eyes of the elect see it, if not the rod of paternal reproof* and a cleansing of the heart? There, there will be violent suffering and a very just cause for grief, when someone, awakening out of the sleep* of lamentable passion, begins to perceive the inner leprosy which he worked so hard to contract. It is true that no one hates his own flesh;* but how much less then shall a soul hate itself?*

Sg 5:3

Num 12:10

Pr 29:15

Jn 11:11

Eph 5:29
Jn 12:25

IV. IF A PERSON LOVES EVIL HE PROVES THAT HE HATES NOT ONLY HIS SOUL BUT EVEN HIS FLESH

5. Perhaps one of you has been struck by this verse of the psalm: 'The man who loves evil hates his soul.'* I would go on to say: he hates

Ps 11:6

his flesh as well. Does a man not hate his soul when by his hard and impenitent heart he stores up wrath for himself on the day of wrath,* trafficking today in hell's stocks? Moreover, it is not so much in the dispositions as in results* that this hatred of body and soul is discovered. There is no doubt that a madman hates his body when he inflicts injury on himself in a frenzied delusion of mind. But is there any greater madness than that of the unrepentant heart and the obstinately sinful will? For now it is not the flesh which his hand attacks but the very mind which it tears and gnaws to pieces.* If you have ever seen a man scratching at his hand and rubbing it until it bleeds, then you have a clear and distinct picture of a sinful soul.* For craving gives way to suffering and mental itching yields to torment. And all the while he was scratching he was well aware that this would happen, but he pretended it would not. We tear our wretched souls to pieces the same way and make them sore with our own hands; only this is all the more serious in that our spiritual being is more precious and more difficult to heal. We act not so much out of a kind of obstinate enmity, as under a kind of numbness brought on by inner insensitivity. The mind* sloshed out of itself does not feel the inward condemnation, for it is not at home,* but probably in the belly, or still lower. Some minds dwell on stewpans, others on purses. The Lord says, 'Where your treasure is, there will your heart be also.'* Is it any wonder that the soul* should feel her own wounds so little when she has forgotten who she is and is inwardly estranged from herself, having taken

Rm 2:5

non in affectu sed in effectu

Jb 13:14

Rm 8:3

animus

Jn 11:12

Mt 6:21
anima

Lk 15:13
Lk 15:17

her journey into a far country?* Yet there will
be a time when, coming to herself,* she will realize how cruelly she has mutilated herself just
to get a miserable piece of game. But she was
not able to feel that as long as she was burning
to lay hands on some vile prey of flies, like a
spider spinning its web out of its own viscera.

The pain of both body and soul
which will follow after death,
and useless penance

Dan 13:17

1 Cor 7:31

Mt 24:28

Lam 3:41

6. She will come home to herself, of that there
is no doubt, but after death has closed all those
physical doors* by which she used to go out
after the figure of this world which passes
away* and wander about outside, busying herself with useless occupations. When that time
comes she will be obliged to remain within herself, having no longer any means of going outside. But it will be a very sorry homecoming
indeed; it will be eternal misery, for though she
repents she will not be able to do penance.
Where there is no body, there can be no activity.* And, obviously, where there is no action,
there can be no satisfaction either. So she will
repent yet suffer, for penance is the balm of suffering. The person who has no hands can no
longer lift up his heart to heaven* with his
hands. The person who does not come to himself before his physical death will be obliged to
remain within himself for all eternity. What
kind of self will that be? What a man has made
for himself in this life, he will find when he
leaves this life, except perhaps it may be still

worse, certainly never better. This very body which he now lays aside he will take up again, not in order to do penance, but to suffer his penalty. The state of his body will be somehow in keeping with the state of his sin: just as his crime will be eternally punished and yet never purged, so also his body will be in constant torment without being consumed by the torments. Nothing is more fitting than that this vengeance should rage forever, for the guilt can never be effaced; nor shall the substance of the flesh vanish, lest someone even think that affliction of the flesh* may come to an end. My brothers, anyone who dreads this, should be wary. Anyone who is careless, stumbles.

Qo 12:12

V. The worms of the conscience are to be discerned and destroyed in this life, not nursed along and nurtured for immortality

7. But to get back to the word where we started: really, it is best for us to return to our hearts,* for this is where he who calls transgressors back with such anxious solicitude shows us his salvation.* In the meantime it must not vex us to feel the worm devouring us within; we must not try to appease it out of delicacy of spirit and a dangerous irresolution, as though we hoped to cover up our present affliction. It is better to feel the worm now when we can still stifle it. Let it eat away now so it will decay, being gradually eaten up by its own over-eating. Let it gnaw away at our corruption, and by its gnawing let it be itself consumed rather

Is 46:8

Ps 50:23

than nursed along to immortality. Scripture says: 'Their worm shall not die, their fire shall not be quenched.'* Who can abide† their gnawing? There is now many a consolation to relieve the torment of a guilty conscience. God is kind and does not let us be tempted beyond our strength;* he will not let this worm harm us beyond repair. Especially at the beginning of a conversion, he anoints our wounds with the oil of mercy so that the acute nature of our sickness and the difficulty of the cure is perceived only to the extent that is expedient. On us seems to smile a sort of easiness, which later disappears when the senses have been trained by practice to fight,* so that one may overcome and come to learn that wisdom is more powerful than anything.* Meanwhile, anyone who has heard the voice of the Lord saying, 'Return, transgressors, to the heart,'* and has discovered such foul things in his inmost chamber will set out like some assiduous detective to investigate them; he will examine each thing and search for the opening by which it filtered in. He will easily discover not just one but many holes. This will cause him no little sorrow, for he will realize that it is through his own windows that this death has entered.* He realizes that the wantonness of his eyes has let many in, the itching of his ears, many,* and the urge for gratifying touch and taste and smell yet many more. Because he is still carnal, he has great difficulty discerning the spiritual vices* of which we spoke earlier. So it happens that though they are more serious, he is less conscious of them, perhaps altogether unconscious. He will be less afflicted by

*Is 66:24
†Ps 147:17

1 Co 10:13

Heb 5:14

Wis 10:12

Is 46:8

Jer 9:21

2 Tm 4:3

1 Co 2:14

his pride and jealousy than by the memory of the more notorious and wicked deeds he has done.

VI. It is easily seen by some that the human will complies with the divine voice

8. And listen, again the voice from the cloud says, 'You have sinned, refrain'. This is to say, 'The drain is overflowing and is making the whole house stink intolerably. It is vain for you* to attempt to empty it while the filth is still seeping in, vain to repent when you have not stopped sinning'. Now who can approve the fastings of those who fast only to quarrel and fight and strike out with disrespectful fist,* those who hold to have their own will and gratifications?* 'It is not such a fast that I choose', says the Lord'.* Close the windows, lock the doors, block up the openings carefully and then, when fresh filth has ceased to flow, you can clean out the old.* As long as a man is without experience in the spiritual combat, he thinks that what is asked of him is easy. He says, 'Who can stop me from controlling my members?' So he prescribes fasting for his palate and proscribes drunkenness; he stops his ears from hearing* about bloodshed, he turns away his eyes from looking at vanities,* he withholds his hands from gain* and instead holds them out to give alms, and he may even set them to work, forbidding them robbery, as it is written, 'Let the thief no longer steal, but rather let him labor with his hands, that he may be able to give to those in need'.*

Ps 127:2

Is 58:4

Is 58:3
Is 58:6

1 Co 5:7

Is 33:15
Ps 119:37
Ps 119:36

Eph 4:28

9. But while he is laying down laws and decrees in this way to his members, even while he is still issuing orders, they suddenly interrupt, screaming in a concerted onslaught, 'May we know what this new teaching is?* It is easy for you to give orders to suit your pleasure. But there is someone who is going to resist these new decrees and contest these new laws.' 'And who may that be?' he asks. And they say, 'None other, of course, than the paralytic lying at home in terrible distress;* that's the woman in whose service you first engaged us — in case you have forgotten — so that we might obey her desires.'* At these words the poor man has gone all pale and been struck dumb with confusion. His spirit is vexed within him.* Whereupon his members scuttle off to their wretched mistress to rouse her cruelly against the master and to clamor for more savage power. The palate complains of being invited to cheap fare and denied the pleasure of getting drunk. The eyes moan that they are condemned to weeping and forbidden all titilation. Provoked and violently enraged by these and other similar hostile critics, the will says, 'Is this a dream* or some tale you are spinning?' Then the tongue, finding the moment ripe for complaint, says, 'It is just as you have heard tell. I too have been ordered to restrain myself from story-telling and lies,* and from now on I may say nothing but serious things and, worse yet, nothing but necessary things.'

Ac 17:19

Mt 8:6

Rm 6:12

Ps 143:4

Gen 37:9

1 Tm 1:4

MAN'S WILL RESISTS THE DIVINE VOICE BY
GLUTTONY, CURIOSITY, PRIDE AND ALL
THE BODILY SENSES

10. Then the crazy old hag leaps up and,
completely forgetting her ailments, storms out
with her hair standing on end, her clothes torn,
her breast bare; she picks at her sores, grinds her
teeth,* goes rigid† and infects even the air with   *Ps 35:16
her poisonous breath. Anyone still keeping his   †Mk 9:17
reason would be disconcerted at such insult and
assault by the wretched will. 'Is this all the faith
you keep with your partner?' she says. 'Is this
the way you show compassion for someone
who puts up with so much? Is this the way
you devise for afflicting still more my grievous
wounds?* Maybe you intend to snatch away   Ps 69:26
what you think is an excessive dowry; but if
you take this away, what will be left? This is
all you offered this feeble wretch, and you realize how all her services have been rendered up
till now. But now, even if you had been able to
cut out the triple tumor of the terrible illness
which lays me low, I cannot. I am passionate,
inquisitive, ambitious; because of this triple festering sore, there is no soundness in me from the
soles of my feet up to the top of my head.'* And   Is 2:6
so the palate and the privy parts of this body
have been handed over to passionate pleasure —
I insist yet again because it seems I must. My
roaming foot and roving eyes are enslaved to
curiosity. My ear and tongue are the servants
of vanity; the one causes the oil of the wicked
to anoint my head* and the other leads me to   Ps 141:5

heap praises on myself when others apparently forget to do so. I have great pleasure both in being praised by others and, when I conveniently can, in boasting in the presence of others. I am always anxious to be vaunted by my own mouth or by that of other people. Even you yourself are powerfully inclined to heap coals on this evil state of affairs. Even my hands, free to move about all over the place, are no longer set to a single occupation, but they busy themselves fiddling about with curiosity or with passionate pleasure. But even though these members have been appointed to such service, never have they succeeded in giving me satisfaction on even a single point. The eye is not satisfied with seeing, nor is the ear sated with hearing.* Yet, I long for the whole body to become an eye for seeing,* or all my members so many gullets for feasting. Are you going to rob me then of this small consolation which I beg you to give me?' With those words she retreats in fury and indignation, screaming, 'I have you in my clutches and will keep hold of you for a long time to come.'

Qo 1:8

1 Co 12:17

THE REASONING POWER OF THE SOUL, HAVING BEEN SO LONG DISTRESSED, IS NOW DOWNCAST AT THE DIFFICULTY OF A TASK IT HAD THOUGHT EASY

11. In the long run, however, this distress comes to enlighten the reason and makes it realize something of the difficulty of the undertaking which it had presumed would be an easy job. It sees the memory clogged with dirty

things; it sees more and more bilge still flowing in; it sees itself incapable of closing the windows thrown wide open to death,* and the will, though ailing, still in supreme command and spreading the suppuration of her festering wounds all over the place. Finally, the soul sees that it is itself contaminated and that the source of this contamination springs not from outside, but from its own body, and not from elsewhere but from itself. It is something in the soul: as the memory, which is tainted, as the very will which injects it. For, in fact, the soul itself is nothing but reason, memory, and will. Now, however, the reason, greatly reduced and, as it were, blind (for so far it has failed to see this state of affairs) is acutely sick; it has come to recognize its malady but finds no remedy; it discovers that the memory is both foul and fetid, and that the will is sick and festering with terrible sores.* And so that his whole humanity should be taken, the body itself rebels: the members become like so many windows by which death enters into the soul* and confusion springs up like weeds.

Jer 9:21

2 Mac 9:9

Jer 9:21

VII. The gentle breeze of consolation which comes from hearing of the blessedness of the promised kingdom of heaven

12. Let the soul which is in this state harken to the divine voice, and to its own amazement and wonder it will hear it say, 'Blessed are the poor in spirit, for theirs is the kingdom of heaven.'* Who is poorer in spirit than the man whose

Mt 5:3

Lk 11:24   spirit finds no rest* and who has nowhere to lay
Mt 8:20   his head?* This also is a counsel of devotion,
that the man who is displeasing to himself is
1 Co 7:32   pleasing to God,* and he who hates his own
house, that is to say a house full of filth and
wretchedness, is invited to the house of glory,
a house not made with hands, eternal in the
2 Co 5:1   heavens.* It is no wonder if he trembles with
awe at the greatness of this honor, and finds it
Rm 10:16   hard to believe what he has heard,* if he starts
in astonishment and says, 'Is it possible for such
wretchedness to make a man happy?' Whoever
you are, if you are in this frame of mind, do not
despair: it is mercy, not misery, that makes a
man happy, but mercy's natural home is misery.
Indeed it happens that misery becomes the
source of man's happiness when humiliation
turns into humility and necessity becomes a
virtue. As it is written, 'Rain in abundance, O
God, you shed abroad; you restored your heri-
Ps 68:9   tage as it languished.'* Sickness has real utility
when it leads us to the doctor's hands, and he
whom God restores to health gains by having
been ill.

THE PERSON WHO STILL HAS SIN RULING HIS
FLESH CANNOT HOPE FOR THIS KINGDOM AND
IS OBLIGED TO THINK ABOUT WHAT FOLLOWS:
BLESSED ARE THE MEEK, AND SO ON

But since there is no way to the kingdom of
God without the first fruits of the kingdom,
and since the man who does not yet rule his own
members cannot hope for the heavenly kingdom, the voice goes on to say, 'Blessed are the

meek, for they shall inherit the earth.'* Put
more clearly, this means, 'Tame the savage
movements of your will and take pains to tame
this cruel beast. You are all tied up; endeavor to
untie what you cannot break outright. [Your
will] is your Eve. Never will you be able to do
her violence or overcome her.'

Mt 5:5

VIII.   13. Then, when the man hears these
words, he breathes more easily and, thinking
that his task will not be so hard, comes forward,
though not without some shame, and sets about
charming this fiery viper. He rebukes his flesh-
ly lures and reproves the consolations of this
flighty world as being trifling and unworthy of
him, and also the shallowest and most fleeting of
all his lovers.

THE HUNGERING GULLET AND THE HANKER-
ING CAPRICE AND THEIR END; THE VANITY OF
CURIOSITY AND THE LOVE OF MONEY
AND THEIR OUTCOME

'I condemn you,' he says, 'out of the very
mouth* of your worthless and wicked servant.†
You cannot deny that in spite of all his obsequious services he has never been able to give you
the slightest satisfaction.' The gullet whose pleasures he rates so highly nowadays is scarcely
wider than two fingers, and yet you go to no
end of pains to procure the slightest delight for
such a tiny member, and in return it only causes
discomfort. The hips and shoulders broaden
grotesquely, the belly swells up as though preg-
nant, not alas with healthy fruit but burdened

*Lk 19:22
†Mt 25:30

with corruption, and this engenders all sorts of maladies because the skeleton cannot support the weight of the flesh. It is the same with the enticing whirlpool of lust: it calls for great expenditures in energy and money; it endangers reputation, honor and even life itself, and its only effect is to fan with the fumes of burning brimstone our already flaming senses. And, like the honeybee, it leaves its sting firmly planted in the heart in which it once distilled its fey sweetness.* Lust's appetites are anxiety and silliness; its actions an abomination and disgrace; its outcome remorse and shame.

Cf. Boethius, *Consol. Phil.* III, metr. 7 (CCh 94:47)

14. I ask you, then, what good do all these frivolous images do the body, what use are they to the soul? Then again, you'll find that a curious man is an empty man. All curiosity brings is frivolous, vain, fleeting consolation. I cannot think what harsher curse I could call down upon a man than that he should always get what he asks for when he tears away from sweet repose out of a curiosity which revels in restlessness. The proof that these pleasures are unsatisfying lies in the very transitoriness which is so diverting. As for the vanity of vanities,* it is nothing, as its very name demonstrates. It is vain labor indeed,* to search after vanity. As a wise man once said, 'O praise! O praise among thousands of mortals thou art nought but vain flatulence in the ear!'* You cannot imagine how much unhappiness this brings forth; it is not so much blissful vanity as vain bliss. From it comes hardness of heart,* as we find it written, 'O my people, they who call you blessed mislead you.'* From it comes the stubborn fury of

Qo 1:2

Ps 127:1

Boethius, *Consol. Phil.* III, pr. 6. Cf. Euripides, *Andromache* 319-20

Mk 3:5

Is 3:12

enmity, the anxious laborings of suspicion, the cruel torment of spite, the torture — more pitiable than pitiful — of burning jealousy. So an insatiable love of riches, far from refreshing the soul by its exercise, racks it with desire. Acquisition is fraught with toil, possession with terror, and loss with remorse. Finally, 'When goods increase, they increase who devour them.'* The exercise of wealth goes to others; all that the rich man reaps from his possessions is excise and anxiety. And for so little, or rather, not even for so little but for nothing at all, he despises the glory which eye has not seen, nor ear heard, nor the heart of man conceived, which God has prepared for those who love him.* This seems not so much foolishness as faithlessness.

Qo 5:10

1 Co 2:9

THE BASENESS OF SERVITUDE TO VICE, THE UNCERTAINTY OF THE HOUR OF DEATH AND THE MISFORTUNE OF AMASSED FORTUNES

15. Surely it is not extraordinary that the world, set in wickedness,* deludes with vain promises souls forgetful of their own condition and noble birth, unashamed at being reduced to slopping swine and sharing their cravings but without being satisfied on their wretched fodder.* How did such faintheartedness and such miserable abjection come to be in so excellent a creature as man? He is capable of eternal blessedness and the glory of our great God.* By his breath he was created, with his likeness he has been stamped, and by his blood he has been redeemed: he has been endowed with faith, adopted in the Spirit; how is it then that he does

1 Jn 5:19

Lk 15:15-16

Tt 2:13

not blush to live in abject servitude beneath this corruption of bodily senses? It is not surprising that, having left such a spouse, this creature pursues such lovers without being able to over-take them.* It is only right that he should hun-ger for husks without getting any,* for he chose to feed swine rather than feast at his father's banquet.* It is crazy labor indeed to feed a bar-ren and fruitless lover while refusing to support a widow, to neglect the care of the heart and yet care for the flesh, gratifying its desires,* to fatten and feed a rotten carcass,* which one knows full well will soon become food for worms. Who does not know that to serve mammon,* to worship avarice, which is to serve idols,* or to pursue the search for vanity is the sign of a degenerate soul?

Hos 2:7
Lk 15:16

Cf. Lk 15:15-24

Rm 13:14
Is 14:19

Mt 6:24
Eph 5:5

Temporal works are as seeds of
an eternal reward

16. After all, there are certain great and re-spectable things which the world seems to be-stow for a time upon her lovers. But we all know how fickle they are. That they are short-lived is certain; uncertain is the term of their short life. They desert the living; yet never, not even once, do they follow the dying.* And yet, among all human happenings, what is more cer-tain than death, what more uncertain than the hour of death? It has no pity for poverty, no reverence for riches. It spares neither birth nor breeding nor even age, the only difference is that the old find it on the doorstep and the young fall into its snares. Unhappy is the man,

Cicero, *De se-nectute* 20.74

who, trusting in the slippery ways and darkness of this life, takes up some perishable work, never realizing that he is a mist appearing for a little time,* a vanity of vanities.† Have you finally obtained, braggard, the dignity you have so long coveted? Hang on to what you have. Is your safe filled with riches, money-bags? Take care or you will lose it. Has your field produced copious fruit? Pull down your barns to build larger ones.* Turn everything upside down; say to your soul, 'You have ample goods laid up for many years'. But you will hear someone say, 'Fool! This night your soul is required of you; and the things you have prepared, whose will they be?'*

17. How I wish it were only your savings which will perish and not the saver, who will perish worse. It would be far more tolerable to sweat in labors to be lost than to be snatched away. But the wages of sin is now death,* and he who sows in his own flesh will from his own flesh reap corruption.* Our works do not pass away, as they seem to do; rather they are scattered like temporal seeds of eternity. The fool will be astonished when he sees a great harvest shooting up from a little seed—good or bad harvest according to the differing quality of the sowing. A man who thinks about all this will never consider any sin little, for he does not value so much the sowing as the future harvest. Humans sow without even knowing it. They sow when they conceal the mystery of lawlessness,* or hide the counsel of vanity,† going about the business of darkness in the dark.*

*Jm 4:15
†Qo 1:2

Lk 12:16

Lk 12:19-20

Rm 6:23

Gal 6:8

*2 Th 2:7
†Ps 26:4
Ps 91:6

IX. IT IS IMPOSSIBLE FOR THE SINNER
TO LIE HIDDEN

18. A man may say to himself, 'The walls
hide me, who sees me?'* Maybe no one sees
you, but even so something does. The wicked
angel sees you, the good angel sees you, and he
who is greater than either the wicked or the
good angels, God sees you, your accuser sees
you, a host of witnesses sees you, the Judge
himself sees you, he before whose judgement
seat you must stand* and under whose eye it is
just as foolish to sin as it is fearful to fall into the
hands of the living God.* Do not think yourself safe: there is many a lurking snare which
you cannot escape. Yes, I tell you, there are
lurking snares from which you cannot escape
and which yet escape you. Surely, he who
plants the ear hears all, and he who forms the
eye sees all.* A mere heap of stones cannot obstruct the rays of the Sun who made them; nor
can the walls of the body block the gaze of
truth. It is as though they did not exist before
his eyes, which are sharper than a two-edged
sword. Not only do they pierce, they also perceive the ways of our thoughts and the marrow
of our intentions.* Moreover, were it not true
that He sees the deepest abyss of the human
heart and all that lies in it and round about it,
the person unaware of anything against himself
would not have been in such fear of the Lord's
judgment. 'It is a very small thing that I should
be judged by you or by any human court,' it
says. 'I do not even judge myself. I am not

Sir 23:25

Rm 14:10

Heb 10:31

Ps 94:9

Heb 4:12

aware of anything against myself, but I am not thereby acquitted. It is the Lord who judges me.* 1 Co 4:3-4

19. If you flatter yourself that you can frustrate human judgment by throwing up a wall or by making excuses, be sure that you cannot cover up the real crimes you commit or hide them from him who is accustomed falsely to accuse you. If you are so afraid of your neighbor's opinion — who probably cares not a hoot about yours — how much less ought you to despise those witnesses who have a much greater hatred of evil and horror of corruption. If you do not fear God, and dread only the gaze of men,* remember that Christ who became man Lk 18:4 cannot ignore the deeds of men; then you will never dare to do in his sight what you would hesitate to do in mine. If the Lord were looking on, you would be horrified even to think of doing deeds you would never carry out in presence of a fellow servant. Moreover, if you fear the eye of the flesh more than the sword which is able to devour the flesh,* what you fear most Dt 32:42 will come upon you and what you dread will befall you.* Nothing is covered up that will not Jb 3:25 be revealed, or hidden that will not be known.* Lk 12:2 The works of darkness,* once come to light,† *Rm 13:12
†Jn 3:20 will be confounded by the light; not only the secret abominations of lewdness, but also the wicked negotiations of those who traffic in sacraments, the deceitful whisperings of those who plot wrongdoing, and the judgments of those who subvert everything, will he who knows everything* make known to everyone on the 1 Jn 3:20 day when the searcher of hearts and reins* be- Ps 7:9 gins to search Jerusalem with lamps.* Zeph 1:2

X. THE FATE OF EVILDOERS AND WHETHER THOSE WHO NEGLECT TO DO GOOD WILL PERISH

20. What are those who have committed crimes going to do, or rather what will they endure, when those who have not done good works shall hear it said to them, 'Depart into the eternal fire?'* How can a man who failed to gird up his loins* to give up doing evil, or failed to hold his lamp to do good, be admitted to the marriage feast when neither the integrity of virginity, nor the brightness of the lamp can make up for a shortage of oil?* Surely they must expect untold anguish, they who, not content merely to do harm during their life, perpetrated heinous crimes,* if those who received good things here must there be in such anguish that in the midst of the flames they shall not have even the tiniest drop of water to cool their parched tongues.* Let us steer clear of evil works then, let us not, confident of being in the net,* willingly be derelict within the Church. We know that not everything gathered in by the net will be put in the fishermen's baskets, for when they come ashore they sort the good into baskets and throw away the bad.* Nor must we be content merely to gird our loins,* we must also light our lamps* and do good† purposefully, thinking over the fact that every tree which does not bear good fruit — not just the one which bears bad fruit — will be cut down and thrown into the fire,* the 'eternal fire prepared for the devil and his angels.'*

Mt 25:41
Lk 12:35

Cf. Mt 25:1-13

Qo 8:11

Lk 16:24-5

Mt 13:47

Mt 13:48
Lk 12:35
*Mt 5:15
†Ga 6:10

Mt 3:10
Mt 25:41

21. Again, let us so turn away from evil and do good* as to seek peace rather than pursue glory. That belongs to God, and he will not give it to another. He has said, 'My glory I give to no other.'* And a man after God's heart has said, 'Not to us, O Lord, not to us, but to your name give glory.'* We remember too what Scripture says: 'Even if you offer rightly but do not rightly divide the offering, you sin.'* Ours is the right division, brothers; let no one depreciate it. However, if anyone should find it not to his liking, let him know that it is not our invention but comes from the angels. Did not the angels first sing, 'Glory to God in the highest, and peace on earth to men of good will'?* Let us therefore keep oil in our lamps, lest — God forbid — knocking in vain at the already-closed door* of the marriage feast, we receive from the bridegroom the bitter answer 'I do not know you.'* Death has taken up its post close to wickedness, barrenness, and vainglory; it follows on the heels of pleasure. So we need fortitude against the temptings of sin in order to resist the roaring lion, firm in the faith* and manfully fending off his fiery darts with this shield. We need justice to do good works.* We need prudence lest we be rejected with the foolish virgins. Finally, we need temperance lest we indulge in pleasures and some day hear said to us what that wretched fellow heard when his feastings and fine clothes had come to an end and he begged for mercy: 'Son, remember that you in your lifetime received good things, and Lazarus in like manner bad things, but now he is comforted here, and you are in anguish.* Surely

Ps 34:14

Is 42:8

Ps 115:1

Gen 4:7 (LXX)

Lk 2:14

Mt 25:4

Mt 25:12

1 P 5:8-9

Gal 6:10

Lk 16:25

God is terrible in his determinations upon the sons of men!* But if he is terrible, he is also found merciful, for he does not hide from us the plan of the judgment to come. 'The soul that sins shall die';* the branch that bears no fruit* shall be cut away; the virgin who has no oil shall be excluded from the marriage feast,* and he who receives good things in this life shall suffer anguish in the life to come.* If these four should happen to be found in one and the same person, clearly he has reached the depths of despair.

Ps 66:5

Ezk 18:20
Jn 15:2
Mt 25:12

Lk 16:25

XI. THE SPIRIT IS CORRECTED BY THE FEAR OF GOD AND THE FLESH RESISTS DOING GOOD

22. The reason suggests inwardly to the will all these and similar things, more insistently as it is perfectly instructed by the light of the spirit. Happy indeed in the person whose will gives way and follows reason's advice, so that, conceiving in fear she may bear heavenly promise and give birth to the spirit of salvation. But it may happen that the will is rebellious and recalcitrant. After all these warnings she is not only impatient in the face of these threats but, worse still, callous. And after basking in blandishments, she is still sour. Far from being moved by the suggestions made by reason, she may be stirred up to even greater fury and retort, 'How long am I to bear with you?* Your words find no place in me.* I know you are shrewd, but your shrewdness finds no place in me.' She may even summon each of her members and order them to be more obsequious than

Mt 17:16
Jn 8:37

usual in obeying her lusts and in serving her villainy. Daily experience teaches us that those who are bent upon conversion find themselves goaded more sharply by the lust of the flesh* and those who have come out of Egypt, determined to flee from Pharaoh,* are driven to work harder at making mortar and brick.*

1 Jn 2:16

Ex 2:15

Ex 1:14

WHILE WE STRUGGLE WE WEEP; AFTER THE STRUGGLE WE HAVE COMFORT, FOR BLESSED ARE THEY WHO WEEP . . .

23. Would to God, however, that the man who has turned away from evil in this manner might also be on his guard against that terrible depth of which we read, 'The wicked man, when he has come into the depth of sin, sneers.'* He can, of course, be cured, but only by the most drastic remedy, and he will easily run risks unless he takes great pains to follow the doctor's instructions and do very carefully what he says. The temptation is violent, near to hopelessness,* unless he pulls himself together and takes pity on his soul, which he sees to be in so pitiful and pitiable a state that he turns his natural affection [to God] and listens to his voice say:* 'Blessed are those who mourn for they shall be comforted.'* He must mourn greatly for the time of mourning has arrived and to swallow down an ever-flowing stream of tears only these suffice. He must mourn, but with deeply-felt piety and ensuing comfort. Let him consider that within himself he will find no rest* for himself, because he is full of misery and desolation. Let him consider that there is no good in his flesh* and that

Pr 18:3

Heb 6:8

Rev 10:4

Mt 5:5

Lk 11:24

Ps 38:3

Gal 1:4 the present evil age* contains nothing but van-
Qo 1:14 ity and affliction of spirit.* Let him consider, I
repeat, that he will find no comfort — not within
nor under nor around himself, until he at last
Col 3:1 learns to seek it from above* and to hope that it
will come down from above. Meanwhile let
Jb 10:20 him mourn and lament his sorrow,* let his eyes
Ps 119:136 well with tears* and his eyelids find no slum-
Pr 6:4 ber.* Tears will wash the darkness from his
Jb 16:17 eyes,* his sight will become keen so he will be
able to turn his gaze towards the brightness of
Ac 22:11 glistering light.*

XII. AFTER MOURNING AND COMFORT, THE KINDLING DESIRE FOR HEAVENLY CONTEMPLATION

24. All this will enable him to peer through
Sg 5:4/†Sg 2:9 the keyhole, to look through the lattices† and
in sweet regard to follow the trail of that guid-
ing ray, seeking light by the light, like some
Mt 2:1ff. eager imitator of the Wise Men.* He shall then
Ps 42:4 discover the place of the wonderful tabernacle,*
Ps 78:25 where man shall eat the bread of angels;* he
shall discover the paradise of pleasure planted
Gen 2:8 by the Lord;* he shall discover a flowering and
thoroughly lovely garden; he shall discover a
place of refreshment and he shall exclaim: 'Oh!
if only this wretched will of mine would heed
Jn 10:17 my voice,* that she might come here and visit
Gen 28:17 this place.* Here surely she would find great
rest, and she would be less troublesome to me,
being herself less troubled? He did not lie who
said: 'Take my yoke upon you, and you will
Mt 11:29 find rest for your souls.'* Buoyed up by trust in

this promise, let him speak more soothingly to
his angered will and, putting on a smile, let him
approach her in a spirit of gentleness,* and say: — 1 Co 4:21
'Turn away your indignation.* I will do you no — Gen 27:45
harm; I could not. This body is yours, I myself
am yours; have no fear, there is nothing to be
afraid of.' He must not be astonished if she
should retort even more bitterly, and say 'much
thinking is driving you mad.'* Let him for now — Ac 26:24
endure all this calmly, carefully dissimulating
what he intends to do and then, while they are
chatting, let him seize a suitable opportunity to
put in another word and say: 'Today I have
found a very beautiful garden, a really lovely
place. It would be good for us to be there;* it is — Mt 17:4
not good for you to lie on this sick-bed, tossing
about on this mattress in pain and eating your
heart out in grief in your room.'* The Lord is — Ps 4:3, 5
near to those who seek him, near the soul that
hopes in him.* He is near you who call upon — Lam 3:25
him and he lends efficacy to your words. The
will's desire shall be stirred not only to see the
place,* but even to go in a little way. And she — Mt 28:6
will long to make her home there.* — Jn 14:23

XIII. In this contemplation lies rest,
and in savoring him lie sweetness
and instruction

25. You must not suppose this paradise* of — Gen 2:8
inner pleasure is some material place: you enter
this garden not on foot, but by deeply-felt affections. You will be enchanted not by a copse of
earthly trees, but by gracious and seemly* beds — Ps 147:1
of spiritual virtues. A garden enclosed, where

*Is 17:10
†Gen 2:10

Sg 2:12

Sg 1:11, 2

Sg 4:16
Gen 2:9

Sg 2:3

Eph 1:18
Sg 2:14
Ps 50:10

Gen 27:29

Is 10:17

Ac 23:1
1 Co 9:7

Mt 19:29

1 Co 2:10

the sealed fountain* flows out into four streams,†
and from this single vein of wisdom flows fourfold virtue. There, too, the most splendid lilies
bloom, and as these flowers appear, the voice of
the turtledove is also heard.* There the bride's
nard breathes forth its utterly fragrant per-
fume* and other aromatic oils flow when the
south wind blows, and the north wind hies
away.* In the midst of the garden is the tree
of life,* the apple tree mentioned in the Song,
more precious than all the trees of the woods,
whose shadow refreshed the bride and whose
fruit was sweet to her taste.* There the radiance of continence and the beholding of un-
blemished truth, enlighten the eyes of the heart;*
and the sweet voice* of the inner comforter
gives joy and gladness to the hearing as well.*
There the nostrils inhale the exquisite scent of
hope, of a rich field which the Lord has blessed.*
There eagerly we have a foretaste of the incomparable delights of charity, and, once all the
thorns and briers which earlier pricked the soul
have been burnt,* the spirit is pervaded with the
balm of mercy and rests happily in good conscience.* But these are not yet the rewards of
eternal life, but only the wages* paid for mili-
tary service; they have nothing to do with the
future promise made to the Church, but concern rather her present due. This is the hundredfold* tendered already in this world to
those who scorn the world. Do not hope to
hear me sing the praises of all that. That is revealed through the Spirit alone:* you will consult books to no avail; you must try to experience it instead. That is wisdom, and man does

not know its price. It is drawn from things hidden, and this delight is not to be found in the land of those who live delightfully.* Yes, it is the Lord's own delight and unless you taste it, you shall not see it. Has it not been said: 'Taste and see that the Lord is delightful'?* This is hidden manna, it is the new name which no one knows except him who receives it.* Not learning but anointing teaches it;* not science but conscience grasps it. He is holy, they are pearls,* and he will not do what he forbade us to do when he began to do and teach.* No longer does he treat like dogs or swine those who have renounced their crimes and evil deeds. He even consoles them with the words of the apostle: 'And such were some of you. But you were washed, you have been made holy.'* Take care that the dog does not turn back to its own vomit, or the scrubbed sow wallow again in the mire.*

Jb 28:12-13

Ps 34:8

Rev 2:17
1 Jn 2:27

Mt 7:6
Ac 1:1

1 Co 6:11

2 P 2:22

XIV. THOSE WHO HAVE HAD THIS TASTE KNOW THEY ARE REFRESHED, FOR BLESSED ARE THOSE WHO HUNGER AND THIRST FOR RIGHTEOUSNESS. . . .

26. At the gate of paradise* a voice is heard† whispering an utterly sacred and secret plan which is hidden from the wise and prudent and revealed to little ones.* The sound of this voice reason now not only grasps, but happily transmits to the will. Blessed are those who hunger and thirst for righteousness, for they shall be satisfied.* Deep indeed is this plan and unfathomable the mystery. This word is sure and

*Gen 3:24
†Sg 2:12

Mt 11:25

Mt 5:6

1 Tm 1:15
Wis 18:15

Lk 15:14

Ps 49:12

Lk 15:16

worthy of full acceptance.* It came to us from heaven, from the royal throne.* A great famine has struck the earth, and not only have we all begun to be in want,* but we have come to extreme destitution. We have even been compared to senseless beasts and have become like them.* We even hunger greedily after the swine's husks.* Anyone who loves money is dissatisfied; anyone who loves luxury is dissatisfied; anyone who loves glory is dissatisfied; in short, anyone who loves this world is always dissatisfied. I have myself known men sated with this world and sick at the very thought of it. I have known men sated with money, sated with honors, sated with the pleasures and curiosities of this world, sated not just a little, but to the point of repugnance. Yet, one can have satisfaction only through the grace of God. Satisfaction is born not of repletion, but of scorn. So, foolish sons of Adam, when you devour the husks of swine, you are feeding not your famished souls, but their very famine. Yes, this fodder fosters your starvation, this unnatural food does no more than sustain famine. And to put it more clearly, let me give just one example taken from among the many things which human vanity covets: the human body will be sated with air before the heart of man is sated with gold. The miser need not take offense. This is true for the ambitious man, the self-indulgent man and the vicious man. If any of you does not perhaps believe me, let him believe experience, either his own or that of many others.

27. Is there someone among you, brothers, who desires to be satisfied and would like this

desire to be fulfilled? Then let him begin to be hungry* for righteousness, and he cannot fail to be satisfied. Let him yearn for those loaves which abound in his father's house, and he will immediately find he is disgusted with the husks of swine. Let him endeavor, however little, to experience the taste of righteousness that he may desire it more and thus merit more; as it has been written: 'He who eats me will hunger for more, and he who drinks me will thirst for more.'* This desire is more akin to the spirit, and because it is natural to it, the heart is more eagerly preoccupied with this and manfully shoves out all other desires. In this way a strong man fully armed is overcome by one stronger than he;* in this way one nail is driven out by another.* 'Blessed are they who hunger and thirst for righteousness.' Then, 'for they will be satisfied.'* Not yet by that one thing by which man is never sated, the one thing by which he lives, but by everything else, all those things for which he previously longed insatiably, so that thereafter the will ceases delivering up the body to obey its former passions,* and delivers it over to reason, urging it to serve righteousness for holiness' sake* with no less zeal than it formerly showed in serving evil for iniquity's.

Lk 15:16

Sir 24:29

Lk 11:21-2
Cf. Cicero, *Tusculan Disputations* 4:35:75, Aristotle, *Politics* 1314ª5
Mt 5:6

Rm 6:12

Rm 6:19

XV. ONCE OUR SINS HAVE BEEN PUNISHED AND FORGIVEN, THEY NO LONGER HARM US IF THEY ARE NOT REPEATED, BUT THEY WORK TOGETHER FOR OUR GOOD

28. Once the will has been turned and the body subdued to service,* as if the fountain

1 Co 9:27

were dry and the breach filled up, a third and
very serious thing remains still to be done: the
memory must be purified and the bilge water
drawn off. But how am I going to cut my life
out of my memory? The dark ink has drenched
my cheap, flimsy parchment: by what technique
can I blot it out? It has not only stained the sur-
face, it has soaked into the whole thing. It is
useless for me to attempt to rub it out: the skin
will be torn before the wretched characters
have been effaced. Forgetfulness might perhaps
efface the memory if, for example, I were
touched in the head and did not remember what
I had done. But to leave my memory intact and
yet wash away its blotches, what penknife can I
use? Only that living and effective word sharper
than a two-edged sword:* 'Your sins are forgiven you.'* Let the Pharisee mutter and say:
'Who can forgive sins but God alone?'* To me
it is God himself who speaks, and no other can
be compared to him. He it was who devised the
whole way of discipline and gave it to Jacob his
servant and to Israel whom he loved, and afterwards appeared on earth and lived among men.*
His forbearance wipes away sin, not by cutting
it out of the memory, but by leaving in the
memory what was there causing discoloration,
and blanching it thoroughly. We then remember many sins, which we know to have been
committed either by ourselves or by others, but
only our own stain us; those of others do us no
harm. How is this? Surely it is because we
blush only for our own sins, and it is only for
these that we fear reproach. Take away damnation, take away fear, take away confusion; full

Heb 4:12
Mk 2:5
Mk 2:7

Bar 3:36-8

remission takes all of these away, and our sins no longer harm us, but even work together for our good,* enabling us to offer devout thanks to him who has remitted them.

Rm 8:28

XVI. The mercy which has been prom-ised to those who repent and are merciful, as has been said: blessed are the merciful . . .

29. Anyone who asks for pardon is fittingly answered with these words: 'Blessed are the merciful, for they shall obtain mercy.'* If you want God to be merciful to you, then, you must yourself be merciful towards your soul. Flood your bed every night with your tears, remember to drench your couch with your weeping.* If you have compassion on yourself, if you struggle on in groanings of penance – for this is mercy's first step –, then you will arrive at mercy. And if you are perhaps a great and frequent sinner and seek great mercy and frequent forgiveness,* you must also work at increasing your mercy. You are reconciled to yourself whereas you had become a burden to yourself,* because you had set yourself up against God. Once peace has been restored this way in your own house, the first thing to do is to extend it to your neighbors so that God may come at last to kiss you with the very kiss of his mouth.* In this way being reconciled to God*, as it has been written, you may have peace.* Forgive those who have sinned against you, and you will be forgiven your sins when you pray to the

Mt 5:7

Ps 6:6

Ps 51:1

Jb 7:20

Sg 1:1
Rm 5:10
Rm 5:1

Father with an easy conscience and say: Forgive us our trespasses, as we forgive those who
trespass against us.* If you have defrauded
someone,* restore the exact amount: what is
left over you must distribute to the poor,* and
because you have been merciful you will obtain
mercy. 'Though your sins are like scarlet, they
shall be white as snow; though they are red like
crimson, they shall become like wool.'* Give
alms so you are not put to shame by all the chi-
caneries by which you have gone astray* and
for which you are now ashamed.* If you are
not able to do this from your earthly substance,*
do it out of good will, and everything will be
wiped clean.* Not only is the reason enlightened and the will straightened, but the memory
too is cleansed so that you may now call upon
the Lord and hear his voice say:

Mt 6:12
Lk 19:8
Lk 18:22

Is 1:18

Zeph 3:11
Rom 6:21
Tob 4:7

Lk 11:41

XVII. THE HEART MUST BE PURIFIED IN ORDER TO SEE GOD, FOR BLESSED ARE THE PURE IN HEART . . .

30. 'Blessed are the pure in heart, for they
shall see God.'* A great promise, my brothers,
and one to be responded to* with our whole
desire. This vision is also our assurance, as John
the Apostle said: 'We are now God's children.
It does not yet appear what we shall be, but we
know that when he appears we shall be like him,
for we shall see him as he is.'* This vision is eternal life,* as Truth himself said in the Gospel:
'This is life eternal, to know you the one true
God, and Jesus Christ whom you have sent.'*
It is a hateful blotch which deprives us of this

Mt 5:8
affectanda

1 Jn 3:2
Jn 12:50

Jn 17:3

vision, and a damnable negligence which makes us meanwhile neglect to cleanse our eye. Just as our bodily sight is blurred by some inner fluid or some outer speck of dust, so spiritual insight is impeded either by the lust of our own flesh or by worldly curiosity and ambition. This we learn as much from our own experience as from Holy Scripture, where we find it written: 'A perishable body weighs down the soul, and this earthly tent burdens the thoughtful mind.'* Wis 9:15
In both instances, however, it is sin that dims and blurs the eye, and that alone screens the light from the eye, and God from man. Yet while we are in this body, we wander apart from the Lord,* and the fault lies not in our body it- 2 Co 5:6
self, but in the fact that our flesh is still a body *Rm 7:24
of death,* or rather a sinful body,† in which †Rm 6:6
there is no good, but only the law of sin.* It Rm 7:23
sometimes happens too that the physical eye seems to remain dim* for a little while even after Gen 27:1
the speck has been taken out or blown away. And it is the same with the inner eye, as the man who walks in the Spirit* has often experienced. Gal 5:16
Even when you have taken out shrapnel, a wound does not immediately begin to heal, but you must then first apply fomentations and nurse it. Let no one imagine he is cleaned up right away, once he has emptied out the bilge water. Washing with water is not sufficient; you must also be purified and refined with fire,* so Ps 12:6
you may say: 'We have gone through fire and water; and you have brought us forth into a place of refreshment.'* 'Blessed are the pure in Ps 66:12
heart, then, for they shall see God.'* Now we Mt 5:8
see in a mirror dimly, but in the future we shall

1 Co 13:12
see face to face,* once our face shall have been cleansed of all smut and he shall present it to himself resplendent, without spot or wrinkle.*

Eph 5:27

XVIII. The pacified, the pacifying, and the peacemaker: blessed are the peacemakers . . .

31. This leads us immediately to add: 'Blessed are the peacemakers, for they shall be called sons of God.'* It is a pacified man who repays good for good, as far as in him lies, and wishes harm to no one. Someone else may be patient and repay no one evil for evil,* being even able to bear with the man who hurts him. There is also the peacemaker: he is always ready to repay good for evil and to help the man who hurts him. The first is one of those little ones who is easily scandalized;* for him it will not be easy to win salvation in this present evil age* so full of stumbling blocks. The second possesses his soul in patience, as has been written.* As for the third, he not only possesses his own soul, but wins many more.* The first, as far as he is able, is in peace. The second keeps peace. The third makes peace. Appropriately therefore is he blessed with the name son, for he accomplishes the duty incumbent on the son: that once he has himself been acceptably reconciled, he in turn reconciles others to his Father.* Now someone who serves well gains good standing for himself,* and what better standing could there be in the father's house than that of the son? For, 'if sons, then heirs, heirs of God and fellow heirs with Christ.'* And so it is, as he

Mt 5:9

Rm 12:17

Mk 9:41
Gal 1:4

Lk 21:19

1 Co 9:19

2 Co 5:18

1 Tm 3:13

Rm 8:17

himself has said, that where he is, there shall his
servant be also.*

Jn 12:26

But I am tiring you by this rambling sermon,
and I have already detained you longer than I
should. So I will come to the end of my chatter,
not because I am shamed into it, but because I
see that time is getting short. But remember
that the Apostle once went on preaching until
midnight.* I wish then — to use his own words —

Ac 20:7

that you would bear with me in a little foolishness, for I feel a divine jealousy for you.*

2 Cor 11:2

XIX. A REBUKE TO THE AMBITIOUS WHO PRESUME TO MAKE PEACE BETWEEN GOD AND OTHERS WHEN THEY THEMSELVES ARE NOT YET PURE IN HEART

32. Little children, 'who warned you to flee
from the wrath to come?'* No one deserves
greater wrath than the enemy who pretends to
be a friend. 'Judas, you betray the Son of man
with a kiss.'* You, a familiar friend, who used
to hold sweet converse with him,* who have
dipped your hand in the same dish!* You have
no share in that prayer which He prayed to the
Father when he said: 'Father, forgive them, for
they do not know what they do.'* Woe to you
who have taken away the key not only of knowledge but also of authority, for you did not enter
yourselves, and you have hindered variously
those whom you ought to have led in.* Yes, you
have taken, you have not received, the keys. Of
such people the Lord said by his prophet: 'They
made kings, but not through me; they set up

Mt 3:7

Lk 22:48
Ps 55:13-4
Mt 26:23

Lk 23:34

Lk 11:52

Hos 8:4 princes, but without my knowledge.* Where does this great zeal for the prelacy come from? Whence this ambitious impudence? Whence this lunacy of human presumption? Would someone who did not uphold any of our territorial laws but actually hindered them, dare to busy himself in their service, snatch at their benefits or regulate their business? Do not suppose that God approves all this, who in his great home endures the vessels of wrath fit for de-

Rm 9:22 struction.* Many come, but consider who is called. Notice the conditions laid down in the Lord's own statement: 'Blessed are the pure in

Mt 5:8 heart', he said, 'for they shall see God';* and then: 'Blessed are the peacemakers, for they

Mt 5:9 shall be called sons of God.'* The heavenly

Mt 5:48 Father* calls pure of heart those who do not look to their own interests but those of Jesus

Ph 2:21 Christ,* those who do not seek their own ad-

1 Co 10:33 vantage, but that of many.* 'Peter', he asked, 'do you love me?' 'Lord, you know I love you.'

Jn 21:16-7 And he said, 'Feed my sheep.'* Would anyone confide beloved sheep like this to a man who did not love them? No wonder what is required

1 Co 4:2 of stewards is that they be found trustworthy.* Woe to those untrustworthy servants who busy themselves like justices of the peace with reconciling others when they themselves have not

Eph 2:3 been reconciled. Woe to the children of wrath* who set themselves up as ministers of grace! Woe to the children of wrath who are not ashamed to usurp the rank and title of the peacemakers! Woe to the children of wrath who pretend to mediate peace in order to feed upon people's sins. Woe to those who walk in

the flesh; they cannot please God* and yet they
aspire presumptuously to reconcile others.

Rm 8:8

ASTONISHMENT THAT CERTAIN MEN USURP
THE SUPREME DIGNITY OF PEACEMAKERS
WHEN THEY HAVE NOT REACHED EVEN
THE LOWEST RANK

33. We should not be bemused, brothers, when
we bemoan the present state of the Church, we
should not be bemused at seeing a petty prince
growing up from the serpent's root.* We
should not be bemused at seeing how anyone
who passes along the path* set out by the Lord
can gather grapes in the Lord's vineyard. Impudently a man arrogates the rank of peacemaker and the standing of the Son of God, a
man who has not yet heard the Lord's voice first
calling him back to his heart or who, if he did
begin to hear it, at once hopped back to hide
himself behind the bushes.* This is why he has
not yet given up sinning and still trails a long
tether. He has not yet come to be a man who
sees his own poverty,* but he says 'I am rich and
need nothing', whereas in fact he is poor, naked,
wretched, and pitiable.* There is in him nothing of the spirit of gentleness* which would
enable him to edify those given up to sin and
yet to look out for himself, lest he too be
tempted.* Unacquainted with tears of compunction, he rejoices more in doing evil and
delights in utterly perverse things.* No wonder
that it was to one of these that the Lord said:
'Woe to you who laugh now, for you shall
mourn and weep.'* It is money, not justice, he

Is 14:29

Ps 79:13
Is 5:7

Gen 3:9-10

Lam 3:1

Rev 3:17
1 Co 4:21

Gal 6:1

Pr 2:14

Lk 6:25

is looking for; his eyes look at everything high

Jb 41:25

up.* Insatiably he hungers for honors, he thirsts for human glory. He is far removed from ten-

Lk 1:78

der mercy,* taking his pleasure in venting his wrath and strutting about like a tyrant and im-

1 Tm 6:5

agining that godliness is a means of gain.* What shall I say about purity of heart? How I wish that it were not forgotten, as if dead at heart. How I wish it were not a dove led astray yet

Hos 7:11

having no heart.* How I wish what is outside were clean, and what is physical were not found to be a soiled garment, so that purity of heart could say, 'You have been purified, you who

Is 52:11

bear the Lord's vessels.'*

XX. It is to be regretted that the impure are not ashamed impudently to defile sacred orders

34. I do not accuse everyone, but I cannot excuse everyone either. God has kept many

Rm 11:4

thousands for himself.* Otherwise — were their justice not there to excuse us, had the Lord of

Rm 9:29

Sabaoth not left us a holy seed* — we should already have been overthrown like Sodom of old;

Jer 50:40

we should have perished like Gomorrah.* The Church has increased, and the clerks in sacred

Ps 40:5

orders have multiplied beyond number.* Truly, Lord, even though you have multiplied the na-

Is 9:3

tion, you have not magnified its joy,* for its merit seems to have decreased as its numbers increased. People rush into holy orders all over the place, and, without awe, without stopping to think, men appropriate for themselves the ministry which awes angelic spirits. They are not even afraid to grab the sign of the kingdom of heaven or to wear the imperial crown; them avarice reigns over, ambition commands, pride dominates, iniquity sits in, luxury lords over, and perhaps, were we to dig under the wall as the prophet Ezekiel suggests,* within these very walls we should see vile abominations, horrors in the house of God. Beyond fornication, adultery* and incest, there are even some who have given themselves up to dishonorable passions and shameless acts.* Would that they not commit those acts which are unbefitting the Apostle to put into writing or me into words. Would that when someone hints that human spirits are given to such abominable passion he could be called a liar.

Ezk 8:8-10

1 Co 6:9

Rm 1:26

35. Were not in times past those cities which nutured such foul deeds condemned by divine judgment and destroyed by flames?* Did not the flames of hell, not brooking delay, lick that detestable nation whose crimes were so flagrant as to advance the judgment? Did not coals of fire, brimstone and scorching wind devour that land which was accomplice to so much confusion?* Was not the whole lot reduced to a single horrible quagmire? The five heads of Hydra have been cut off, but alas! they sprout again without number. Who rebuilt these sordid cities? Who widened the walls of wickedness? Who spread abroad the deadly virus? Woe! Woe! The enemy of mankind has scattered the wretched remains of that fiery brimstone all over the place. He has strewn the body of the Church* with those damnable ashes, and even spattered some of her ministers with that stink-

Gen 19:1-29

Ps 11:6

Col 1:18

ing, putrid discharge! Alas! 'Chosen race, royal
priesthood, holy nation, God's own people';*
who could believe that such things should have
come to pass in you when he thinks of your
godly origin and the beginnings of the christian
religion and the spiritual gifts which accompanied it?

36. Stained like this, they go into the tabernacle* of the living God.† They dwell in the
temple with these stains, profaning the Lord's
holy place,* calling down upon themselves
manifold judgment because no matter how
weighed down they are with an overburdened
conscience, they push themselves into the sanctuary of God.* Not only do such men fail to
please God, they irritate him far more, for in
their hearts they say, 'He will never see it.'* Of
course, they irritate him, they enrage him
against themselves, I am afraid, through the
very things by which they ought to placate him.
If only they would sit down to count the cost
of the tower they have begun, in case they have
not the means to finish it.* If only those who
are incapable of remaining continent would
fear to profess perfection rashly and to assume
the title of celibacy. This is a costly tower, a
great precept which not everyone can accept.*
It would without doubt have been better to
marry than to burn,* to be saved in the humble
ranks of the faithful than to live less worthily in
the lofty ranks of the clergy and be more severely judged. Many, not everyone but certainly
many, such a crowd that they cannot pass un-
noticed — and they are so unabashed they do
not even try to do so — many use the freedom to

1 P 2:9

*Ex 28:43
†Dt 5:26

Lev 19:8

Ps 73:17

Ps 10:13

Lk 14:28

Mt 19:11

1 Co 7:9

which they have been called as an opportunity for the flesh.* They abstain from the remedy afforded by marriage and give themselves up to all forms of vice.

Gal 5:13

XXI. An exhortation to penance: as they taste first of lowly things, so may they then worthily move up to loftier

37. Spare your souls, brothers, I beg you, spare, spare the blood which has been poured out for you.* Beware of the terrifying danger, turn away from the fire which has been made ready.* Let your profession of perfection not be found later to be a mockery and let its power now appear in the form of godliness.* Let it not be an empty appearance of the celibate life, and void of truth. Can chastity remain unscathed amid delights, or humility among riches, or piety in business, or truth amid much talking, or charity in this present evil age?* Flee from the midst of Babylon.* Flee and save your souls!* Flock to the city of refuge,† where you can do penance for the past, obtain grace in the present, and confidently wait for future glory. Do not let the consciousness of your sins hold you back, for where they abound, grace always superabounds.* Do not let the austerity of penance deter you: the sufferings of this present time are not worth comparing* with the forgiveness to be granted to our past sins, with the present grace of consolation which is now given to us or with the future glory which has been promised us. For nothing is so bitter that the

Mt 26:28

Mt 25:41

2 Tm 3:5

Gal 1:4
Jer 51:6
*Jer 48:6
†Josh 21:36

Rm 5:20

Rm 8:18

2 S 4:41
Pr 3:18

Jn 10:38

flour of the prophet* cannot sweeten it and wisdom, the tree of life,* cannot make it savory.

38. If you do not believe my words, believe the works;* acknowledge the examples of many. Sinners flock from everywhere to do penance, and even though they are delicate by nature or training, they do not mind roughing it outwardly if only they can soothe their rasping conscience. Nothing is impossible to believers, nothing difficult to lovers, nothing hard to the meek, nothing arduous to the humble; to them grace lends its aid, and devotion gentles a command to the obedient person. Why occupy yourselves with things too great and marvellous for you?* Indeed it is a great and marvellous thing to be the servant of Christ and a steward of the mysteries of God.* The rank of peacemakers is far above you, unless perhaps, skipping the aforementioned steps, you prefer to leap rather than to climb up. If only someone, if it were possible, were to get in in such a way and minister as faithfully as confidently he intruded! But it is a difficult, probably even an impossible, thing for the sweet fruit of charity to burn on the bitter root of ambition. If you are willing to listen, I will tell you, or rather not I but the Lord: 'When you are invited to a marriage feast, go and sit in the lowest place,* for everyone who exalts himself will be humbled, and he who humbles himself will be exalted.*

Ps 131:1

1 Co 4:1

Lk 14:8-10

Lk 14:11

XXII. THE PERSECUTION WHICH WE MUST SUFFER ACCORDING TO THE LAST BEATITUDE: BLESSED ARE THOSE WHO ARE PERSECUTED . . . BLESSED WILL YOU BE . . .

39. 'Blessed are the peacemakers', he has said, 'for they shall be called sons of God.'* Consider attentively that it is not the peace-preachers, but the peacemakers, who are praised. For there are some who preach but do not practice it.* Just as it is not the hearers of the law who are righteous, but the doers,* so it is not those who proclaim peace who are blessed, but those who practise it. If only those among us who today seem to be pharisees — and perhaps they are — could at least preach what they ought, even if they do not practise it. If only those who are not willing to set forth the Gospel free of charge,* might at least offer something for the charge! If only they would preach the Gospel to earn their bread. 'The hireling', he said, 'sees the wolf coming and flees.'* If only those today who are not shepherds would at least show themselves hirelings and not wolves. If only they would not devour [the sheep], if only they would not flee when no one is chasing them. If only they would not leave the flock unprotected until they see the wolf coming. Perhaps, after all, it would be better to support them, especially in times, of peace, when they are found receiving their reward,* and in return for their wages, working at keeping the flock, as long as they do not trouble the flock and lead it astray from the pastures of righteousness and truth. For any

Mt 5:9

Mt 23:3

Rm 2:13

1 Co 9:18

Jn 10:12

Mt 6:2

Mt 25:32

persecution will soon separate and distinguish the hirelings from the shepherds.* How will the man who pursues temporal gain be able to support passing pain? How will the man who prefers an earthly reward to righteousness be able to endure persecution for the sake of righteousness? 'Blessed are those who are persecuted for righteousness' sake', he said, 'for theirs is the

Mt 5:10

kingdom of heaven.'* This is the beatitude of shepherds, not hirelings, still less of robbers and wolves. Never yet having been persecuted for righteousness' sake, they choose to put up with persecution rather than justice. This is opposed

Wis 2:12

to their efforts* and it is even hard for them to hear tell of it.

40. Yet for the sake of their greed, for the sake of ambition, you will see them ready to support all sorts of dangers, to cause scandal, to endure hatred, to mask shameful doings, to ignore curses. In the end, such ill will is no less harmful than the cowardice of hirelings. The Shepherd, the Good Shepherd who did not spare his life for his sheep says therefore to real shepherds: 'Blessed are you when men hate you, and when they exclude you and revile you, and cast out your name as evil, on account of the Son of man! Rejoice in that day, and leap for

Lk 6:22

joy, for great is your reward in heaven.'* Indeed, why should people fear thieves while they

Mt 6:19

are laying up treasure in heaven?* They are not disturbed by increasing tribulations while they anticipate an increased reward. In fact, they are even more pleased — as is only right — because the recompense increases more than the suffering. They leap and dance for joy because they suffer many things for Christ's sake and lay up for themselves thereby an even greater reward close to him. 'Why are you afraid, O ye of little faith?'* A sure statement of undeniable truth has it that adversity will not harm a person on whom no evil has a grip. But it is not enough to say 'it does no harm', for it brings great and ever-increasing benefit, as long as we have justice in our intention and Christ in our cause, with whom the 'hope of the poor shall not perish for ever.'* To him be the glory, both now and in the day of eternity.*

Mt 8:26

Ps 9:18
2 P 3:18

LENTEN SERMONS ON THE PSALM 'HE WHO DWELLS'

[IN THE SHELTER OF THE MOST HIGH]

INTRODUCTION

IN THE PAST when one set out to write something, it was the thing to do to say that one was incapable. And the finished work was to be rounded off by a plea for pardon for its imperfections. Today I am obliged to do just that. The only difference between now and then is that with me this is not just a literary cliché, but a simple truth. Anyone who knows anything about the existing state of bernardology will realize that obscure folk like myself have one common source of knowledge: the extensive writings of Jean Leclercq osb who, since over twenty years ago he first discovered a bernardine manuscript at Engelberg between two falls in the snow, has never ceased to enlighten us on the texts and writings of St Bernard. His waters are poured abroad for strangers to drink. Instead of giving at every step the precise reference to these studies, therefore, I prefer to indicate a select but substantial bibliography available to those who not only read French, but also have both the taste and the leisure for diving into what may at first glance appear dry sources. Experts will recognize when I am referring to one or other of these authorities. Those who are not experts, or who do not read French will, I hope, be pleased to have at least something to go by in English.

It was only after great hesitation that I set out on the venture of writing an Introduction to the texts which I have translated. Not much experience was needed to convince me that it was highly clownish of me to introduce the first two works, the four homilies *In Praise of the Virgin Mother* [published as *Magnificat: Homilies in Praise of The Blessed Virgin Mary* in 1979], and *On Conversion. A Sermon to Clerics*. I resolved for the future to mind my own business of translating, and to let someone more qualified get on with the introducing. However, man proposes and God disposes. Circumstances being what they are, and a more qualified authority having begged off for legitimate reasons, the love of Christ incites me and has the upper hand. May it cover the multitude of imperfections in this and the other introductions, and may the Holy Spirit convey to the reader that inner sweetness which springs from experience and leads to a deeper, existential understanding of Bernard's message. That having been said, let us get on with the business to hand.

The translation presented here goes by the title *Lenten Sermons on the Psalm 'He who dwells'.* The Latin text is to be found in *Sancti Bernardi Opera IV*, edited by Jean Leclercq osb and Henri Rochais (Rome, 1966) pages 383-492. In commenting upon this work, the first thing I must do, following Bernard's own example, is to examine the title.[1] According to it we would seem to be in presence of a series of spoken exhortations given to monks during a specific liturgical season. The group of seventeen sermons which forms a commentary on Psalm 90[2] is not only one of the most famous texts composed by Bernard, but also one of the most beautiful. Together with the homilies In Praise of the Virgin Mother, this group of sermons is considered one of the jewels of medieval christian literature. These sermons contain more than a doctrine of the spiritual life: they also offer us a typical example of St Bernard's style at its purest and loftiest. Its sprightliness might mislead the reader into thinking that this text as a whole is the fruit of improvised, spontaneous preaching and that they were uttered in a close time sequence. Any attentive reader, however, and even more any translator, cannot help wondering how Bernard managed to give forth such exquisite and untranslatable eloquence, even if we make allowances for the gift of the gab, as an English poet once called it. This leads us to ask whether the sermons were indeed preached. Are they not more akin to written sermons like the four homilies In Praise of the BVM, which in fact make up a sort of treatise written in the literary style of sermons but never pronounced by Bernard *viva voce* to any audience, monastic or other. This first question being set, we may widen the breach of critical assessment and ask whether the group of 'sermons' on psalm ninety does not form instead a treatise, written at ease and over a longer time space than would be allowed by a single lenten season. The various references which Bernard makes to his multiple occupations seem, if not to substantiate this query, at least to bring it within the realm of possibility. To pose these questions is to pose not only the problem of the genesis of the sermons on psalm ninety — to ask for the story of the text, if you like — but also that of the literery genre of the complete series, seventeen sermons in all, preceded by a preface.

Before tackling technical details, let us try to get some idea of St Bernard's basic insight. The fundamental theme of these sermons is the christian pilgrimage from conversion to consummation, the *consummatum est* of the divinized soul led by grace to the threshold of the eternal city. This journey is the natural pathway of the soul who sets out to follow Christ. We follow in the steps of the Master as he goes up secretly to Jerusalem for the feast. The journey starts in the wilderness where Christ was tempted. Out of this trackless waste, paths emerge. It is in the valley of death that there begins the long and winding uphill path which connects with the royal road, the way of the Cross leading to the City of the King of heaven and earth. But though we walk in the valley of the shadow of death, we have no reason to fear: God is there to protect those who hope in him and run forward by prayer, sustained by faith and humility. There are snares hidden along the way; the enemy lies in ambush. Prudence, humility and obedience will safeguard our steps; the lamp of God's word will enlighten our eyes. We must have recourse to the sacraments, penance and the holy eucharist, sharing in Christ's sufferings and imitating his life. The food of angels, the bread come down from heaven will be our viaticum. The only hurdle which might discourage us from setting out, i.e., the length of the journey, is thus forestalled. Yet in the desert even the bread of angels may become a source of temptation, as it was for Jesus. Let us but follow his example, resist the demon, and angels will come and minister to us, sojourners that we are in a foreign land. We know that the life of man on earth is one long temptation; therefore we pray our heavenly Father that we may not be led into temptation. Once we have turned back to the Lord in our hearts, we shall be beset by trials from all sides. Yet we have nothing to fear in our journey, neither during the night of adversity nor in the light of day, unless perhaps we are for a brief moment afraid and thus purified, for fear is a fiery furnace. And when all fear has been driven out, we are children of light walking by day and progressing along the path of salvation. But a terrible and subtle danger lies in the way: pride. If pride does not trip us up, then the crafty enemy will attack us with the love of money: this is the business that walks about in the darkness disguised as an angel of light. He waits in ambush for the heedless runner.

At all times, now and at the hour of our death, we have need of the invisible protection of truth. Christ remains hidden and absent, as it were. But this seeming divine absence must not perturb us. God will not abandon us. We must not worry, but carry Christ humbly in our bodies: he is a gentle weight. Along the road to Jerusalem, let us be like that little ass upon which the Saviour once graciously deigned to sit: 'Happy is the man who carries Christ in this way and merits to be led into the holy city by the Holy of holies himself. He has nothing at all to fear, he will suffer neither obstacles on the way nor rejection at the gate.' (QH 7.4) Whether we journey by land, sea or air, we have nothing to fear for he has given his angels such charge of us to guard us in all our ways that the enemy cannot even approach us. God our Father watches over his faithful until they arrive at that perfect and holy city whose borders are peace (QH 8:5). Faith, hope and charity are there to preserve us, if we will (QH 10.1). We need discernment as well to distinguish the way to go. We need help from on high because all the ways of the sons of Adam are corrupt, oriented to the necessity and avarice which lead to destruction and unhappiness (QH 11.3).

We must turn away from the pernicious heights of vanity and cruelty and follow the humble, lowly paths of mercy and truth (QH 11.8), directing our steps in these ways of the Lord. The first step along the path to the heavenly Jerusalem is the tender mercy which inclines a man to lament and repent, to weep and thus to reap the harvest of eternity. This first act of mercy is the first step of a man's return to the heart. It enables him to enter the secret places of the soul. All that remains for him now is to link up with the royal road. He must bring his actions into line with his thoughts. He must become as a little child; otherwise he will never enter the kingdom of heaven. 'In this way man will enter the ways of the Lord, ways of mercy and truth, the ways of life. And the end of all these ways is the salvation of the wayfarer' (QH 11.9). Although we are children and have a long and dangerous way to go, there is no need to fear: our angels, our guardians and trustees, are faithful, prudent, powerful. Even after death, they will carry us in their hands into Abraham's bosom, that is heaven, the bosom of the Father where dwells the eternal Son. Here below we must walk on the asp and the basilisk, trample underfoot the lion and the dragon, opposing the four virtues — courage, prudence, temperance, and humility — to these four dangers.

And then, sweet Lord Jesus, full of compassion towards his saints in tribulation, towards those who are running the last lap of the course, encourages us gently, saying, 'Come to me, all who labor and are heavy laden and I will refresh you.' (QH 15.1) We weep no longer for sin, but for joy and glad surprise. Tears well up in the eyes which are suddenly illumined and perceive, beyond the disguise, Christ who has purified his saint, substituting a burden of kindliness for the burden of sin. A man remains a beast of burden all his life long even though he may be a saint: God burdens us when he pardons us (QH 15.1). No longer content with the company of angels, such a soul aspires to the Lord of angels himself. He prays for this, longs that God who speaks to him should no longer be content to be present in his messenger, be no longer content to kiss him as it were by an intermediary, but to kiss him with the very kiss of his mouth (QH 15.2).

The fight is nearly over, the journey's end in sight: 'because he hoped in me, I will deliver him', says the Lord. We are approaching the end of our life-long Lent, we are drawing near the eternal Paschal Feast when God himself will be with us, when he will wipe away every tear from our eyes. Already we are assured of our resurrection, for Christ our Lord is risen. God is going to fill us with length of days, for tribulation leads to glory. He came down that he might be near the broken-hearted, the time is coming, *dies venit, dies tua in qua reflorent omnia*, when we shall 'be caught up together in the clouds to meet the Lord in the air; and so we shall always be with the Lord.' This happens on the condition, that here below we are anxious to have him as our fellow traveller, 'he who will restore the homeland to us in the future, or rather, who will be the way to the homeland.' (QH 17.4) Let us strive then for peace and holiness, for without these no one can see God (QH 17.6). And it is precisely that which is our journey's end: the face to face encounter with the Risen Christ, the blessed vision of peace accorded to the pure of heart.

Should anyone, entirely devoid of spiritual experience, wonder whether or not St Bernard's message is still relevant today, let him read these lines of a monk of the Russian Orthodox Church:

> Innumerable crowds of people have lovingly, obediently, walked in the footsteps of Christ, treading the long way, the tragic way which is shown by our Lord, a way tragic but which leads from this earth to the very throne of God, into the Kingdom of God. They walk, carrying their

crosses, they walk now for two thousand years, those who believe in Christ. They walk on, following him, crowd after crowd, and on the way we see crosses, innumerable crosses, on which are crucified the disciples of Christ. Crosses, one cross after the other, and however far we look, it is crosses and crosses again. We see the bodies of the martyrs, we see the heroes of the spirit, we see monks and nuns, we see the priests and pastors, but many, many more people do we see, ordinary, simple, humble people of God who have willingly taken upon themselves the cross of Christ. There is no end to this procession. They walk throughout the centuries knowing that Christ has foretold us that they will have sorrow on the earth, but that the Kingdom of God is theirs. They walk with the heavy cross, rejected, hated, because of truth, because of the name of Christ. They walk, they walk, these pure victims of God, the old and the young, children and grown-ups. But *where are we?* Are we going to stand and look; to see this long procession, this throng of people with shining eyes, with hope unquenched, with unfaltering love, with incredible joy in their hearts, pass us by? Shall we not join them, this eternally moving crowd, that is marked as a crowd of victims, but also as little children of the Kingdom? Are we not going to take up our cross and follow Christ? Christ has commanded us to follow him. He has invited us to the banquet of his Kingdom and he is at the head of this procession. Nay, he is together with each of those who walk. Is this a nightmare? How can blood and flesh endure this tragedy, the sight of all these martyrs, new and old? Because Christ is risen, because we do not see in the Lord who walks ahead of us the defeated prophet of Galilee as he was seen by his tormentors, his persecutors. We know him now in the glory of the Resurrection. We know that every word of his is true. We know that the Kingdom of God is ours if we simply follow him.[3]

This is the message which Bernard transmitted to his monks. It is the eternal theme of exodus, exile, and repatriation, the alternation of sorrow and joy, light and darkness. It is the divine command given to Abram, 'Go from your country to the land that I will show you', echoed across the centuries. Exodus, exile, repatriation, enacted by the mighty Word of God who leapt down from heaven, who came to his own who received him not. Christ, come from his Father and, going back to his Father, is the perfect model for every exile, every member of the pilgrim Church wandering and wondering here below till He come again. In that day night shall be no more, for the Lord God will be our light. He, the bright morning star, is coming, bringing his recompense, to repay every one of us for what we have done. Behold, he is coming soon. Such, in substance, is Bernard's experience.

THE LITERARY GENRE

The Middle Ages inherited from the ancient world of classical Latin certain rules to be followed depending whether one intended writing a sermon, a letter, a treatise, or any other of the then commonly accepted literary forms. In monastic literature — and thus *a priori*, in St Bernard's works — the sermon is the most frequent literary genre. We have the type of sermon which is strictly a homily, e.g. the style Bernard chose for writing his homilies on The Virgin Mother, in which the author was bent on explaining a given scriptural passage and on directing the sermons, spoken or written, or both, to some pastoral end. The sermon, which could be one of several types, was part and parcel of the monastic observance. We must not forget that many sermons were spoken, and have been lost to posterity. Of those which were written, the first copy often consisted of notes taken down by someone in the audience. And as the art of tironian shorthand known in patristic times had been lost and the system adopted in the thirteenth century had not yet come into being, these notes were more often than not only fragmentary. All that the auditor could hope to do was to take down more or less faithfully a sentence here and there. These fragmentary, skeletal sermons were sometimes left in this form and sometimes called in by the preacher who proceeded to correct them and occasionally to add his own profuse afterthoughts. Another possibility was that the preacher himself prepared his sermon on tablets of wax, jotting down the guidelines, often using mnemonic devices. He later completed and revised these block-note jottings, which were then copied in their emended form by a notary, a copyist, or, more rarely, the author himself.

In this connection, the examination of the manuscripts of St Bernard and his biographers reveals two tell-tale words: *dictare* (to dictate) and *scribere* (to write). In the twelfth century of St Bernard *dictare* meant in general to write, to compose, whereas *scribere* meant to recopy. The first step, the composition, was done on wax tablets which permitted numerous modifications; the second copy was definitive and therefore done on parchment. After it was finished only minor changes could be made. *Dictare*, when applied to St Bernard or any other author could mean one of two things: to dictate a rough copy or to dictate the finished text. The same word applied to a notary meant either to take notes from dictation or to compose a complete and full text with the help of these dictated notes. In order to understand this distinction, we must realize that in those days the sense of 'dictate' was not as restricted as in our time. Today we dictate to someone else a text which we may or may not have composed, whereas in the twelfth century one dictated to oneself or to someone else a text in the process of composition. An author composed aloud in such manner that his mouth dictated to a hand, his own or that of another person. In modern parlance we could compare the medieval 'dictation' to the elaboration of the manuscript (or first typescript) composed by an author.

The medieval *scribere*, 'writing', would be equivalent to work done by the modern copy-typist or printer. An example of this is offered us by the preface of the homilies on The Virgin. The Latin text begins *Scribere me aliquid et devotio iubet, et prohibet occupatio.* ('My devotion has been urging me to write something but so far my occupations have hindered me.') It would seem that we have here an instance in which Bernard himself was the copyist. Perhaps he had already 'dictated' a rough copy, an outline of something in praise of the Virgin Mother, but he had never found time to copy, or have it copied, that is to write or to have it written, on parchment. But now that illness prevented him from being in night choir, he had found a suitable opportunity for saying something by writing. (*Scribere me aliquid . . . loqui videlicet aliquid . . .*) If this supposition is true, there must have existed a no longer extant autograph of St Bernard in praise of the Virgin Mother. Whatever may be the case, there is no doubting that Bernard's oratorical activity is made up not only of sermons which he actually spoke, but also of those which he composed in writing without preaching them and still others which were composed more or less under his supervision but which again he never preached. In this last case, Bernard would have prepared a short outline giving the major themes and certain key-words, perhaps even paragraph headings followed by a brief summary which he wrote on wax and then confided to a faithful disciple well-acquainted with his styles — for he had more than one — and the lines along which his mind and heart worked. Some of these written sermons were then never preached, at least in their final form. Such seems to be the case with the final draft of the present work, which is really a sort of treatise dressed up as a series of sermons. Put more scientifically, this means that we have here a work whose literary genre is that of the sermon.

What, we may wonder, distinguishes the sermon from the treatise? Putting forward a tentative hypothesis we can suggest that the major distinction is rooted in the history of the development of expressed thought, and even in the history of thought itself. Man spoke before he wrote, and consequently he heard before he read. Originally the spoken word, the *sermo*, must have been direct spontaneous speech expressing the thought of one person and destined to seize the mind of one or more persons by the instrumentality of the ear. Being spontaneous, the original *sermo* would scarcely have had any preconceived structure. Its spontaneous regeneration and development would have blended with the hearer's reaction. A treatise, *tractatus*, on the other hand, would seem to have marked a development in the organization of thought leading to a preconceived structure and classification into mental categories. With the progress of time and the development of man's æsthetic senses there came to be certain rules of eloquence as well as certain norms for composing correctly. In the past, one never wrote without composing, without first drawing up a plan. Bernard inherited this art of composition from the great masters of classical Latin who in turn had inherited it from ancient Greece. Remember that originally literature was a *spontaneous* work of authors of genius: after them others, commenting on their works, drew up the laws of literary genre and principles of composition. As we have already seen, the sermon came to be one such genre and this itself was subdivided into various species. As for the treatise, it is difficult to define it precisely for it varied not only according to its source, but also according to the subject treated. But whatever the case, a treatise is always a *methodical* written discussion of some matter.

We are now in a position to understand the literary genre of QH. St Bernard refers to 'sermons' and we do seem at first appearance to be dealing with seventeen sermons. Yet some ancient manuscripts classify them as a treatise, and indeed when you take the thing to pieces, or try to translate it, you readily see that on the whole it is a methodical discourse on the spiritual combat revealing refinements of style which could hardly have been uttered on the spur of the moment. What then? We have a work which may be a 'hybrid'[4] – without this word being abusive. QH is neither a series of sermons nor a treatise nor a scriptural commentary. The intrinsic structure is that of a methodical plan of the spiritual combat, but the extrinsic form is that of the sermon. St Bernard had learnt rhetoric, the art of speaking well. He had the gift of eloquence, the gift of persuading by speech; he had learnt the art of writing in the school of the masters of ancient latinity. He loved God and his brethren. It was Lent, a season of unusual hardship and labour. And all that put together accounts for the commentary in the form of sermons which is QH, a treatise written in the literary genre of the sermon.

GENESIS OF THE TEXT

We have already seen that a more than cursory reading of QH poses the problem of the history of the text as we have it today. In order to solve it we must examine the manuscript tradition, which is extremely rich and complicated. The text was frequently copied, but the evidence afforded by one copy is sometimes contradicted by that of another manuscript, so much so that the editor of the 1966 edition found himself confronted with what seemed to be an inextricable tangle. After patient unsnarling it emerged that these sermons had been written in three stages: there are three recensions, from a first rough draft to the final complete series. Reading through the sermons, one readily conjectures that they cover a complete lenten period, even though this may have been made up of three successive Lents. Another conjecture, more probable, is that the 'writing' of the complete series had been interrupted, even though Bernard may, or may not, have dictated to himself or to a secretary the rough drafts.

Before going further into this delicate and possibly tedious question of manuscript evidence concerning the existence of three authentic recensions, let us settle the date of the finished product. This may be done on the basis of the internal evidence offered by the text itself.

Date

The Preface and the first sermons suggest the beginning of Lent. Paragraph 2 of the Preface mentions 'these days during which, as is only right, your fatigue is somewhat greater', and this is a reminiscence of chapter 49 of the Rule of St Benedict, concerning the observance of Lent. In this chapter St Benedict advises monks to add something to their usual ascetical practices. St Bernard's Preface is a sort of commentary on this chapter of the Rule, customarily read in cistercian monasteries on the first Sunday in Lent. Another witness in favour of this Sunday is found in the same paragraph of the Preface, 2[16:5] 'I have chosen that very psalm from which the enemy took occasion for tempting', says St Bernard referring to the Gospel narration for the first Sunday in Lent. Again, in paragraph one there are certain reminiscences of St Paul's second letter to the Corinthians, part of which was read on this same Sunday. Sermon 2.1[10] refers to the sheep and the goats mentioned in the Gospel for Monday of the first week of Lent. Sermon 3.1[3], 3.2[11], 3.5[1] contains quotations and reminiscences of (Vulgate) Psalms 48, 56, 54,[6] all three of which are chanted at divine Office on Tuesdays in keeping with the plan suggested by the Rule of St Benedict. Sermon 4.1[5,7] refers to an event in the life of Elijah as told in 1 Kings 19 and read on Ember Wednesday in Lent, the first week. All this evidence seems to point to the fact that the first four sermons make up a homogeneous group. In the introductory paragraph of Sermon Eight St Bernard in 'a few words of introduction' excuses himself for 'the length of yesterday's sermon' which seems to have caused him some trouble with the monks. And in Sermon 9.8[4] he cites from a paragraph of Lamentations which used to be read in cistercian monasteries on Thursday of the second week in Lent. Again, in Sermon 10.6, Bernard cites an incident in the life of St Bene-

dict as related by St Gregory in his *Dialogues* II,11 formerly
read during the third nocturn of Benedict's feast [21 March].
There is no reason to suppose for certain that this passage had
been read on the day Bernard preached this sermon, but it lies
within the realm of possibility, and even probability. Were this
to be the case, it would offer us a valuable factor towards finding an exact date. If we now refer to Sermon 6.7[20], we see that
Bernard winds up his preaching about the four temptations
with the words: 'That is all I wanted to say about these temptations, for I remember having dealt with them in one of the sermons on the Song of Songs when the occasion cropped up in
connection with the noonday rest of the bridegroom after
which the bride was inquiring.' Now, this theme is developed
in Sermon Thirty-three on the Song of Songs, and we know
that sc 24 was given after Bernard's return from Rome in the
fall of 1138: Sermon Thirty-three was probably written shortly
afterwards. It so happens that in the years between 1139 and
1153, the year Bernard died, if we exclude the years when he
was away from Clairvaux during Lent, the feast of St Benedict,
21 March, coincided with the second week of Lent — on Tues-
day, to be precise — only in 1139. This then may be taken as the
probable date for the completed manuscript of QH. It is under-
standable that Bernard would not have repeated his teaching on
the four temptations, but simply referred to a sermon written
a few months previously.

There is more such exciting evidence. If we take QH Sermon
Eleven, for example, we find that it opens with a reference to
the same pericope of Lamentations III read on Thursday in the
second week of Lent and mentioned in Sermon 9.8[4]. This same
Sermon 11.11[2] comes back again on this scriptural passage. The
following day Bernard gave Sermon Twelve — at least if we
may assume that he spoke the truth when he began: 'Yesterday,
if you remember . . .' In Sermon 13.11[1] he brings in witnesses
to testify to the fact that in the life to come the angels bear us
up on their hands. The first witness is St Benedict: 'Only a

little while ago you read of our blessed Father Benedict . . . ?

Jean Leclercq points out that although this passage of St Gregory's *Dialogues* (II, 31) is not to be found in MSS 114 at Dijon as part of the allotted office readings for the feast, it could well have been read in the refectory that day. Moreover, the eighth responsory and the *Benedictus* antiphon mention Germanus, bishop of Capua. In Sermon 16.2 Bernard connects the threefold help which we are to receive 'with the great triduum which we are soon going to celebrate.' But it was not yet Holy Week, for the sermon closes with two lines from the hymn *Summi largitor praemii* which was sung at Compline during Lent according to the hymnary of St Bernard. Finally, at the beginning of Sermon Seventeen, the last of the series, St Bernard says that 'we are about to celebrate the resurrection of the Lord.'

Recensions

Having settled by internal evidence and cross references to SC the date of the final recension of QH, let us now tackle the problem of the three different forms, the three recensions, in which these sermons are found. The study will seem a bit 'speleological', so to speak, but the results will be worth the trouble.

There are seventy-five primitive, i.e. twelfth and thirteenth century manuscripts of QH. They reveal that the series existed in three forms: a short one (S), a longer one (L) and a final perfect form (PF). The major characteristics of each group may be summarized as follows:

I. The Short Form (S)

1) The Preface is slightly shorter than in the final edition and the opening word is not *Considero* (I consider, rendered in this translation by the present participle Considering) but *Scio* (I know); the rest of the text has minor variations from L and PF.

2) The entire commentary comprises only the first six sermons which are presented as thirty fairly short fragments — sort

of sentences distinguished by their initials and often separated by titles such as, *On the first verse: He who dwells in the aid of the Most High.* This presentation will not surprise us if we recall that a preacher prepared his sermons, jotting down ideas and making use of mnemonic devices. Nor must we forget that people in the audience sometimes took down notes as best they could.

3) The text has many variants from the second and third editions. Sermon Six is particularly different, being a shortened version of sc 33.11-16 on the four temptations of the Church.

There exist nine ancient manuscripts of this short form, five of which were retained with a view to the establishment of the critical edition. Generally these manuscripts are found in collections of the liturgical sermons among those for Lent; often they are sandwiched between the sixth sermon for Lent and the Sermon for the Feast of St Benedict, 21 March.

II. The Longer Form (L)

1) The opening word of the Preface is *Considero.*

2) The text for Sermons One–Six is, on the whole the same as that in the short edition; it has the same divisions, but some specific modifications.

3) A kind of summary of Sermon Three is inserted between the closing words of this same sermon and Sermon Four. The gist of the sentence is that according to St Paul (Tm 6:9) the snare of the hunter means riches, and whoever flees and spurns them will be out of reach of the sharp word. But if someone should have become entangled in riches, he can strive to shake himself free by doing works of mercy and thus escape the sharp word of damnation.

4) The reference to sc 33.11-16 at the end of Sermon Six is followed by a short recapitulation of the passage referred to.

5) The commentary is continued up to verse 10, 'No evil shall befall you, no scourge come near your tent.' This supple-

ment to the short recension coincides with Sermons Seven–Ten of the final edition, except for minor variants.

III. *The Complete and Perfect Form* (PF)

This is the one edited form and is the basis of the 1966 edition. The opening word is *Considero;* the sentence inserted after Sermon Three (see II, 3 above) is suppressed. Sermons Four and Five are longer, but the recapitulation of SC 33.11-16 (see II, 4 above) is omitted. The commentary is carried through to the end giving a total of seventeen sermons. Two sermons, Thirteen and Fourteen, are devoted to verse 13: 'You will walk on the asp and the basilisk; you will trample underfoot the lion and the dragon.'

A glance at the accompanying map will show that QH manuscripts found their way to or were copied in over forty different monasteries in Europe. The perfect text was the only one kept at Clairvaux and this is quite normal. During the last years of his life, Bernard set to work on a careful literary revision of the greatest of his works. Once this editing had been done, there was no reason for the librarian to keep the two incomplete copies.

Provenance of early manuscripts of Lenten Sermons
on the Psalm 'He Who Dwells' (see p. 99)

BERNARD AS A WRITER

Without going into too much detail, let us take just a few examples from the Preface to show how Bernard proceeded with the very important stage in editing which is called in Latin *emendatio*. The examples, few as they are, testify to the presence of a cloud of other witnesses to Bernard's care to leave to posterity a work where, as he might have said, beauty and truth kiss each other in perfect harmony.

We have already seen that the first draft began with *Scio*, which became *Considero* in the second and the third versions. This change is significant: the use of the verb *to consider* suggests that Bernard was not only aware of the rough time his monks were having at the beginning of Lent, but was even preoccupied by it, turning it over in his mind and wondering what he could do for them. This change in the choice of the opening word gives an insight into Bernard's psychology as well as into his carefulness in expressing the full depth of his thought. Another, slighter, change is to be noticed in the substitution of *intrinsecus* (within) for *extrinsecus* (without). All Bernard did was to change the prefix (*in* for *ex*) but the new word alters the whole balance of meaning of the phrase. Today we read: '. . . you are being killed all the day long by much fasting and frequent labors in unusual watchings, in addition to *all that is going on within you*, contrition of heart and a multitude of temptations'. In the first draft the meaning of the text is '. . . by much fasting and frequent labors in unusual watching; in addition to *all those things going on without*, there is contrition of heart and a multitude of temptations'. The difference is slight but meaningful. In this same phrase we have another variant: in the first version there was temptation, whereas we now read about temptations, in the plural. The elegance of the change does not appear so clearly in English, but in Latin it helps reveal Bernard's artistry, for the use of the Latin plural ending in *um* not only gave greater force to the sentence but allowed a rhyme: the phrase also acquired swing—rhythm, if you prefer. Then again, a minor addition made for the final edition emphasizes the reason for everything that had gone before. Bernard, towards the end of paragraph one of the Preface explains that since what the brethren are putting up with is above their strength, then it must be because of the help of divine power that the enemy is defeated. The words *ex hoc* (in this way), which he added for the third edition make it evident that our victory against the devil is due to grace. This minor addition suggests a theology of the christian combat. Again, a little further on in this same first paragraph of the Preface we read, 'Who is it who upholds (*sustinet*) the entire bulk of the earth?' Had the translation been done on a manuscript of the first or second recension, we should have, 'Who is it who carries (*portat*) the entire bulk of the earth?' The verb 'to uphold' is certainly more apt in this context than 'to carry'. Moreover, it provides a logical internal lead for the twice-repeated use of *sustinere* in the Latin where we read, '*Nam si est aliquid quod sustineat cetera, ipsum a quo sustinetur?*' In the English rendering the repetition of the verb is a trifle ungracious, but shows Bernard's sense of sonority retained: 'And if there exists one single being *upholding* all the others, then by whom is he himself *upheld?*' The *portat* (carries) ousted by *sustinet* (upholds) in the first of these phrases comes into its own at the last: *Non invenitur nisi verbum virtutis omnia portans*: It is none other than the word of power which bears up all things. Here, the English 'bears up', selected on account of its use in the RSV of the Bible at Hebrews 1:3, is intended to get over to the reader a triple sense of carrying (conveyed by the Latin *portare*), upholding and sustaining (both suggested by *sustinere*).

Just one more example of Bernard's artistry, if you will. To sense more easily the finesse of the Latin, let us set out from the English. The phrase we have translated as 'Who is it that upholds the entire bulk of the earth?' (cf. Is 40:12) could just as well have been rendered, 'Who is it who upholds the earth's entire bulk?' The inversion allowed by the use of the genitive helps us to understand why Bernard in his final edition inverted the *totam terrae molem* of the first and second and wrote *totem molem terrae*: the inversion brought his sentence more into line with the biblical reminiscence he had in mind; another possible cause is that, for reasons of euphony, his sensitive ear rejected the succession of dentals in *totam terrae molem*. It would be out of place, and tedious too, to continue dissecting texts testifying to Bernard's talent as a writer. There is however more to good writing than just fiddling around with words; there is also the art of composition. Bernard knew this. He knew that a careful, though flexible, framework or skeleton was necessary to good prose. Let us lay bare the bones of Sermon Two, which is built up on a succession of binary factors, and we shall see how he used his talent and his learning.

The doctrine of St Bernard in Sermon Two may be schematised in the following way:

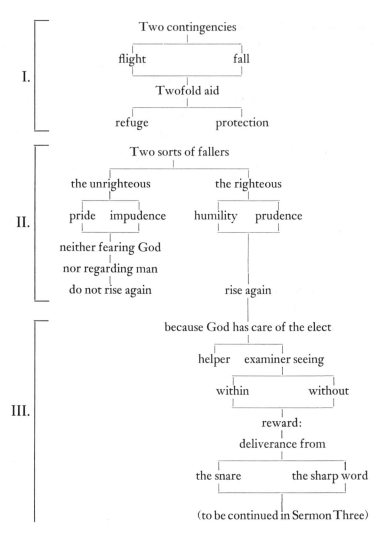

This enables us to distinguish three major sections: I. the introductory section in which Bernard treats of the sorry plight of man here below and God's twofold aid. This introduces the theme of the divine protection afforded those who stumble on the path of life and merit either salvation or damnation at the final judgement. II. These are the goats, the unrighteous on the left hand, and the sheep, the righteous on the other. The goats are condemned because of their self-sufficiency, the pride and impudence of those who neither fear God nor regard men. This God-man couplet recalls part I on the economy of salvation, God saving fallen man, which is the dominant note of the sermon. Parallel to the fall of the wicked is that of the righteous who, because of their humility and prudence, fall into God's hands and thus rise again. This comparison completes section II and Bernard takes the notion of God as his springboard for section III dealing with the recompense of the righteous. God's all-seeing eye perceives man's inward and outward reactions to grace. The reward is deliverance from temptation and damnation, which is what is meant by the snare and the sharp word — as Bernard goes on to explain in Sermon Three.

THE DOCTRINE OF QH

When Bernard set out to preach to his monks he had in view their salvation in Christ through the Church and the sacraments. He devoted the complete series of sermons to God's will to save and our will to be saved, our readiness to share in Christ's passion and cross and thus share if possible in the glory of his resurrection.

Our first step along the way of salvation is to dwell in the aid of the Most High, not trusting in our own strength (1.1[1]) but giving ourselves up to watching, fasting and prayer. Our eyes must be firmly fixed on God so that we are not led to morbid introspection, to seeing our own weakness instead of counting on grace (1.2). Once we are under the protection of the God of heaven — which is not to be confused with his presence, enjoyed only by the angels (1.4) — we may confidently expect that in temptation God will be our refuge and our protector, provided we remain humble and prudent, knowing that temptation lies on every side. We must be constantly mindful that

God looks down upon the righteous and the unrighteous (2.3). Temptations lie on every side, up and round and down and about, but if we are like prudent harts we shall long after flowing streams and live on in God's love by humbling ourselves under his mighty hand and obeying our superiors (3.1). Avoiding avarice by the practice of poverty we shall live in thanksgiving, being delivered from the sharp word, eternal damnation, by the merits of Christ's sufferings. But this implies our hearing with a ready ear the hard word calling us to do the penance (3.3) which will make us worthy to share in Christ's passion, to eat his flesh and drink his blood in the Sacrament of the altar, living for God by faith and abiding in him through love. We have every right to rejoice in the grace thus proposed to us, but we may not yet feel secure like St Andrew running to meet his cross. We are a long way from our passion, and we might fall back before the end of our lifelong Lent, failing to cross the Red Sea and turning back in our hearts to Egypt.

We know the way. It is long and beset with dangers, but there is nothing to fear. Besides the bread of angels received in the Sacrament of the altar there is the bread of the word of God to comfort us. This should encourage us to resist the temptations which our divine Lord underwent before us (3.2). Our hidden life of penance and prayer is a holy mystery (4.3). And the promise of the future life is assured us if we live the hidden life totally content to be rebuffed and rebuked, if we dwell under the shadow of the Holy Spirit by whom Blessed Mary bore fruit for the salvation of the world.

Satan is ready to sift us as wheat (5.1), but no temptation will overcome us if we watch and pray, for we are shielded by divine grace. However dark may be the night of temptation and adversity (6.1) the shield of grace is always there to protect us, especially at the beginning of our conversion. Like little children in a storm, we may sometimes be afraid, but even this fear will work for our purification (6.2). Even those of us who are in the illuminative way (6.3) must be on our guard against the swift flying arrow of vainglory. There will be no danger if we shelter behind the shield of truth, the greatest enemy of vanity. Examination of conscience will help us fight this vice (6.3). A final ruse of the enemy of mankind is illusion (6.6) but truth will have the upper hand.

We need the protection of truth during our life and at the moment of death; hope gives us confidence. Yet we must do our bit during life's journey and manfully carry our luggage like some beast of burden. Our burden is Christ himself riding into the Holy City — how could we go astray? (7.4). Christ is on our backs and yet he has already gone ahead to prepare a home for us.

The way to Heaven is sure. God himself has predestined us to glorification. No devilish trick can mislead us for God has given his angels charge to guard us in all our ways, to be to our right and to our left, behind and before, as long as we ourselves do not become drowsy and fall asleep, but keep to the hard ways for God's sake. And there is no special merit here, for God loved us before we loved him; and he loves us so much that at the resurrection of the dead he will render to every man his due so that, like the stars in the firmament, each one will shine with an eternal light differing from all others in brightness.

Whatever may be the circumstances here below, however dark the night, however stormy the sea, God is our hope (9.5). For him we count everything as loss, we throw everything away, for God is our great and only hope. To live by hope, in hope, is faith. Our hope, our faith are founded on the rock of Christ's passionate love. He said, 'Greater love has no man than this, that a man lay down his life for his friends.' Perfect love thirsts after the Most High (9.8) and the singleness of purity leads the soul to seek him. This is perfection, and perfect detachment. Ardent love rejoices that the Beloved ascends to the Father, where he will take his place as the co-equal of the Most High.

Although Christ has ascended on high, we must never forget

that we are still pilgrims and therefore able to lose our way, to
wander about here and there instead of keeping to the king's
highway. Discernment is necessary for us if we are to select the
right path, to avoid not only our own ways but also those of the
demons: presumption and obstinance. Therein lies the danger
of contempt, impenitence and a hardened heart (11.5). The
remedy is humility and self-knowledge. In contrast to the demonic ways there are the ways of the angels, ascending and descending: ascending to the contemplation of God; descending
for man's protection. Then there are the ways of the Lord:
mercy and truth. When he comes again he will bow down the
swollen hills, trampling down the pernicious heights of vanity
and cruelty, treading lightly on the paths of mercy and truth.
Men and angels may also walk along these holy ways. For man,
mercy is the beginning of the return to his heart, and is thus the
path of salvation (11.9). To return to one's heart is to become
like a little child and to walk in the ways of humble truth. For
angels, the path of truth is contemplation of the divine face, the
path of mercy is to keep us in all our ways. This is the charge
they have received from God, a singular proof of his esteem and
love (12.4). Little children though we may be, we have nothing to fear under such guardians. They will help us over the
dangers of this mortal life and carry us up to heaven, provided
we ourselves are vigilant to the very end, watching against the
obstinance which is the ruin of all true religion (13.3). We
must be pure, peaceable and gentle, free of envy and anger, and
giving place to meekness and longanimity (13.4-6).

All these things are a gift of grace for which we must thank
the Father from whom comes every perfect gift. Is not man as
great as the gift itself? (14.1). We have every reason to be
grateful, for the two gifts, being and having, are entirely gratuitous, received without either our meriting them or toiling for
them (14.2). Finally, there is the gift of redemption. O happy
fault! And the blessed Incarnation. Four free gifts and ten holy
commandments (14.4). Fourfold thanks be to God. Let the

hosts of wickedness not prevent us from giving thanks or lead us to seal God's graciousness with our ungraciousness. Beware the sins of the flesh, vain glory, deceit and all root of bitterness, anger, rebellion, greed and vanity (14.9).

But this makes heavy going! The road is long and winding. 'Come to me, all who labor and are heavy laden, and I will refresh you', says the Lord (15.1). Christ's burden is sweet, and grace is the greatest burden he lays upon us. It is the burden of his kindness that weighs us down: no wonder that we weep! We are accustomed to sin and unkindness, and the gentle Lord Jesus gives grace and kindliness. No longer content to kiss us by an intermediary, whether sinful man or winged messenger, he kisses us with the very kiss of his mouth. The road was long and wound uphill all the way, but at dawn, the Sun of righteousness has risen for us, pledge of the fruit of our own participation in his paschal mystery. He will fill us with length of days and show us his salvation. The hope of glory lies in present tribulation, 'this slight momentary affliction is preparing for us an eternal weight of glory'.

Emmanuel, God with us, let me be with you in tribulation; break my heart that I may have you near me in my tribulation; let me embrace you in tribulation: for who have I in heaven but you and there is nothing I desire on earth beside you. Fill me with length of days. God eternal, show me your salvation, your Jesus so that for all eternity I may see him in whom I have believed, whom I have loved, for whom I long, your Jesus, our Lord, who is God blessed for ever.

MARIE-BERNARD-SAÏD OSB

Abbaye du Sacre-Coeur
Oriocourt

NOTES

1. SC 1: IV.6: '*Sed quid? Titulum praeterimus?*'.

2. Psalm 90 in the Vulgate enumeration familiar to St Bernard is by the Hebrew numbering psalm 91. While direct references to it in the sermons have been left in the form by which Bernard knew the psalm, scriptural citations in the margins here, as elsewhere in this volume, conform to the numbering of *The Jerusalem Bible*, which follows the Hebrew text.

3. Anthony Bloom, *Meditations on a Theme. A Spiritual Journey* (London: A. R. Mowbray, 1972) 124-5.

4. I would like to thank Monsieur Robert Bultot, researcher at the Institut Interfacultaire des Études Médiévales of the University of Louvain, for the *Note* which he communicated to me on the subject of literary genres. I found his word 'hybrid', applied to QH, very enlightening.

5. Because QH contains so many biblical references, I have adopted a method of reference using Sermon, paragraph, and number of citation within that paragraph. For example, 3.1^3 means Sermon Three, paragraph one, the third citation.

6. As cited, Ps 49:12, 57:5, 55:6.

LENTEN SERMONS ON THE PSALM
'HE WHO DWELLS'

THE PSALM

1. He who dwells in the shelter of the Most High will abide under the protection of the God of Heaven.

2. He will say to the Lord: you are my protector and my refuge; my God, in him will I hope.

3. For he has delivered me from the snare of the hunters and from the sharp word.

4. He will overshadow you with his shoulders: and under his wings you will hope.

5. His truth will cover you with a shield: you will not fear the terror of the night;

6. Nor the arrow that flies by day, nor the bogy that prowls in the darkness, nor assault, nor the noonday devil.

7. A thousand may fall at your side, ten thousand at your right hand, but you it will not approach.

8. You will but consider with your eyes and see the sinners' recompense.

9. Because you, O Lord, are my hope: you have made the Most High your refuge.

10. No evil shall befall you, no scourge come near your tent.

11. For he has given his angels charge of you to guard you in all your ways.

12. On their hands they will bear you up, lest you dash your foot against a stone.

13. You will walk on the asp and the basilisk; you will trample underfoot the lion and the dragon.

14. Because he hoped in me I will deliver him, I will protect him because he has known my name.

15. He will call to me and I shall answer him; I am with him in trouble, I shall rescue him and honor him.

16. With length of days will I satisfy him and show him my salvation.

PREFACE

1. CONSIDERING YOUR EFFORTS,
brothers, not without great stirrings
of compassion, I wonder what comfort I may offer you, and there comes to my mind something to do with the flesh. But this would be of no profit,* and in fact may even be harmful. For, however slight the cheating we do in sowing, the loss in harvesting is not slight, and if I were to lessen your penance out of cruel compassion, your crown would gradually come to lose its jewels.

Jn 6:64

What are we to do then? Where is the prophet's tidbit?* For there is death in the pot,† and you are being killed all the day long* by much fasting and frequent labors* in unwonted watchings,* in addition to all that is going on within you, contrition of heart and a crowd of temptations. You are being killed, but for the sake of him who died for you. In this way, if for him you share abundantly his sufferings, you will also share abundantly in comfort through him,* and thus your soul will come to delight in him and refuse to be comforted by anything else.* Close to him, this great tribulation* will discover sure consolation. Are you not, in fact, enduring something beyond human strength, beyond nature, and quite different from what you are accustomed to? Someone else is bearing it for you, therefore, and without any doubt it is he who bears all things by his

*2 K 4:41/†*Ibid.*
Rm 8:36
2 Co 11:27-8
2 Co 11:23

2 Co 1:5

Ps 77:2-3
Rev 7:14

Heb 1:3

word of power.* The enemy is now being struck down by his own sword, and the greatness of the tribulation by which he usually tempts you is instead overcoming temptation; is this not the surest proof of divine presence? For what need have we to be afraid when he who upholds all things is with us? The Lord is the defender of my life; of whom shall I be afraid?* For even though I walk through the valley of the shadow of death, I fear no evil, for you are with me.* Who is it that upholds the whole weight of the earth?* And upon whom does the whole world rest? Now if there exists some being who upholds all others, then by whom is he himself upheld? It is none other than the word of power which bears all things.* For by the word of the Lord were the heavens made and all their power by the breath of his mouth.*

Ps 27:1

Ps 23:4

Is 40:12

Heb 1:3

Ps 33:6

2. Therefore, that you may find consolation in God's word, particularly in these days during which, as is quite right, your fatigue is somewhat greater, I trust it will be not unuseful to talk to you about something in Holy Scripture, as some of you have already asked me to do. To this purpose I have chosen that very psalm by which the enemy seized an opportunity for tempting,* so that thereby the arms of the wicked one will be crushed* with the passage which he presumed to usurp to his own ends. And here, brothers, I want you to know* that those people who usurp for unholy purposes any part of Holy Scripture and hold back the truth of God by lies,* as some are sometimes given to doing, are clearly imitators of the

Mt 4:10-11

Ps 74:14

Rm 1:13

Rm 1:18

enemy. Beware of this, dear ones, for it is a very devilish thing, and those who, for their own ruin, attempt to pervert the saving writ prove that they are on his side. But I will not linger over this. It is enough, I believe, to have touched upon the matter briefly. Now, with the Lord's help, let us try to examine and explain something about the psalm we have chosen.

SERMON ONE

On the First Verse:

HE WHO DWELLS IN THE SHELTER OF THE
MOST HIGH WILL ABIDE UNDER THE
PROTECTION OF THE GOD OF HEAVEN

1. THE BEST MEANS of recognizing someone who dwells in divine shelter is by looking at those who do not dwell there. You will find they are of three types: the first do not hope; the second have given up hoping; and the third hope in vain. For if anyone fails to make God his refuge, trusting in his own strength and the abundance of his riches,* he does not dwell in the shelter of God. He turns a deaf ear to the advice of the prophet, 'Seek the Lord while he may be found, call upon him while he is near.'* And seeking only temporal goods, he is envious of wrongdoers;* seeing the prosperity of the wicked† he is far removed from the help of God,* which he supposes he does not need.

But what have we to do with judging outsiders?* My fear, brothers, is that among us there may be someone who is not dwelling in the shelter of the Most High, but trusting in his strength and in the abundance of his riches. Possibly someone who is zealous and much given to

Ps 52:8, 49:6

Is 55:6

Ps 37:1/†Ps 73:3
Cf. Ps 22:9

1 Co 5:12

119

watching, fasting, and labors* and other such
things, but who thinks that he has long since
amassed a whole wealth of merits and, trusting
in this, has grown less than careful about the
fear of God.* In this dangerous security he has
slipped into idle and curious habits and goes
about grumbling, slandering, and criticizing.
Had he but made a habit of dwelling in the shelter of God, he would now look to himself and
fear to offend Him whom he would realize full
well is still necessary to him. He ought to fear
God* all the more, and be all the more careful,
in that he has received so many more of His
gifts. Without Him, we cannot hold or preserve
what we have received from Him. But—and this
is something which I am unable to speak of or
regard without sorrow—there are some people
who at the beginning of their conversion are
fairly god-fearing and careful until they have
made a good start in their new way of life, and
then, although they ought to yearn for much
more—in keeping with the words, 'Those who
eat me will hunger for more'*—they start be-
having as if to say: 'Why should we go on doing
our service when we have now received all that
is to be given?' Oh, if you only knew* how
little what you have is and how quickly you
will lose it if he who gave it to you does not also
preserve it for you. Those two thoughts are
salutary and can make us careful and subject
enough to God* as not to be among those who
do not dwell in the shelter of the Most High
just because they fail to consider how necessary
it is to them. These are the people who do not
hope in the Lord.*

2 Co 6:5

2 Co 7:1

Cf. Tob 1:10,
Sir 1:20

Sir 24:29

Jn 4:10

Ps 62:2, 6

Pr 16:20

2. But there are also some who have lost hope. At the sight of their own weakness, they falter and stumble from faintness of spirit,* dwelling in their own bodies and always harping on their own frailty and ever ready to pour out all their woes. As soon as you take notice of them, their imagination flares up. They certainly do not dwell in the shelter of God, and they do not even know what it is because they are unable to stretch up far enough to think about it. There are still others who, though they hope in God, do so in vain because they flatter themselves in the hope of his mercy so much that they neglect to mend their sinful ways. Altogether vain is this hope.* It leads to their downfall because there is no love in it. Against these the prophet says: 'Cursed the man who sins in hope.'* And another says: 'The Lord takes pleasure in those who fear him, and those who hope in his mercy.'* Before saying 'those who hope', he expressly mentions 'those who fear him'. A man's hope is vain indeed when he rejects grace out of contempt and empties his hope out completely.

3. None of these three dwells in the shelter of the Most High. The first dwells in his merits, the second in his woes, and the third in his vices. The third person's dwelling is unclean, the second's is uneasy, the first's is foolish and reckless. What could be more foolish than to take up one's dwelling in a house which has hardly been begun? Do you think it has already been finished?* But when a man has finished, he is just then beginning.* What is more, this dwelling place is crumbling to ruins. What you ought to do is to prop it up and reinforce it rather than

Ps 55:8

Sir 34:1

not scriptural

Ps 147:11

Lk 14:30
Sir 18:6

Lk 6:49

live in it. Is not this present life frail and un-
stable? And anything founded upon it must
necessarily resemble it. Does anyone think he
can build a solid building on a shaky foundation?* So the dwelling of those who place their
hope in their own merits is dangerous; dangerous because falling to ruins. As for those who
despair when they think about their own infir-
mities, their house is uneasy and, as we have
said, they dwell in torments. For besides suffering from troubles which beset them day and
night, they are tormented still more by troubles
which have not yet fallen on them, and to such
an extent that the day's trouble is not sufficient

Cf. Mt 6:34

to the day,* but they are overwhelmed by trouble which they will probably never experience.
Can anyone think of a more unbearable hell?
Especially when they are overwrought with so
much effort and take no comfort in the bread

Jn 6:31

from heaven?* These people do not dwell in
the shelter of the Most High because they
despair. The first do not even seek to do so,
because they feel no necessity for it. But the
second are far from it because they seek God's
help in such a way they can never get to it. The
only people who dwell in the shelter of the
Most High are those whose sole desire is to receive it, whose sole fear is to lose it, and who

Augustine, *De
Trinitate* XII.14;
Cf. William of St
Thierry, *Ep aur*
279; CF 12:100

ponder it carefully and diligently—which surely is piety, the worship of God.* Happy indeed
is he who dwells in the shelter of the Most High,
for he will abide under the protection of the

Gen 1:9, Jb 28:24

God of heaven. Is there under heaven* anything that can harm the person whom the God

Gen 24:7

of heaven* has decided to protect and preserve?

The powers of the air are under heaven, this
present evil age* is under heaven and also the
spirit lusting against the flesh.*

4. Nothing better could be said than 'under
the protection of the God of heaven', because
anyone who deserves to have this protection
will be able to fear nothing under heaven, and
thus, as the prayer goes on in the next verse:
HE WHO DWELLS IN THE SHELTER OF THE
MOST HIGH WILL ABIDE UNDER THE PROTEC-
TION OF THE GOD OF HEAVEN. HE WILL SAY
TO THE LORD, 'YOU ARE MY PROTECTOR.'
And in this way, the words 'he will abide under
the protection of the God of heaven' explain
the preceding ones: HE WHO DWELLS IN THE
SHELTER OF THE MOST HIGH. Perhaps more than
that it is meant to teach us that we should
seek not only shelter in order to do good, but
also the protection which will deliver us from
evil.* Pay careful attention,† too, that it says
'under the protection' and not 'in the presence.'
An angel rejoices in His presence; all I ask is to
be able to abide under his protection! The angel
is happy in his presence; all I ask is to be secure
under his protection. And [the psalmist] says
'the God of heaven.' There is, of course, no
doubt about his being everywhere, but he is in
heaven in such a way that, by comparison, he
does not seem to be on earth. So when we pray,
we say, 'Our Father, who art in heaven.'* So it
is with our soul: for though it is in the whole
body, it is more especially localized in the head
where all the senses meet, whereas in the rest of
the members there seems to be only one sense —
namely, touch — and insofar as it is in some way

Gal 1:4

Gal 5:17

*Mt 6:13/†Pr 23:1

Mt 6:9

in the head, it seems rather to govern the other members than to dwell in them. So, in the same way, when we think of that presence which gives joy to the angels, we can scarcely put the same name to the protection of God. And 'he will say to the Lord, you are my protector'. But let us hold that over for another sermon.

SERMON TWO

On the Second Verse:

HE WILL SAY TO THE LORD: YOU ARE

MY PROTECTOR AND MY REFUGE:

MY GOD, IN HIM SHALL I HOPE

1. HE WHO DWELLS in the shelter of
the Most High, says the prophet, will
say to the Lord, 'you are my protector
and my refuge: my God, in him shall I hope.'* Ps 91:1-2
He will say it with thanksgiving,* praising God 2 Co 4:15
and his mercy* for his twofold shelter. Every- Ps 107:8
one who is still dwelling in this shelter, and not
yet in the Kingdom, often needs to take flight,
and yet sometimes he falls. Yes, I tell you, while
we are in the body,* we have to flee from the 2 Co 5:6
presence of pursuing temptation. And if we
sometimes do not flee quickly enough, as happens, we are buffeted and thrown down, but the
Lord protects us.* When someone comes along Ps 3:5
to pelt us in our pressing flight with the dung
of plodding oxen, He is our refuge, and we are
enabled to escape the filthy stoning.* He is our Sir 22:1-2
protector, too, so that, even when we fall, we
are not bruised, because the Lord stays us with
his hand.* Therefore, when we feel the urge to Ps 37:24
temptation in our thoughts, let us at once flee
to him and humbly ask help. And if it should

125

happen, as it sometimes does, that we flee to him less swiftly than we ought, let us be all the more solicitous that the Lord's hand may hold us up.* For everyone, as long as he is detained in this present age, must necessarily fall sometimes, but whereas some are bruised in their falling, others are not because the Lord upholds them with his hand.* And how may we distinguish the one from the other so we may, following the Lord's own example, separate the sheep from the goats,* the righteous from the unrighteous? Even the righteous man falls seven times a day.*

Ps 18:35

Ps 37:24

Mt 25:32
Pr 24:16

2. In fact, the only difference in their falls is that the righteous is protected by the Lord, and therefore rises again stronger than before, whereas when the wicked stumbles, he finds no help in arising again.* Truth to tell, he falls either into shameful harm or into shamelessness. Either he makes excuses for what he has done — and this is shame bringing in sin* — or else he has the harlot's brow* and neither fears God nor regards man,* but proclaims his sin like Sodom.* But the righteous falls into God's hands, and in some marvelous way even his sin works for his justice. For we know that everything works for the good of those who love God.* Does not that very fall work for our good, when by it we become more humble and more cautious? Does not the Lord protect anyone who falls, who is protected by humility? 'I was pushed hard and falling', says the prophet, but he who pushed me gained nothing because the Lord protected me.'* Thus may the faithful soul say to the Lord: 'You are my protector'. All creatures may say, 'You are my creator'; even

Ps 41:8

Sir 4:25
Jer 3:3
Lk 18:4
Is 3:9

Rm 8:28

Ps 112:13

the animals may say, 'You are my shepherd'; all
men may say, 'You are my redeemer.'* But only
he who dwells in the shelter of the Most High
may say, 'You are my protector.' So he adds,
'And my God.' Why not 'our God'? Because,
though he is the God of all* in creation, redemption, and other benefits common to us all,
yet in their temptations it is the elect alone who
have him, as it were, as their own. For he is
ready to protect the falling soul, to draw to
himself the fleeing soul in such a way that he
seems to have left everything else,* to take care
of that single soul.

3. Therefore every soul should look upon
God as being his very own, not only helper, but
also examiner. Who could ever become careless
if he had his eyes constantly fixed upon God
whose eyes are constantly turned towards him?
Again, when God is looking down on him,
never at any moment failing to see what is going
on both within and without, searching and
judging not only his actions, but even the most
subtle motions of his soul, how could he fail to
consider him specifically his God? And therefore, not without grounds can he say, MY GOD,
IN HIM WILL I HOPE. Notice that he did not say,
'I hoped', or 'I hope', but 'I will hope.' As much
as to say, this is my vow and my resolution, this
is the intention of my heart.* This is my hope,
laid up in my bosom,* and in this will I persevere, for 'In him will I hope.' I shall not despair,
nor shall I hope in vain, for 'woe to the man
who sins in hope',* and no less to him who sins
in despair. I will not be one of those who do
not hope in the Lord: in him will I hope. This

Ps 19:15

Sir 36:1

Lk 5:11

Heb 4:12
Jb 19:27

Cf. I.2 *supra*

is what he says. But now, what about the fruit, the reward, the prize? HE SHALL DELIVER ME FROM THE SNARE OF THE HUNTERS, AND FROM THE SHARP WORD. But we will put off explaining this snare and this word to another day and, if you do not mind, to another sermon.

SERMON THREE

On the Third Verse:

FOR HE HAS DELIVERED ME FROM THE
SNARE OF THE HUNTERS AND
FROM THE SHARP WORD

1. BROTHERS, BY THIS WORD,* 'he has delivered me from the snare of the hunters', I am stung to kindness towards myself and I take great pity on my own soul.* Does this mean that we are beasts? Beasts through and through, for man when he was in honor did not understand: he is compared to senseless beasts.* Yes, men are beasts, straying sheep without a shepherd.* How can you be proud, O man?* How can you puff yourself up for your smattering of knowledge? Look, you have become a beast for whom the hunters lay snares. And who are these hunters? They are the worst and most wicked, the most callous and cruelest hunters. They are hunters who, in order not to be heard, never sound the horn but shoot the blameless from ambush.* They are the leaders of this present darkness,* so extraordinarily cunning in their slyness and wicked in their devilish deceit that in comparison to them even the most astute man is like a beast before hunters. Those who, like the apostle, are not ignorant of their designs,* and those whom

Rm 13:9

Sir 30:24

Ps 49:12
Mt 9:36
Sir 10:9

Ps 64:10
Eph 6:12

2 Co 2:11

1 Co 1:21

*2 Co 2:8
†Ps 144:12

Heb 5:14

Rm 14:5

*Cf. Augustine,
*En.in Ps.*41:3;
CCh 38:461
†Ps 42:1

Est 16:6

1 P 5:6

Gen 27:8

2 Co 2:11

1 Tm 6:9

the wisdom of God* has allowed to discover the wiles of the wicked, are the exception. I beg you,* new plants of God,† you have senses not yet trained to distinguish good from evil,* do not follow the judgment of your heart, do not luxuriate in your senses,* lest the wily hunter deceive you, as yet inexperienced. For the beastly beasts of the forest — I mean men of the world — he lays his snares fairly openly, because he never doubts he will easily catch them. But for you, who are like warier harts, deadly* serpents longing after flowing streams,† he hides his snares with greater skill, and beguiles you with the false trickery of his arguments.* I beg you, then, humble yourselves under the mighty hand of God* your shepherd, and obey the words* of those who, having been taught by daily practice and long experience — both their own and many others' — have come to know better this hunter's craftiness.

2. But now that we recognize both hunters and beasts, let us examine the snares. I do not want to make up anything, or pass along anything doubtful. The apostle points out this snare to us; he is not ignorant of the hunters' designs.* Tell us, I beg you, holy Paul, what is this snare of the devil from which the faithful soul rejoices to have been delivered? 'Those who desire to be rich in this world', he answers, 'fall into temptation and into the devil's snare.'* Does this mean that this world's riches are the devil's snare? How few there are, alas, who would rejoice for having been delivered from this snare! How many there are who regret not being more caught up in it and who strive with might and

main to become more ensnarled and entangled!
But you, you who have left everything* to follow the Son of Man who has nowhere to lay his
head,* rejoice and say, 'He has delivered me
from the snare of the hunters.' Give thanks to
him* with all your heart and with all your soul,
and with all your strength* and give him thanks
from the very marrow of your heart, saying,
'He has delivered me from the snare of the
hunters.' And in order to grasp how great are
these benefits and to know they are given you
by God, listen to the next words: AND FROM
THE SHARP WORD. O man, or rather, O beast, are
you not afraid of the snare? Then fear the axe!
Did he not say, 'From the sharp word'? And
what is this word if not that of insatiable hell:
'Bring them along, bring them along, cut them
down, tear them to bits, kill them off quickly,
hasten to drag away the spoils.' What else is
this, if not a sharp word: 'Let the wicked be
carried off so he may not see the majesty of the
Lord'?* Is this not how hunters gloat over a
captured beast, crying out and saying, 'Away
with it, away with it! Poke in the spit, bring
along the coals and dump it into boiling caul-
drons'? Again, it was a sharp word which the
rebellious house,* the people the Jews,† howled:
'Away with him, away with him!'* How terrible that word, how sharp, how cruel! Their
teeth are indeed spears and arrows, and their
tongues are sharp swords.* Lord, you bore this
sharp word. Why did you do it, if not to deliver us from the sharp word? Of your kindness, grant that we do not endure what you
deigned to endure for our sakes.

Mt 19:27-8

Mt 8:20

Ps 100:3
Mk 12:30

Is 26:10

*Ezk 2:5
†1 Mac 8:20
Jn 19:15

Ps 57:5

Mt 3:2

Jn 6:61

Mk 4:11

Jn 6:54

Jn 6:67

1 P 4:13

Eph 3:17

1 Co 1:30
1 Jn 4:16

2 Co 4:17

Mt 3:2

Ps 112:7
Mt 25:41
Lk 12:5

Mt 11:30

3. When we encourage them to do penance,* men of the world may answer, 'This is a hard saying.'* This is what we read in the Gospel. The Lord was speaking of penance, but in parables, as though to those to whom it is not given to know the secret of the kingdom of God.* And when they had heard him say, 'Unless you eat the flesh of the Son of Man, and drink his blood,'* they answered, 'This is a hard saying!', and they drew back.* But what does it mean to eat his flesh and drink his blood, if not to share in his sufferings* and to imitate the way of life he led in the flesh? So the holy Sacrament of the altar in which we receive the body of the Lord teaches us that just as the bread enters our body, so our Lord enters us, in order to dwell in our hearts through faith.* For when justice enters, he whom God the Father made our righteousness* enters. And he who abides in love abides in God, and God in him.* But there are still many who say to us, 'This is a hard saying.' But is this hardness not merely a slight, momentary affliction working within us an eternal weight of glory beyond comparison?* Is it so hard to buy back by a very brief and fleeting labor those torments and sufferings which will last eternally and which no mind can ever conceive? Does it seem sharp to you to be told 'Repent'?* You are mistaken. Listen to another sharp word, another hard saying, an evil tiding:* 'Depart, you cursèd, into eternal fire.'* Yes, I tell you, fear this,* consider this a hard saying and you will find that the yoke of the Lord is sweet and his burden light.* If you are not yet able to believe that it is sweet in itself, then at least ac-

knowledge that by comparison it is very sweet indeed.

4. But as for you, my brothers, you who are winged and before whose eyes* the snare has been cast in vain, you who have entirely abandoned the riches of this world,* what have you to fear from the sharp word, now that you have already been delivered from the snare? Happy are you, O Jeduthun, for whom some of the psalms were written,* you who have leaped over the snare, and are thus far removed from the sharp word. For to whom will it be said, 'Depart, you cursèd, into eternal fire, for I was hungry and you gave me no food'?* To whom, I say, will this be said, if not to those who have enjoyed this world's goods?* At this word do your hearts not exult and become filled with spiritual joy?* Is your poverty not more precious than this world's treasures which you left behind? Surely it is your poverty that sets you free from the sharp word. For how can God demand of you what you have left for love of him? And yet you give him this too, and by the labor of your hands Christ is fed and clothed, and so wants for nothing. Give thanks, therefore, rejoice and say, 'He delivered me from the snare of the hunters and from the sharp word.' Rejoice, I tell you, but still for a while with trembling.* I want you to feel joyful, but not yet secure, rejoicing in the Holy Spirit,* yet still fearful and on your guard lest you slide back.

5. Is there anything you ought still to fear? Just one thing, something very serious, the sin of Judas, the sin of apostasy. It is a good thing that you have received wings like the dove and

Gal 3:1

1 Tm 6:17

Cf. Pss 39, 62, 77

Mt 25:41-2

1 Jn 3:17

Ac 2:28

Ps 2:11
Rm 14:17

have flown away to be at rest.* But on earth there will be no rest, only toil and trouble* and affliction of spirit.* For the soul that flies away what is there then to fear, if not that he may perhaps see a dead body or something of the sort on the ground, stretched out by these wicked hunters to stir his appetite, that he be captured in the snare they have set, and that the last state of that man be worse than the first.* This, I tell you, is profoundly to be feared, lest someone by his heart alone, or even by his body, turn back to his own vomit.* We read of the children of Israel that in their hearts they went back to Egypt.* They could not return in body because they were prevented by the Red Sea closing in on their heels. This is what each one of us must fear to the core, that we somehow offend God to such an extent that we come to be manifestly repudiated and vomited up by him.* And if shame prevents us from apostasizing in body, lukewarmness will gradually cause apostasy of the heart and the heart will live like a secular in religious habit and embrace whatever worldly consolations it can find. We are not holier than the apostle, who was afraid that, after having preached to others, he might himself become a castaway.* And this is something to be afraid of until the snare is broken,* until the soul has laid aside this body. The body itself is a kind of snare, which is why we read that the eye causes grief to the soul.* It behooves a man therefore to feel secure when he carries his own snare about with him. But it is good to dwell in the aid of the Most High and so through him be capable of avoiding the snare.

Ps 55:6
Ps 90:10
Qo 1:14

Mt 12:45

Pr 26:11, 2 P 2:22

Nb 14:3

Rev 3:16

1 Co 9:27
Ps 124:6

Lam 3:51

SERMON FOUR

On the Fourth Verse:

HE WILL OVERSHADOW YOU WITH HIS SHOULDERS AND BENEATH HIS WINGS YOU WILL HOPE

1. GREATER BLESSINGS should deservedly be promised the man who humbly praises and devoutly gives thanks. Now, he who has been faithful over little is by right set over much,* just as, on the contrary, he who is ungrateful for what he receives is unworthy to receive more. Therefore the Spirit will answer devout thanksgiving, saying, 'Not only will he do this, but he will also overshadow you with his shoulders.' I believe that these shoulders must be taken to mean the Lord's double promise, that is to say, for this life which now is and the life which is to come. Had he simply promised the kingdom without giving us food for the journey, men would complain bitterly and say, 'It is indeed a great thing you have promised us, but we have no means of getting to it.' And that is why he who has promised eternal life after this age has also promised that he himself will, by his very provident kindness, give us the hundredfold even now in this age.* What excuse do you still have, O man?†

Mt 25:21

*Mk 10:30
†Rm 2:1

135

For the mouth of him who speaks lies has been
stopped.* What else could the enemy bring up
to tempt you except that your life lies far ahead
of you?* And why should you be afraid if a
great journey lies ahead, you who have received
the food of the strong so you do not faint on the
way?* Elijah was served food by an angel, food
which by human standards is the most common:
bread and water. And yet he gathered so much
strength from that food that he walked for forty
days without feeling fatigue or hunger.* Would
you like the angels to minister* this food to
you? It will surprise me if you do not.

2. But if you long for this food, and seek it
simply by an ambition more humble, and not
in order to boast of angelic service, then listen
to how it is written of the Lord that, when the
devil tempted and coaxed him to change stones
into loaves of bread,* he resisted and said, 'Man
does not live by bread alone, but by every word
that proceeds from the mouth of God.'* Then,
once the temptation had been overcome and the
tempter put to flight, angels came and minis-
tered to him.* So you, too, if you want to be
served by angels, fly the consolations of this
world and resist the temptations of the devil.*
Let your soul refuse to be comforted by other
things if you want it to take pleasure in the remembrance of God.* When you are hungry
the devil coaxes you to run off for bread; but
you ought rather to listen to him who said, 'Man
does not live by bread alone.' Apart from the
sole necessity of sustaining the body, what other
reason have you to be so distracted by so many
things that you look now for food, now for

Ps 63:12

1 K 19:7

Mt 15:32

1 K 19:5-8
Mt 4:11

Mt 4:3-4

Mt 4:4

Mt 4:11

Jm 4:7

Ps 77:2-3

drink, and now for clothing or a bed, when you are able to find all that you need in a single thing: the word of God. This is the manna having all sweetness* and a delicious smell; it is a rest true and sincere, sweet and savoury, joyful and holy.

Wis 16:20

3. This is the promise made for this present life. But who can disclose the promise of the life to come? If the anticipation of the righteous is joy,* and such joy that everything that can be desired in this world is not worthy to be compared to it, what will be that joy which we anticipate? Eye has not seen, O God, beside you, what things you have prepared for those who love you.* Beneath these shoulders we receive then four benefits: beneath them we are hidden; beneath them we are protected from the attacks of hawks and kites — the powers of the air —;* beneath this saving shadow we are refreshed and shaded from the excessive heat of the sun; beneath them too, we are fed and nurtured. For in another psalm the prophet has said, 'He hid me in his tent in the day of trouble,'* that is to say, while these days are still evil* and we are sojourners in a foreign land* given into the hands of the wicked,* where there is no reign of peace, and where the God of peace* does not reign. If he does reign, why do we say, 'Your kingdom come'?* And so it is necessary for us in the meantime to lie hidden if we have a precious thing, for it is the treasure of the kingdom of heaven which a man found and hid away.* This is why we hide bodily in cloisters and in forests. Do you wonder what we gain by this hiddenness? There is no one here, I believe,

Pr 10:28

Is 64:4

Eph 2:2

Ps 27:5
Eph 5:16
Ex 2:22
Jb 9:24
2 Co 13:11

Mt 6:10

Ibid.

who, were he to do in the world a quarter of
what he does here, would not be revered as a
saint, reckoned as an angel, whereas now he is

2 Tm 4:2 daily rebuked and chided* as negligent. Do you
think it no small advantage not to be taken for

Cf. RB 4:62 a saint before actually being one? Would you
not be afraid that, having already received this
cheap reward, you would have no future re-

Cf. Mt. 6:1-2, 5 ward?* So it is necessary for all this to lie hidden not only from other people's eyes but from
your own as well, and even more necessary.
For there is a saying of the Lord: 'When you
have done all that is commanded you, say, "we
are worthless servants; we have only done what

Lk 17:10 was our duty". '* Woe to us indeed if we did
1 Co 9:16 not do this!* In this lies great virtue and the
Tt 2:12 best security: that while you live faithfully,*
forgetting what lies behind and straining for-
Ph 3:13 ward to what lies ahead,* you do not so much
see what you have already obtained as wait for
what you still lack. This hiddenness, which we
have already said is afforded beneath the Lord's
shoulders, is something very similar to the over-
shadowing which came upon Mary from the
Lk 1:35 Holy Spirit* to conceal an incomprehensible
mystery.

4. And this same prophet also says of this
protection, 'You have covered my head in the
Ps 140:7 day of battle'.* For just as the mother, when
Dt 32:11 she sees the hawk coming, spreads her wings*
to let the little birds come under them and find
sure refuge, so for us also, in some way, the
immense and ineffable kindness of our God is
spread out in an ever-widening embrace. And
this is why it was said further up, 'You are my

refuge.'* Now truly, under his shoulders we
have both saving shade and protection. The
physical sun, although it is good and very necessary, yet if it is not shaded, its heat will harm the
weak head and its brightness affect weak eyes;
and this is not the fault of the sun, but of weakness. And it is the same with the Sun of justice.
This is why it is said, 'Be not righteous over-
much,'* not because righteousness is not good,
but because while we are still weak* we need to
moderate that good grace lest perhaps we fall
into the vice of pride or indiscretion. Why is it
that though we pray and entreat without ceas-
ing we cannot receive that abundance of grace*
we desire? Do you think that God has become
miserly or needy, powerless or merciless? No
indeed, certainly not! But he knows our frame,*
and he overshadows us with his shoulders. Yet
we must never on that account cease from en-
treaty, because even though he does not give
enough to satisfy us, he gives what is necessary
to sustain us. And even though he guards against
too great a fervor, he nevertheless enfolds us
with his warmth like a mother.* And this is the
fourth thing which we said stands ready for us
beneath his shoulders, that we may be enfolded
like chicks in the warmth of their mother's
body, lest we wander outside* and die as grows
cold the love* which cannot be poured out in us
save through the Spirit who is given us.* Secure
beneath these wings, therefore, we shall hope,
because the sight of present gifts strengthens
our anticipation of those to come. Amen.

Pss 31:4, 71:2

Qo 7:17
Rm 5:6

Rm 5:17

Ps 103:14

1 Th 2:7

Jb 38:41
Mt 24:12
Rm 5:5

SERMON FIVE

On the First Part of the Fifth Verse:

HIS TRUTH WILL COVER YOU
WITH A SHIELD

Mt 26:41

1. 'WATCH AND PRAY that you do not enter into temptation.'* You know who said this, and when, for these were the Lord's words as his passion approached. And notice how, though it was he who was about to suffer, and not his disciples, he prayed not for himself, but for them. This was why he said to Peter, 'Behold, Satan sought to have you, to sift you like wheat, but I have prayed for you that your faith may not fail; and when you have turned again, strengthen your brothers.'* And if it behooved them to be so afraid of the Lord's passion, how much more ought we to be afraid, brothers, in our passion. Watch, therefore, and pray, that you do not enter into temptation, for you are hemmed about by temptations. This is why you read that the life of man on earth is a temptation.* Therefore, if our life is so full of temptations that it can deservedly be called a temptation, we must keep constant watch warily and prayerfully, lest we fall into it. This is why we say in the Lord's prayer, 'lead us not into temptation.'* Yet, even though you are surrounded

Lk 22:31-2

Jb 7:1

Mt 6:13

140

by temptations, his truth will surround you with
a shield,* so that just as there are wars on all   Ps 91:5
sides, so on all sides there are strongholds, too.
And this makes it quite evident that this shield
must be a spiritual one which can surround us
on all sides. Truth surrounds us because it was
truth who made the promise, and he proves
himself to be as he promised. The apostle says,
'God is faithful, and he will not let you be
tempted beyond your strength.'*   1 Co 10:13

2. And it is not incongruous that the grace of
divine protection be compared to a shield which
is broader and bigger at the top, in order to
cover the head and shoulders, but narrower
at the bottom, so that it weighs less, especially
as the legs, being slenderer, are not so easily
wounded, and anyway, it is not so dangerous
to be wounded in these limbs. It is for the same
sort of reason, if I may say so, that Christ gives
his soldiers* scant and scarce temporal supplies   2 Tm 2:3
to guard their lower parts, that is to say the
flesh; for he does not want them to be weighed
down with a lot of such things, but wants them
to have food and clothing,* as the apostle says,   1 Tm 6:8
and to be content with that. But for the higher
parts he gives spiritual gifts* in greater abun-   Rm 1:11
dance and breadth. So you read: 'Seek first
the kingdom of God and his righteousness and
everything will be given you,'* including the   Mt 6:33
food and clothing for which he said we were
not to be anxious.* Our Father in heaven† in   *Mt 6:25-31
†Mt 6:26
his gracious kindness gives them to us for two
reasons; lest thinking he is angry with us if he
refused us these things, we should despair, or
lest excessive anxiety about them should be

harmful to our spiritual exercises. Without
them one cannot live or serve God.* But the
scantier they are the better.

3. His truth will surround you with a shield
then: YOU WILL NOT FEAR THE TERROR OF THE
NIGHT, NOR THE ARROW THAT FLIES BY DAY, NOR
THE BOGY THAT PROWLS IN DARKNESS, NOR AS-
SAULT, NOR THE NOONDAY DEVIL. These are the
four temptations by which we are surrounded
on all sides, and we need to be surrounded by
the Lord's shield in such a way that it is to the
right and to the left,* at the back and at the
front.* Furthermore, I want you to be fore-
warned that no one can live on earth without
temptation, so when one is perhaps taken away,
we may be sure that another will come along.
Rather than feel secure, we ought to be wary
of temptation and so beg to be delivered from it.
I dare not promise perfect liberty or rest as long
as we are in the body of this death.* And in
connection with this, we should consider how
God's kindness is so well-disposed towards us
that he sometimes allows us to suffer certain
temptations for a while lest more dangerous
ones perhaps beset us. But he delivers us more
speedily from some so we may be tried by different ones which he foresees will be more useful to us. It now remains for us to consider—but
not right now—the four temptations we have
mentioned. I believe that it is in the order they
are enumerated that they beset those who have
turned [to God]* and that they are, so to speak,
the chief of all other temptations.

Ph 3:3

Ex 14:29
1 Mac 13:27

Rm 7:24

Ps 85:8—*qui
convertuntur*

SERMON SIX

*On the Second Part of This Verse,
and on the Sixth:*

YOU WILL NOT FEAR THE TERROR OF THE
NIGHT; NOR THE ARROW THAT FLIES BY
DAY, NOR THE BOGY THAT PROWLS IN
THE DARKNESS, NOR ASSAULT, NOR
THE NOONDAY DEVIL

1. IN HOLY SCRIPTURE adversity is usually betokened by night, and we know
that against those who turn to God* the   Ps 85:8
first struggle is generally against vexations of
the body. The flesh, never hitherto subdued,*   1 Co 9:27
will never with good will put up with being
chastised and brought into servitude. But remembering still the liberty only recently lost, it
will lust bitterly against the spirit,* especially   Gal 5:13
amid those pains by which you die every day,*   1 Co 15:31
or rather by which you are being killed all day
long,* for they are not only above your strength   Rm 8:36
and beyond nature, but also contrary to what
you are accustomed. Is it astonishing that they
cause you trouble, particularly those among
you who are not yet used to them and do not
have recourse to prayer quickly enough, and do
not take refuge in holy meditations in order to
lighten the burden of the day and the scorching

Mt 20:12

heat?* The shield of the Lord is plainly necessary to us at the beginning of our conversion
so that we do not fear the terror of the night.
Furthermore, it is exact to say the terror of the
night, and not night itself, because this affliction
is not so much temptation itself as the fear arising from it. We all struggle, but this does not
mean we are all being tempted, and those who
are tempted suffer more from the fear of pain
to come than from present grief.

2. Because fear itself constitutes the temptation, it is appropriate to say that anyone who is
surrounded by the Lord's shield will perhaps be
attacked, will perhaps be tempted, will perhaps
be afraid of the night, but this fear can do him
no harm. Moreover, if it does not dominate

Ps 19:14
Jb 41:25

him, then he will be blameless* and cleansed, as
it is written, 'the terrified will be made pure.'*
This fear is a furnace, but truth brings it about
that it does not sear but refines. This fear is
surely dark and nocturnal, but the ray of truth
easily overcomes it. This allows the eyes of the
heart to see the sins we have committed in such
a way that, as the prophet said of himself, we
are even ready to be whipped, declaring our

Ps 38:18
Mt 25:46

iniquity and thinking upon our sin.* Sometimes
we think about the eternal punishment* which
we have deserved until, by comparison with
what we have escaped, we consider delightful
everything we are now undergoing. Sometimes, too, — frequently — we think about the
heavenly reward towards which we are straining, for the sufferings of this present time are
not worth comparing with the glory that is to

Rm 8:18

be revealed to us.* Sometimes, again, we think

about the things Christ bore for us, in order that, frequently meditating upon all that his majesty endured for his worthless servants,* we may blush at not being able to suffer even a little on our own behalf.

Lk 17:10

3. But perhaps truth has prevailed, already surrounding us in so many ways and on so many sides that it enables us not only to push this fear away, but even to cast it out* altogether. The night is now far gone,* but still, as a child of light* now walking honestly as in the day,† fear the arrow. It flies lightly and pricks lightly. Yet I tell you, it inflicts no slight wound; it kills fast. This arrow is none other than vain glory, which is why it does not attack the wavering and the careless. It is those who appear more fervent who must look out for themselves; they must be afraid on this score, and be extremely cautious never to leave the invincible shield of truth.* For what could be more opposed to vanity [than truth]? We are not required to protect ourselves from this arrow with the hidden and intimate secrets of truth. The soul should know itself and be conscious of the truth about itself. For, unless I am mistaken, a man cannot easily be misled by someone who praises him during his lifetime, and thus become top-lofty,* if he carefully examines himself within in the light of truth. Surely if he thinks about his own condition, he will say to himself, 'How can you, who are but dust and ashes, be proud?'* Surely, if he considers his own corruption, he must necessarily admit that there is no good in him. Or, if he does perhaps seem to find some good,* he will not, I think, be able to argue

1 Jn 4:18
Rm 13:12
*Eph 5:8
†Rm 13:13

Wis 5:20

Rm 11:20

Sir 10:9

Pr 25:27

against the apostle when he says, 'What do you
have that you have not received?'* and elsewhere, 'Let him who stands look out lest he
fall.'* Finally, if he reckons faithfully, he will
have no difficulty in acknowledging that he
cannot go out with ten thousand men to meet
someone coming against him with twenty thousand,* and that all his righteous deeds are to be
thought of as filthy rags.*

4. Furthermore, truth must be opposed to
the temptations which ensue. Our ancient enemy is not going to cease for all that: he will
have recourse to craftier arguments. He has
verified that the tower is firm on every side: he
cannot get at it either on the left by the indeci-
sion arising from fear, or on the right by batter-
ing it with human praise, but is frustrated in
both attempts. So he says, 'Well, if I cannot
overthrow it by force, then perhaps I shall be
able to deceive it by the traitor's ruse.' Who do
you think will be this traitor? Obviously the
love of money, the root of all evils;* ambition,
a subtle evil, a secret virus, a hidden pest, the
craftsman of deceit; the mother of hypocrisy,
the begetter of spite, the source of vices, the
tinder of crimes, the rust of virtue, the moth* of
holiness, the blinker of hearts,* producing sickness from remedies, and begetting illness from
medicine. 'He has spurned vain glory because
it is vain. Maybe he will conceive a fondness
for more solid food: honors, perhaps, or maybe
riches.' That is what he says. How many people
have been thrust into outer darkness* by this
bogy prowling in the darkness, stripping them
of the marriage garment* and emptying the

Margin references:
1 Co 4:7
1 Co 10:12
Lk 14:31
Is 64:6
1 Tm 6:10
Mt 6:19
Is 6:10
Mt 22:13
Mt 22:11

exercises of virtue of any fruit of piety? So many have been wickedly deceived by this pest and shamefully overthrown that others for whom he lies in ambush should tremble at the thought of sudden ruin. But what fosters this worm, if not estrangement from reason and obliviousness to truth? And what else but truth will disclose this looming enemy and show it up as a bogy of darkness? Surely that was meant by the words: 'What will it profit a man if he gain the whole world* and loses or forfeits himself?'* And again, 'Mighty men will be tempted mightily'.* It is by such unremitting suggestions that [truth] reminds us how silly is the consolation of ambition, how serious its condemnation, how short-lived its utility, and how uncertain its end.

5. These were the Lord's temptations; the enemy did not dare bring up the fourth. For that springs from ignorance, and he knew only too well that a person who gave answers so measured that he could not trip him up by anything he asked must be extremely wise. By the first temptation [the enemy] tried to persuade a hungry man to change stones into loaves of bread;* but He, without either denying or affirming that He could do so, held out another bread saying, 'Not in bread alone'* and so forth. In the second temptation* the devil coaxed him to throw himself down, promising that if he were the Son of God, he would come to no harm and the whole city would praise and honor him; here again, He neither denied nor affirmed who He was. The third [temptation] was one of ambition, when [the devil] promised

Mt 16:26
Lk 9:25
Wis 6:7

Mt 4:2-3

Mt 4:4
Mt 4:5-7

all the kingdoms of this world, if he would fall
down and worship him.* Do you see now how
ambition leads to worship of the devil, for he
promises the honor and glory of this world to
those who will worship him? He withheld the
fourth temptation from our Lord, as I have said,
because he saw from the prudence of his answers that he was a man of experience.

6. But what does he do against others, those
who love righteousness and hate wickedness?*
What else but dress vice up as virtue? For when
he recognizes perfect lovers of good he attempts
to persuade them to do evil under the appearances of good; not just ordinary good, but
something perfect, so that someone who really
loves to do good may consent more easily, and
in this way he easily trips up the runner. This
devil is not just the day devil, but the noonday
devil. Was not he the one Mary was afraid of
when she took fright at the angel's unusual
greeting?* Was not he the one the apostle was
alluding to when he said, 'We are not ignorant
of their designs?* For this angel of Satan dis-
guises himself as an angel of light.* Lastly, was
not he the one the disciples feared when they
saw the Lord walking upon the sea and cried
out thinking he was a ghost?* And notice how
fitting it is that the disciples were enjoined during the fourth watch to watch against the fourth
temptation. Nor do I think it necessary for me
to say much about this, which is only the simple
truth that discloses veiled fraud.

7. No one who considers them carefully will
have difficulty in discovering these four temptations in the general state of the Church. Did not

Mt 4:8-10

Ps 45:8

Lk 1:29-30

2 Co 2:11
2 Co 11:14

Mt 14:25-6

the terror of the night keep the young plant* of
the Church busy in those days when all who
killed the servants of God* thought they were
offering God service?* Then, when persecution
ceased and day had returned, the flying arrow
troubled her more and afflicted her more grievously; then some people left the Church, puffed
up* by the spirit of the flesh, hankering after
vain and fleeting honor and wanting to make
a name for themselves; they magnified their
tongues* and forged perverse doctrines. And
nowadays, there is peace from pagans, peace
from heretics, yet there is no peace* from her
false sons. You have multiplied the people*
Lord Jesus,* but you have not multiplied its
joy,* for many are called but few are chosen.†
All are christians, and almost all look after their
own interests* and not those of Jesus Christ.
For they even pursue their nefarious quest and
the business of darkness in running after posi-
tions of ecclesiastical dignity, and in this they
are seeking not the salvation of souls, but the
extravagance of riches. This is why they get
themselves tonsured, this is why they go to
church all the time, celebrate masses, and sing
psalms. Today people scrap shamelessly to get
archbishoprics and archdeaconries in order to
dissipate church revenues in wanton waste and
vain pursuits. Now it remains for us to disclose
the man of sin, the son of perdition,* who is no
longer simply the day devil, but the noonday
devil disguised as an angel of light and exalting
himself above all that is called God or that is
worshipped.* How cruelly he waits in ambush
at the heel of Mother Church, grieving at hav-

Ps 144:12

Ac 16:17

Jn 16:2

Gal 5:26

Ps 12:4

Jer 6:14, Ezk 13:10

Is 9:3

Ac 7:59, Rev 22:20

*Is 9:3

†Mt 20:16, 22:14

Ph 2:21

2 Th 2:3

2 Co 11:14

Gen 3:5

ing had his head bruised.* This is clearly going
to be a very serious assault! Yet from this too,

*Jn 8:32
†Ps 89:5
‡Mt 29:22
2 Th 2:8

Truth will free* the Church of the elect,† short-
ening the day‡ for them and destroying the
midday devil by the light of His coming.*

Enough said about these temptations. Now I
remember having dealt with them in one of my

SC 33.8-16

sermons on the Song of Songs,* where mention
was made of the noonday devil in connection
with the noonday rest of the bridegroom after

Sg 1:6

which the bride was inquiring.*

SERMON SEVEN

On the Seventh Verse:

A THOUSAND MAY FALL AT YOUR SIDE,

TEN THOUSAND AT YOUR RIGHT HAND,

BUT YOU IT WILL NOT APPROACH

1. WE LIVE IN HOPE, brothers, and we do not lose heart in this present tribulation* because we are looking forward to never-ending joys. Our expectation is not vain, nor should our hope seem doubtful, for it rests upon the promises of eternal truth. So the very fact of receiving gifts now undergirds the expectation of those to come. And the power of present grace is the surest proof that, beyond all doubt, we are going to receive the promised happiness to come. None other than the Lord of Hosts is the King of Glory,* and to him we also address this prayer in the hymn, *Eph 3:13*

Ps 24:7, 9

> The Father of perennial glory,
> The Father of powerful grace.*

Splendor paternae gloriae 3.3-4: Hymn of Sunday Lauds

Again, in a psalm we sing that 'God loves mercy and truth, the Lord will give grace and glory.'* Therefore let our sense of duty put up manfully with the combat in this world and suffer calmly any persecution. Why indeed should it not bear all this when it makes us strong for all things*

Ps 84:12

Sir 50:31

151

1 Tm 4:8
and holds out promise for the present life and also for the life to come?* Let it courageously resist the assailant, because for him who resists there shall be an unwearied champion and for him who overcomes a surpassingly bountiful rewarder. It is said: HIS TRUTH WILL SURROUND YOU WITH A SHIELD.

2. Clearly we have need of the invincible protection of his truth, not only now while we are still in this base flesh and pummeled with dangers, but also then, when after leaving this life we are assailed by the monstrosities of evil spirits. The enemy horde sought to harm even the most holy soul of glorious Martin,* and the cruel beast, knowing that his time was short,* was not afraid to bring up all the fury of unflagging evil against someone over whom he had no power. He presumed to make a rash and impudent attack on the King of Glory,* as He himself bears witness: 'The prince of this world is coming, but he has no power over me.'* Happy the soul who with the shield of truth so repels the darts of temptation here below, that he need never fear poison taking hold in him. He will never be confounded when he speaks to his enemies in the gate.* 'Fatal enemy, you will find nothing in me.'* Happy the man who is so surrounded with the buckler of truth that it preserves his going out and his coming in:* his going out from this life and his coming into the life to come, where he will no longer be set upon from the rear, and where the enemy can never rush him from the front. But in spite of this, he will still need a guardian. He will still need a faithful leader. He will still need a great

of Tours (†397)
Rev 12:12

Ps 24:8

Jn 14:30

Ps 127:6
Sulpicius Severus,
Ep. 3.16 (on St
Martin), CSEL 1:149
Ps 121:8

comforter because of the horrible visions, no
less than he now needs someone to help and defend him against invisible tempters.

3. Meanwhile, dear ones, glorify and bear
Christ in your bodies.* He is a delightful burden, a gentle weight, a salutary pack even though
sometimes he may seem to weigh heavily and
even though from time to time he whacks your
flanks and whips the laggard, and occasionally
even curbs you with bit and bridle* and urges
you successfully on. Be like a beast of burden,*
you who bear the Saviour,* but do not be just
like a beast. It has been said that 'Man when he
is in honor does not understand; he is compared
to a senseless beast and becomes like one.'* But
why does the prophet strike out so at the man
who has become like a beast of burden, and re-
prove him so, especially when in another place
he says to God, speaking of himself with no little happiness, 'I am made a beast before you, yet
am I always by you.'* I think — or rather I do
not think, I know — that a likeness to beasts is
recommended to man, but this consists not in
being unintelligent, certainly, not in imitating
its stupidity, but rather its patience. Nor do I
detect a note of complaint or irritation in the
words, 'When a man was beneath God's burden,
he did not buck: he became like a beast before
him.' Who would not greatly envy that beast
upon whose lowly back our Saviour graciously
deigned to sit* in order to recommend his own
inexpressible gentleness, if, while it was carrying so precious a burden, it had also understood
the extraordinary honor? Be like a beast of burden, then, but not in everything. Be patient in

1 Co 6:20

Ps 32:10
Ps 73:21
Mt 21:7

Ps 49:12

Ps 73:21-2

Mt 21:7

carrying the burden, but understand the honor; wisely and lovingly ponder less your own comfort than the value of your burden.

4. The great Ignatius,* who used to listen to the disciple whom Jesus loved,* our martyr whose precious relics have enriched our poverty, in several letters which he wrote to her greets a certain Mary as Christophora. This is certainly a wonderful title and an immense acclamation of the honor that was hers. For to bear him, whom to serve is to reign, is an honor rather than an encumbrance. Moreover, need we fear that the little ass we mentioned just now, the one on which our Saviour sat, should ever faint by the way* under such a load? Need we fear a wolf leaping out, or robbers attacking, or any danger or declivity under such guidance? Happy is the person who carries Christ in such a way that he deserves to be led into the holy city* by the Holy of Holies.† He need have no fear that he will suffer any obstacle on the way, or rejection at the gate. For that other beast the faithful people prepared the way,* for this one the holy angels will do it. 'He has given his angels charge of you to keep you in all your ways lest you dash your foot against a stone.' But we must not go into this now; it is better to follow the order of the scriptural narration.

5. A THOUSAND MAY FALL AT YOUR SIDE, it says, TEN THOUSAND AT YOUR RIGHT HAND; BUT YOU IT WILL NOT APPROACH. This, as you are not unaware, is the verse we will be discussing today. In the preceding section we last dealt with, if you remember, we said that the protection of truth will set us free* from the four

Margin notes:

of Antioch
(† *c.* 107)
Jn 19:26

Mt 15:32

*Mt 4:5
†Dan 9:24

Mt 21:8

Jn 8:32

greatest and most serious temptations of this
life, that is to say, 'From the terror of the night,
from the arrow that flies by day, the bogy that
prowls in darkness, and from assault and the
noonday devil.' I think then that what comes
next — A THOUSAND MAY FALL AT YOUR SIDE, and
so on — should be taken more as referring to the
life to come. This was why at the beginning of
this sermon — I suppose you still remember — we
recalled the phrase of the Apostle which says
that godliness counts for everything,* holding   1 Tm 4:8
out promise to the life which now is and is to
come. Listen, therefore, and listen in the glad-
ness of your heart* to what relates to the prom-   Jer 15:16
ise of the life to come and to your expectations.
Where your treasure is, there will your heart be
also.* I have not forgotten how carefully you   Mt 6:21
listened to what I said about present times; yet
you should listen still more carefully to what
concerns the future. For the false prophet — I
mean Balaam: mull over his story,* you who   Num 22:5
already know it — even he, I tell you, though
·wicked, wished for the death of the righteous*   Num 23:10
and prayed that his last end would be similar.
The fruit of godliness is so great, and so great
the recompense of righteousness, that even the
wicked and unrighteous could desire nothing
else. Yet a song of Sion is less comforting than
the willows of Babylon. So we must hang up
our harps among them and lament instead by
the waters of Babylon,* in the hope of persuad-   Ps 137:1-3
ing them to mourn. Clearly I must sing only
where there are those who at the sound of the
psaltry,* at the sound of a song of Sion, leap in   Am 6:5
quickness of spirit and in the ardor of holy de-

Ps 55:6
*exsultare...
ex seipso saltare*
Jo 1:4

sire for it rejoice to fly away, saying: 'Who will give me wings like a dove that I may fly away and be at rest?'* Is rejoicing anything else than leaping out of oneself?* Those who are still in peril at sea,* tossed about by the waves, battered by the billows, take scant pleasure in the promise of the tranquility and pleasantness of the shore, however agreeable it may be, because they are still far away and almost in despair. In the same way, the verse which is proposed to us today does not concern the soul, for it does not yet deserve to hear, A THOUSAND SHALL FALL AT YOUR SIDE, TEN THOUSAND ON YOUR RIGHT HAND. Remember to whom this promise was made, for HE WHO DWELLS IN THE SHELTER OF THE MOST HIGH WILL ABIDE UNDER THE PROTECTION OF THE GOD OF HEAVEN.

Heb 6:19

Ps 106:24

Gen 49:10

6. If someone is approaching the port of salvation by meditation and ardent desire, having, as it were, let down the anchor of his hope* and thus moored himself unwaveringly to that desirable land,* let him listen to this verse throughout every one of his fighting days, waiting until his hoped-for exchange shall come.* This is the surest and straightest approach to port. This present life in which you are placed is a preparation for your leaving, that is to say, of your divine calling and justification. For between these two things there has been set a certain link, a link of eternity to eternity, of glorification to predestination, for just as there is no precise beginning to predestination, so there will never be any end to glory. In case you should think I have invented this middle connection between twin eternities, listen to the

apostle and see whether he does not tell you the same thing even more clearly: 'Those whom he foreknew', he says, 'he also predestined to be conformed to the image of his Son.'* How, or in what order, do you think he will glorify us? Now, anything coming from God is ordered. Do you imagine that you will suddenly jump from predestination to glory? Provide yourself with a middle bridge, or rather step on the one already prepared for you. 'Those whom he predestined, he also called; and those whom he called, he also justified; and those whom he justified he also glorified.'*

Rm 8:29

Rm 8:30

7. This seems a very good way to not a few men. And it is a good way, there is no need to worry over its end. The issue of this way must not cause you suspicion; go along in security, go along more vigorously as you are more sure of drawing near the issue. For if you hold to the means, how can the issue fail to get closer? 'Repent', he said, 'for the kingdom of heaven is at hand.'* And you answer, 'But the kingdom of heaven suffers violence, and men of violence take it by force.'* No approach to it lies open to me, except through the intervening wedges of the enemy. Giants stand in the middle of the road: they hover in the air, they obstruct the passage, they spy on all who pass by. Nevertheless, conduct yourself faithfully;* do not be afraid.* They are great and numerous, but A THOUSAND WILL FALL AT YOUR SIDE, and TEN THOUSAND AT YOUR RIGHT HAND. They will fall on all sides and will never for all eternity harm you. Even more: they will not come near you. Of course, the wicked man sees this and is an-

Mt 3:2

Mt 11:12

Ps 12:6
Lk 1:30

Ps 112:10

Ps 59:10

Ps 23:6

Ps 121:8

Eph 6:12

Ibid.

Ibid.

gry,* but God will come to your side, for His
mercy comes forth to meet you,* and this same
mercy follows you,* guarding your going out
and your coming in,* as you no doubt remember from earlier. Otherwise, what human faculty could withstand the terrible assault of spiritual wickedness* without being shaken to the
core by that unbearable horror?

8. Do you think, brothers, that any faculty
of body or heart could bear it if even a single
one of the many rulers of darkness* were to
rush into your midst in all his fierceness and appear in darksome physical bulk? Only a few
days ago — as you know — one of you woke up
after having fallen asleep. And he had been so
gravely vexed by nocturnal visions that he could
scarcely keep control of himself and be comfortable the entire day. The terror-stricken
fellow even scared the whole lot of you when
he yelled in a terrible voice. It is a great shame
that your faith seems to have slept to such an extent even while you slumbered. But probably
this happened so we would be careful to remember against whom we are fighting, lest we be
found unwary of their hostile enmity* or ungrateful for divine protection. Under the extreme torment of his own spite, his inveterate
malice erupts into fury, especially during these
holy days, showing that he is racked bitterly by
your devotion. In the heat of this same consuming rage, but still more daringly, he attends holy
souls going out of this world; but he is only at
their side; he is not allowed to attack them head
on and take them by force, or to sneak up from
the rear to entrap them.

9. Nor shall he even set snares for you by the wayside,* for HE WILL NOT COME NEAR YOU. Ps 140:5 Not only shall he not reach out far enough to strike you, but he shall not even come near enough to scare you. For I think you are afraid of being overcome with horror at such monstrous spectres and such a multitude of ghostly shapes. But the Paraclete will be there by you, an eminent and most effective comforter, for it is of him you read, 'Ethiopians bow down before him and his enemies lick the dust.'* In his Ps 72:9 eyes the reprobate is despised* and he will there- Ps 15:4 fore honor those who fear him. When you are present, Lord Jesus, however many enemies may rush us, they will not rush us but be routed; they will march in from all sides only to melt away and perish in the sight of God, as wax melts in the presence of fire.* What have I to Ps 68:2 fear from a deserter, what have I to dread from a trembler, why should I be in awe of a fumbler? Though I walk through the valley of the shadow of death, I will fear no evil* while you are Ps 23:4 with me, O Lord my God.* For very soon the Ps 7:1 day will dawn and the shadows bend,* and then Sg 4:6 the rulers of darkness* will fall away. For Eph 6:12 though we now walk by faith* amid their veiled 2 Co 5:7 and wicked suggestions, and not by sight, yet faith triumphs victorious; how much more easily still shall the clear recognition of the truth which is to be revealed blow away those dark and gloomy shadows? Do not bicker about their numbers, nor have the slightest fear of their array. Remember how, at one command from the Saviour, a whole legion of demons left the body of a man who had been possessed and

Lk 8:26-33

obsessed for a long time past, and how not one of them dared without his order to enter swine.* How much more then, under his leadership, however many they may be, will they not fall down on all sides and exclaim in great amazement, 'Who is this who is coming up, rising like the dawn, fair as the moon, bright as the sun,

Sg 6:9

terrible as an army with banners?'* Intrepid and entirely unafraid, yes, rejoicing and giving praise, you will look upon them with your own eyes; no longer suffering attack fearing their rage, you will see the recompense of the wicked.

10. And now, what has already been said today would seem enough; but I think that several of you are waiting in suspense. For, unless I am mistaken, the more zealous among you are anxious to know why ten thousand will fall at your right hand, but only one thousand at the left. For when it says simply 'at your side', I think we may take it to mean the left, especially as the right is immediately and specifically mentioned. And indeed it seems surely to be for some mysterious reason that though many are said to fall at the left, many more fall at the right. Unless of course some one should be so silly and so insipid as to imagine that one thousand and ten thousand signify the appraisal of a fixed number instead of an incalculable comparison. But this is not the usual way in which we

1 Co 11:16

and the Church of God* interpret divine Scripture. They fall, a thousand will fall at your left, but ten thousand at your right hand, therefore, because they always push with greater wickedness and a heavier hand to the right, and grab the right side. And if we consider the great

body of the Church,* we shall easily notice that
the spiritual men in the Church are far more bitterly attacked than are the carnal. I think that
we may not unfittingly take these two sorts of
men to be the two sides, right and left. This is
what proud and ever jealous malice does, hit-
ting harder the more perfect, according to the
saying 'his food is choice'* and, again, that 'the
river is turbulent yet he is not afraid; he is confident though the Jordan rushes into his mouth.'*
He only acts, I tell you, in keeping with the sure
dispensation of the divine plan, which does not
allow the imperfect to be tempted beyond their
strength,* making them grow by temptation;
and thus for the more perfect he prepares not
only more glorious, but even more numerous,
triumphs over the enemy. Therefore the whole
Church of the elect will be equally crowned
because she will have fought on both sides according to the rules,* so powerfully tossing her
enemies with both horns that it will soon be evident that a thousand are falling at her side and
ten thousand at her right. So it was in days of
old when the more perfect virtue of David was
tested* and the repudiation of Saul had not yet
been divulged in Israel: 'They sing in dances,
saying Saul has slain a thousand and David ten
thousand.'*

11. But if you prefer to apply this to each of
you, we lack no means to a spiritual understanding of this verse if only you consult your own
experience. With far greater anxiousness and
craftiness do the enemy hordes try to wound us
on the right than on the left, striving to carry
off the substance, not of our bodies, but of our

Col 1:18

Hab 1:16

Jb 40:18

1 Co 10:13

2 Tm 2:5

Wis 1:3

1 S 21:11

hearts. We all know that they are jealous of any prosperity of the human race, and they struggle to defraud it of any happiness on earth or in heaven, but of the dew of heaven far more than of the fatness of earth.* It is for you to judge whether we can fittingly apply these two sides to the dual substance of mankind. When I set spiritual goods to the right and carnal to the left, I have little fear of being criticized, especially by those of us who are constantly wary of taking right for left or left for right. True wisdom proves just this, that whereas riches and honor are in the left hand, long life is in the right.* It will never do for you to be ignorant of where the determined enemy horde will attack most furiously. It must be resisted all the more earnestly there where the need presses most urgently, where the whole thrust of war threatens, where the entire cause of battle takes its stand. There you will be led into shameful captivity if vanquished, or achieve a glorious triumph if victorious.

12. This is why, and not out of some sort of stupidity, you appear to men more willingly to expose the left flank to enemy batteries: to give all your attention to defending the right. This is nothing but the wisdom of the serpent,* which Christ commended and proposed that all Christians imitate: if need be, one exposes the whole body to keep the head safe. This is true philosophy, the advice of the Sage: 'Keep your heart with all vigilance; for from it comes life.'* And lastly, 'God's grace and mercy are on his servants, and he watches over his chosen ones.'* He remains forever a zealous protector of the

Gen 27:28

Pr 3:16

Mt 10:16

Pr 4:23

Wis 4:15

right, all the while, as it were, feinting with the left. Of this the prophet bears witness when he says of him, 'I kept the Lord always in my sight; because he is at my right hand, I shall not be moved.'* Do you think he was not holding the right hand,* and only the right, of the man whom he allowed to suffer in all his possessions as well as in his flesh anything the enemy liked? 'But yet', he said, 'spare his life.'* O good Jesus, if only you would always be at my right hand! If only you would always hold my right hand! I know and I am sure* that no adversity will harm me if no iniquity holds sway over me. Let my left side be fleeced and flogged; let it be smitten with insults and taunted with shame: willingly shall I expose it while I am kept by you, as long as you are my protection on my right side.*

Ps 16:9
Ps 73:22

Jb 2:6

2 Tm 1:12

Ps 121:5

13. It may be also that these thousand who are to fall at the left are to be understood as men, rather than as demons. For most of them beset us because of temporal and transient goods which they either begrudge our having out of malicious jealousy, or, out of unjust greed, bewail not having themselves. Perhaps they will endeavor to make off with this world's goods,* or man's good opinion, perhaps even physical life. Human persecution can rage even that far, but it can do nothing more* against souls. For we know the demons begrudge us eternal and supernal things, not in order to gain for themselves what they have irretrievably lost, but to keep that poor being raised from dust* from acceding to the place to which they were created in glory and from which they have irretrievably

1 Jn 3:17

Lk 12:4

1 S 2:8

fallen. Obdurate malice is indignant and consumed with spite that human frailty gains what it did not deserve to keep. And if they perhaps attempt, from time to time, to inflict temporal punishment on someone, or rejoice when it befalls him, this is their whole strategem, that the outward loss will be the occasion of an inward, either for himself or for someone else. And in the same way in the human sphere, as often as people take pains to flatter us or to do something harmful to our right hand, they seem to act not chiefly for spiritual ends but in order thereby to acquire some projected temporal profit for themselves or us or someone else, or to ward off some disadvantage. That is, unless they have passed from being men to devils who can now somehow hope to cudgel into eternal damnation man, their worst enemy.

14. Why have we wretches grown drowsy in spiritual zeal, we who are so beset by spiritual wickedness? I am ashamed to speak of this, yet the force of my suffering prevents me from being silent. How many people there are, brothers, even among those who continue in the habit of religion and the intention of perfection, to whom can be applied the prophet's terrible statement: 'If I forget you, Jerusalem, let my right hand be forgotten.'* At brooding attentively on the care of their left they are very expert, but that is the wisdom of this age,* which they ought to have renounced, which flesh and blood have revealed,* to which, according to the apostle, they seem not to wish to give way. They are so keen to grab the lucre of this age, so worldly in enjoying transient advantage, that

Ps 137:5

1 Co 2:6

Gal 1:16

you see them all distraught at even the slightest
loss of temporal possessions, and competing for
them so carnally, chasing them so foolishly, en-
tangling themselves so irreverently in worldly
pursuits* — as if their entire heritage and substance were in them. It is true a farmer tends a
poor plot of land more carefully, but he has no
greater or more precious possession. A beggar
hides a crust of bread on his person* because in
his sack such fodder would get mouldy. But
you, why do you lean towards such extreme
poverty, and wear yourself out uselessly labor-
ing for this? There is another possession awaiting you, though perhaps [you think it] far
away. You are wrong. Nothing is as near us as
that which is within us.* Perhaps you plead
that even if it is not far off, it is useless for you
to trouble yourself about it, so you think you
have already done enough searching here below. You are mistaken: this is where you will
best find it; in fact, you will find it nowhere else.
Or perhaps you think you have no need to work
at it, or that it does not yield enough to your
labor? Or else you believe that it is laid away
safely and you can keep it there without vigilant
care? If you entertain any of these thoughts,
know that you are being extremely foolish. For
here especially 'whatever a man sows, that shall
he also reap.'* And, 'he who sows sparingly will
also reap sparingly, but he who sows bountifully will also reap bountifully,'* — a yield of
thirtyfold, sixtyfold, an hundredfold.* But you
have this treasure in earthen vessels,* if you still
have it at all. I think you may already have
lost it; I think it has already been carried off; I

2 Tm 2:4

Jb 23:2

Lk 17:21

Gal 6:8

2 Co 9:6
Mk 4:8
2 Co 4:7

think that aliens have already devoured your
strength* without your knowing it. And you
are not able to set your heart on your treasure,*
for you do not possess the treasure. Otherwise,
I beg you, if you are so anxious, if you spurn
no triviality, if you so prudently save your chaff,
then remember to guard your barn. Indeed,
you do not leave your treasure exposed when
you hatch it in a dungheap. A thousand may
begrudge you the latter, but ten thousand besiege the former, and they outnumber the others
in craftiness and cruelty no less than in count.
Turn on them the eyes of faith. They may already have breached the gate, they may already
be freely plundering everything, they may al-
read be dividing the spoils.* Why do you, a
careful observer, hold to the left side so badly,
if not because [these treasures] are not at your
side but in front of you; because you keep
them always before your eyes?* Anyone who
touches them, you think has touched not your
side, but the apple of your eye.*

15. Look out for this now, whoever you may
be who neglect the right and foster the left, for
fear you may receive with the goats the place to
the left which you have chosen.* This is a harsh
word, brothers, you have every reason to tremble. Yet you must be as careful as you are fearful. For my Lord Jesus, after having bestowed
so many benefits on me in his inestimable kindness, even suffering his right side to be pierced*
for me, because he wanted me to drink only
from his right, has prepared a refuge for me to
his right. If only I might deserve to be like the
dove which dwells in the cleft of the rock,* in

Hos 7:9

Ps 62:10

Lk 11:22

Ps 16:9

Ps 17:8

Mt 25:33

Jn 19:34

Sg 2:14

the cleft of his right side! Consider that He did not feel this wound inwardly. Nor did he will to receive it before falling asleep in death, in order to warn you that as long as you live you must watch over this right side, and that the soul which pretends — because of some evil numbness — that it has been wounded in the right side, is to be considered dead. Rightly is it said that man's heart is on the left because his affections are forever inclined and tilting earthwards.* Gen 8:21 And anyone knows this who has groaned miserably, 'my soul cleaves to the dust; quicken me according to your word.'* Ps 119:25 But the man who admonished us, 'Let us lift up our hearts and hands to God,'* did not want us to be weighed down Lam 3:41 by our human condition and heaviness of heart. He persuaded us rather to move up from the left side to the right. Brothers, the troops of this world carry their shields to the left. Do not imitate them if you do not wish to be counted among those who agree to fight for this world and not for Christ. No one battling for God gets entangled in civilian pursuits.* This means 2 Tm 2:4 that he puts his shield on the right instead of on the left.

16. And yet, brothers, we must cover both sides, if you remember. WITH A SHIELD HIS TRUTH WILL COVER YOU, says [the psalm],* and Ps 91:5 the apostle says, 'With weapons of righteousness to the right hand and to the left.'* Again, 2 Co 6:7 listen to Righteousness himself. Maybe he will advise a different tactic for each side. On the one hand he commands, 'Beloved, never defend yourselves, but give place to wrath.'* And on Rm 12:19 the other hand he orders us to 'give no place to

the devil,'* and again, 'Resist the devil, and he will flee from you.'* Now listen to how you are to cover both sides: 'Provide what is good not only in the sight of God, but also of men.'* For this is the will of God,* that by doing good you should not only wither the envy of devils but also put to silence the ignorance of foolish men.* Shall the hostile host forever assail us from both sides? There will come a time when they not only will not assail, but will not even abide. A THOUSAND WILL FALL AT YOUR SIDE AND TEN THOUSAND ON YOUR RIGHT HAND. Human malice will then no longer have the power to harm us, and we shall be no more frightened of a thousand devils than of a swarm of worms or gnats. We shall pay no more attention to them than the sons of Israel paid to the dead Egyptians lying all around, once they had crossed the Red Sea and spied the wheels of their chariots sinking into the deep.* Far more securely and delightedly than they, shall we sing to the Lord because he shall have triumphed gloriously, throwing horse and rider down into the abyss.* Amen.

Marginal references:
Eph 4:27
Jn 4:7

Rm 12:17
1 Th 4:3

1 P 2:15

Ex 14:25-31

Ex 15:3

SERMON EIGHT

On the Eighth Verse:

YOU WILL BUT CONSIDER WITH YOUR EYES
AND SEE THE SINNERS' RECOMPENSE

1. I WOULD SPEAK to you more briefly
once in a while, dear ones, if only I had
the opportunity of doing so more frequently, as I believe you have sometimes noticed. How often, the day's own trouble being
sufficient thereto,* have I been obliged, some-   Mt 6:34
times for days, to endure the very vexing silence
of not encouraging and consoling you.* It   1 Co 14:3
never occurred to me that anyone would be surprised if I wanted to make the most of the time*   Eph 5:16
by giving longer sermons less frequently. These
few words of introduction are intended as an
excuse to you for the length of yesterday's sermon and the shortness of today's. I fear some of
you were not very pleased with yesterday's and
some will not be pleased with today's, and perhaps it would have been better had they been of
equal length.

HIS TRUTH WILL COVER YOU WITH A SHIELD,
it says. YOU WILL NOT FEAR THE TERROR OF THE
NIGHT, NOR THE ARROW THAT FLIES BY DAY, NOR
THE BOGY THAT PROWLS IN DARKNESS, NOR AS-
SAULT, NOR THE NOONDAY DEVIL. A THOUSAND
MAY FALL AT YOUR SIDE, TEN THOUSAND AT YOUR

RIGHT HAND; BUT YOU IT WILL NOT APPROACH.
In the preceding sermons I have spoken to you
about all that in the measure that Truth itself
graciously allowed me to do so. I told you how
the faithful soul is guarded against temptations
now and later against difficulties. This is what
the same prophet states more briefly in another
psalm: 'By you I shall be rescued from temptation, and in my God I shall leap over the wall.'*
If God is your guide, no stumbling-block will
get in the way as you go along in this world, nor
shall any obstacle obtrude as you go out from it.
The first psalm shows how often the soul is rescued from danger, and the second how fully
and securely it is set free. Now, in my opinion
the words in the third, YOU WILL BUT CONSIDER
WITH YOUR EYES, contain the promise of very
great happiness. A THOUSAND MAY FALL AT YOUR
SIDE, TEN THOUSAND AT YOUR RIGHT HAND; BUT
YOU IT WILL NOT APPROACH. YOU WILL BUT
CONSIDER WITH YOUR EYES. Let it be so, I pray,
Lord, let it be so. Let them fall, yet may I not
fall. Let them tremble, yet may I not tremble.
Let them be dismayed, yet may I not be dismayed.*

2. Obviously, these few words suggest the
immortality of the soul and affirm our belief in
the resurrection of the body. Surely, when my
enemies have been overthrown, I shall be there
to see them, and in good time I shall even have
eyes with which to see their final recompense.
For he did not say merely 'with eyes', but 'with
your eyes will you consider', with these very
same eyes which now grow dim through debil-
ity* and fail while waiting in hope for your

Ps 18:29

Cf. Jer 17:18

Ps 88:9

God.* And truly, brothers, our eyes do grow
dim while we wait in hope. If someone sees,
what does he hope for?* Is it not said, 'Hope
that is seen is not hope'?* Therefore, you will
consider with those very eyes which now you
do not even dare to lift up to heaven,* these
very same eyes which now gush tears and are
so often rubbed sore in compunction. Do not
imagine that new ones are going to be gener-
ated; your own are going to be regenerated.
But what else is there for me to say about the
eye which, though the smallest part of the human body, is its most eminent and excellent? A
blessed hope is laid up in our bosoms,* on the
promise of Truth himself, that not so much as a
single hair of our head will perish.*

3. Therefore if such a vision is expressly
promised to the eyes, surely it is because the
soul's greatest desire is to see goodness. 'I believe', it is said, 'that I shall see the goodness of
the Lord in the land of the living.'* Anyone
who yearns to walk more by sight than by faith,
longs to have the very best windows of his body
opened to supernal truth.* Faith comes by hearing,* not by seeing. It is 'the assurance of things
hoped for, the conviction of things not seen.'*
And in faith therefore, as in hope, the eye fails
us; the ear alone avails. The prophet said, 'The
Lord God opened my ear.'* But the time will
come when he will also unveil the eye. The
time will come when it will no longer be said,
'Hear, O daughter, and incline your ear,'* but
rather, 'Lift up your eyes* and contemplate.'
What? Surely the gladness and rejoicing* which
your God has stored up for you. What? Surely

Ps 69:3

Rm 8:24
Ibid.

Lk 18:13

Jb 19:27

Lk 21:18

Ps 27:15

2 Co 5:7
Rm 10:17
Heb 11:1

Is 50:5

Ps 45:11
Jn 4:35
Sir 15:6

Is 64:4
animus
1 Co 2:9

not only those things which you may now hear
and believe, but do not yet see, but such things
as God has prepared for those who love him,
things which eye has not seen, nor ear heard,*
which have never been conceived by the mind*
of man.* The eye of the resurrection will grasp
what neither hearing nor the mind itself can
ever grasp here. And I think, too, that in func-
tion of the soul's ardent desire to see what it
now hears and believes, there is in the very mention of the eyes another very evident proclama-
tion of future resurrection: 'I shall be clothed
again with my skin and in my flesh I shall see
God my Saviour, whom I myself shall see and
not another and my eyes shall behold'; and, he
adds, 'This my hope is laid up in my bosom.'*

Jb 19:26

4. Perhaps we should pay closer attention to
the fact that he says 'my eyes', as in the psalm it
is said 'with your eyes will you consider.' But
do my eyes not already seem to be mine? Not
really mine. They once seemed to be mine, for
they were known to be part of the paternal substance which I received, but kept badly. It was
very soon wasted; I quickly dissipated it all.*
The law of sin took hold of my members,*
death came at will through my windows,* and
I, even I, became its slave.* I was a wretched
servant, serving not a man, but foul and unclean
beasts. I did not attend them as a hired servant,
but as a slave. Far from receiving my hire, I
was denied even food, for fear I should be even
hungrier on account of the food. No one gave
me the husks of the swine when I craved them,
so I fell in with swine yet did not fall to with
swine.* Finally, was my eye not my own, when

Lk 15:12-13
Rm 7:23
Jer 9:21
Rm 26:20

vivo-convivo

it plundered my own soul? Being reduced to such extreme necessity, I was obliged to put into the hands of the master the good things given me, that he might protect them from the tyrranical enemy — something I simply could not do.

5. Consider attentively, dear ones, and take note by what power it was that you escaped the unbearable yoke of Pharaoh,* that your members be no more arms of iniquity for sin and that it no longer reign over your mortal bodies.* This is not your doing, brothers: 'The right hand of the Lord accomplishes virtue';* he alone can do this, he to whom nothing is impossible. Do not say, 'our hand is triumphant',* but truly and salutarily confess that it is the Lord who has done all these things.* Finally, let no one of you doubt in the slightest that as long as the days are evil* man is never secure and he will have to be on his guard against presuming to want to take back his possessions from so kind a hand and so provident a tutor to strike out rashly towards a dangerous and delusive freedom. Though yours is a jealous Father, his jealousy for you comes not from envy, but from providence. He orders your whole substance to remain in his keeping for fear you should lose it. When at last you arrive at that great and holy city whose borders are in peace,* where there will no longer be any need to fear enemy incursions; not only will all these things be given back to you, but he will bestow far more, and his very self. Meanwhile then, turn away from your own desires,* and be never so rash as to keep for yourself the members you have consecrated to God, know-

Ex 1:8-10

Rm 6:12-3

Ps 118:16

Dt 32:27

Jb 12:9

Eph 5:16

Ps 148:14

Sir 18:30

ing that since they have been set apart for godliness, it is only with great sacrilege that you use
them for vanity, curiosity, sinful pleasure, or
any other works of this world. 'Do you not
know', says the apostle, 'that your bodies are a
temple of the Holy Spirit which you have from
God and you are not your own?'* And again,
'The body is not meant for immorality.'* Then
for what? Would it be for yourself? Yes, it is
yours to dispose of, but only if you are able by
your own forces to snatch it away from the
onslaught of immorality or, if already snatched
away, to safeguard it. But, if perhaps you cannot do this, or rather because you cannot do it,
let it be 'a body not meant for immorality, but
for the Lord', and let it serve here below in your
sanctification, lest it go on still worse to serve in
your corruption. The apostle said, 'I am speaking in human terms because of the weakness of
your flesh. As once you yielded your members
to serve greater and greater iniquity, so now
yield your members to righteousness for sanctification.'* It was indeed on account of our weakness that he spoke this way. But when God shall
raise up in power what we now sow in weakness,* there will be no need to go on being
slaves. For when we have free security and secure freedom, will not each one of us be given
back to himself? With what greater freedom
could our Mighty Father endow his faithful servant than he does when he sets him over all His
possessions?*

6. In times to come then, YOU WILL CONSIDER
WITH YOUR EYES, if only you acknowledge in
the meantime that they belong to him and not

1 Co 6:19
1 Co 6:13

Rm 6:19

1 Co 15:43

Mt 24:45-7

to you. Now, you think over what I have already said to you, that, renouncing your own will, you have by your vows set apart for divine service the members you were unable to drag away from the tyranny of sin; surely you cannot consider these same members still in your possession when a law contrary to God is still in them, even though it may not reign over them, and when in them your second enemy, the penalty of sin, not only remains but prevails and holds sway? Can you call spiritual a body which is dead because of sin* and which continually weighs down your soul? Surely, if anyone is keen to say this, he is only declaring his own burden, his own prison. Moreover, how can you call your eyes your own when, whether you will or not, sleep completely closes them, smoke stings them, a speck of dust wounds them, harmful fluid clouds them, painful itching torments them, and finally death itself blinds them? Only then when all these other things are no more, will you be able truly to consider with your eyes, for they will be free for you to use freely and safely for any purpose you want. You shall no longer need to turn away your eyes lest they behold vanities,* for they will gaze upon purest truth. Death will no longer come in through these windows,* for even this last enemy* will have been destroyed. But are you perhaps afraid that your eyes will one day be blinded by the intensity of light where each of the righteous shall shine like a sun?* Of course, this would be something to fear if the resurrection were not going to glorify our eyes, just as it shall other members of the human body.

Rm 8:10

Ps 119:37

Jer 9:21
1 Co 15:26

Mt 13:43

7. AND YOU WILL SEE THE SINNERS' RECOM-
PENSE. This surely is going to cause them terrible torment and there will be a great heap of
evildoers. Perhaps if, in their torment, they
could forget those against whom they had so
wickedly fought, or at least keep them out of
sight, they would then have some sort of comfort. Yet even though it may cause them immense suffering to see us observing them, what
good can it do us, of what use or pleasure is it?
However cruel our enemies may be, we cannot
imagine anything more unchristian, indeed more
inhuman and more detestable, than to feast our
eyes on the blood of the wicked or to relish the
sight of poor wretches suffering. But yet, just
as the sinner shall see and be angry, gnashing his
teeth and melting away,* — for the blessed shall
be called into the kingdom before the accursed
are cast into the furnace of fire* — so too the
upright shall see and be glad* when they consider what they have escaped. In that final separation then, as the sight of the lambs will occasion fury in the goats,* so on the other hand the
consideration of the damned will provide the
chosen immense cause for praising and thanksgiving.* Why else would the just be so over-
whelmedly thankful, if not because they compare the unimaginable happiness which they
now enjoy to the recompense of sinners, from
which they remember they have been separated
solely by the Redeemer's most steadfast and devoted mercy? And what greater cause could
wicked souls have to shrivel in anger than to see
others being led before their very eyes into the
kingdom of highest bliss while they themselves

Ps 112:10

Mt 25:34, 41-2
Ps 107:42

Mt 25:32

Is 51:3

are condemned to groan in the misery of undying death, in the stench, the horrors, the agonies of eternal fire? 'There will be weeping and gnashing of teeth':* weeping because of the fire which is never quenched;* gnashing of teeth because of the worm which never dies. Weeping from pain, gnashing of teeth from fury. The intensity of their torments will wrench tears from them; the vehemence of consuming envy* and obdurate evil, the gnashing of teeth. And thus YOU SHALL SEE THE RECOMPENSE OF THE WICKED, lest, unmindful of so great a danger, you should ever become ungrateful to him who set you free.

8. The righteous will see the recompense of sinners not only for this, but also so that they may be perfectly secure. When a thousand have fallen at their side and ten thousand at their right, there will no longer be any need for them to fear human or devilish malice, for they will see them not just falling, but falling into hell. For remembering the serpent, the craftiest of all animals, and knowing only too well how he once seduced the woman in paradise,* do you think they could stop fearing him unless they saw him and all his cohort thrown into the flames and a great chasm fixed* between him and them?

9. There is still a third advantage to your consideration of sinners: that in comparison with their deformity you may shine more gloriously* and more strikingly. Contrasts, when compared, cause each to stand out more clearly, as, for example, when you compare black and white the latter appears more dazzling and the

Mt 13:42
Mk 9:43

Wis 6:25

Gen 3:1

Lk 16:26

Qo 43:9

former more dismal. But listen to an even surer testimony of this, the prophetic word: 'The righteous will rejoice when he sees the vengeance.' And why? 'He will wash his hands in the blood of the wicked.'* Clearly he will not be stained by the blood, but washed; thus whereas one is bloodstained, the other will appear more glistening; whereas one gets filthier, the other shines more beautifully.

10. In the life to come, human sensibility will not shrink from all this as it does now, and it is for none of these three reasons will wisdom laugh* at their ruination, as it assuredly will do. Utterly incapable of deceit, wisdom will say: 'I have called and you refused to listen, I have stretched out my hand and no one paid any heed.' And a little further on, 'I also shall laugh at your ruination; I shall mock when panic assails you, when calamity strikes without warning and ruination sweeps in like a whirlwind.'* What do we believe will be so pleasing to wisdom in the ruination of the foolish, if not the very just disposing and the faultless ordering of events? And what pleases wisdom must needs also please the wise. So do not find so harsh the words, 'You will consider with your eyes,' when you too are going to laugh at the ruination of sinners, not from some sadistic cruelty but from zeal for justice and a love of equity which delights in the exquisite harmony of the divine ordering of things. And when all things are ordered, each one set in its proper place, or rather when you completely and fully* realize by the light of truth that each is in its right place, how will you refrain from giving praise

Ps 58:9

Pr 1:26

Pr 1:26-7

Cf. Heb. 9:11

in all things to the governor of all? Peter the apostle put it prettily when he affirmed that the son of perdition* had gone to his own place,† for he who burst asunder* in mid-air had been the abettor of the powers of the air,* and he who had wickedly betrayed him who was both true God and true man come from heaven* into the midst of the earth* to work our salvation was rejected by heaven and spurned by earth.

*Jn 17:12
†Ac 1:25
Judas: Ac 1:18
Eph 2:2

Jn 3:31
Ps 74:13

11. Therefore, YOU WILL CONSIDER WITH YOUR EYES AND SEE THE SINNERS' RECOMPENSE. First of all, for your escape; secondly, for your complete security; thirdly, for the sake of comparison; and fourthly, for the perfect emulation of righteousness. There will come a time, no longer of mercy, but of judgement, because once all hope of amendment is gone there can be absolutely no question of compassion for the wicked. We shall be far removed from any softness due to human weakness, even though charity, like the open bosom of some widespread net taking in good fish and bad,* that is to say both comfortable and uncomfortable sensibilities, makes use of it for a time here below for the purposes of salvation. This is while we are still at sea. Once ashore, she* will keep only the good fish, rejoicing so much with those who rejoice that she cannot weep with those who weep.* Otherwise, how is this world to be judged by us,* if we are still softhearted and have not been led into the cellar of wine?* Is this not the meaning of the words, 'I will enter into the strength of the Lord. O Lord, I shall speak of your righteousness alone'?* Even now we are not allowed to be partial to the pauper,*

Mt 13:47-8

charity

Rm 12:15
1 Co 6:2
Sg 2:4

Ps 71:14
Ex 23:3

or to take pity on him when he comes to trial. However much it may vex us, we must control this human sensibility and pronounce a just sentence. Once our mind is no longer subject to divided feelings and we can be free of any vexation, then shall these words find their fulfilment:* 'Their judges have been swallowed up by the rock to which they are joined.'* They will be swallowed up, clearly, in their sensitivity for justice and they will emulate the solidness of the Rock to which they are joined. It says that 'they are joined to the Rock.' To follow him alone they left everything else.* When Peter asked what they were going to get, this Rock replied, 'When the Son of Man shall sit on the throne of his majesty, you will also sit on twelve thrones, judging the twelve tribes of Israel.'* This was what the prophet was predicting when he said, 'The Lord will enter into judgement with the elders of his people.'* Do you think there was any flexibility in those judges joined to the Rock? The apostle said, 'He who cleaves to the Lord is one spirit with him.'* And anyone joined to the Rock is one stone with him. It was to this that the prophet aspired when he said, 'For me it is good to cleave to God.'* So then, 'Their judges have been swallowed up by the Rock to which they are joined.' What an intimacy of grace! What a pinnacle of honor! What a privilege of confidence! What a prerogative of perfect security!

12. What more need we fear? Can we think of anything more anxiety-ridden and nerve-wracking than having someday to stand before so formidable a tribunal and wait for the unpre-

Lk 22:37

Ps 141:7

Mt 19:27

Mt 19:28

Is 3:14

1 Co 6:17

Ps 73:27

dictable sentence of so severe a Judge? 'It is a fearful thing', the apostle says, 'to fall into the hands of the living God.'* Brothers, let us judge ourselves now and by present judgement strive to avoid that fearful prospect. 'God will not give judgement twice for the same thing.'* There are certain sins, and certain good deeds, which are conspicuous* prior to judgement. Thus some, not waiting for the sentence,* are at once cast down into the nether regions by the weight of their own crimes, whereas others mount up with no delay at all, in full freedom of spirit to the thrones prepared* for them. How happy is the voluntary poverty of those who leave all things to follow you,* Lord Jesus!* It is indeed happy, for it will make them fully secure, indeed fully glorious, on that day when all creation is being dashed to smithereens and merits severely examined and judgements meted out. Now let us listen to what the devout and faithful soul replies to such promises. You will see that it is neither diffident nor less confident than it ought to be 'For you, O Lord, are my hope,'* it says. What could it say that would be soberer or more godly?* To this there is no more fitting reply than the words which follow: YOU HAVE MADE THE MOST HIGH YOUR REFUGE.

Forgive me once more, brothers. Today again I seem to have gone a little overtime.

Heb 10:31

Nah 1:9

1 Tm 5:25
Jb 29:21

Ps 93:3

Mt 19:27
Ac 7:59, Rev 22:20

Ps 91:9
Tt 2:12

SERMON NINE

On the Ninth Verse:

BECAUSE YOU, O LORD, ARE MY HOPE:
YOU HAVE MADE THE MOST HIGH
YOUR REFUGE

1. **A**ND TODAY, BROTHERS, let us hear something of the promise of the Father,* the expectation of his sons,† the end of this, our pilgrimage, the reward of our labors,* the fruit of captivity. Ours is indeed a very hard captivity; it is not only the one we bear in common with the condition of the human race, but also one by which we surrender ourselves to rigid shackles of discipline and to a prison of hard servitude, wishing to mortify our own wills and even hastening to lose our souls* in this world.† This is obviously a pitiable servitude, but only if it is forced on us, not if it is voluntary. But since you make this offering voluntarily to God,* you do your will no violence except by that same will. There must be some reason for this: and I imagine it is one which surpasses any other. If it is for him we have undertaken something, however great, however laborious it may be, is there any reason to groan and moan? And even if the great hardness of our labor now and then arouses compassion, a consideration of the reason for it will

*Ac 1:4
†Rm 8:19

Wis 10:17

*Mt 10:39
†Jn 10:25

Ps 54:6

occasion congratulations. What good do we do which is not done not only for him but also by him? 'It is God at work in you, both to will and to work his good pleasure.'* He, then, provides our works with their origin and their reward; he is himself our whole reward. And so it happens that this supreme good, perfect simplicity in himself, appears in us to be two-fold, being both the efficient and the final cause of any good we do. It is a good thing, then, brothers, that in all these, your many labors, you should not only persevere, but also overcome, because of him who loves you. Is it not through him? Yes, obviously! As the apostle says, 'As we have abundant trials for Christ, so through him we have abundant comfort too.'*

Ph 2:13

2 Co 1:5

2. 'For God's sake'* is a much-used phrase, a commonplace. But, surely, when it is not uttered meaninglessly, it is an extremely profound phrase. We often hear it in men's mouths, even when it is demonstrably far from their hearts. Every one asks to be helped 'for God's sake'; 'for God's sake' every one solicits support. All too easily things are asked 'for God's sake' which are not according to God; people implore 'for God's sake' that something be done to them which they do not want for God's sake, or want even perhaps in opposition to God. For others, it is a living and powerful word,* when it arises neither perfunctorily, nor unwarrantedly, nor in keeping with a manner of speaking or the art of persuasion, but out of the fullness of devotion, as it should, and the pure intention of the mind. The world passes away, you know, and its lusts,* and none of the things which were

1 P 2:13

Heb 4:12

1 Jn 2:17

done for it will seem advantageously settled or firmly established enough not to fall with it. For when the cause itself fails, how can anything based upon it escape crumbling along with it? For those who sow in the flesh will from the flesh reap only corruption* of the flesh, because all flesh is grass and its beauty is like the flower of the field; and when the grass withers, then the flower too must necessarily fade.* He alone who is the never-failing cause, not the flower of grass, but the word of God will remain for ever.* This was why he said, 'Heaven and earth will pass away, but my words will not pass away.'*

3. Therefore, dearly beloved, it is prudent and useful for you to have chosen to keep to hard ways for the sake of the words of his mouth, sowing there where your share of the seed will suffer the least loss. 'He who sows sparingly' will reap, of course, but 'he will reap sparingly.'* Now if someone sows, he will have a reward.* And we know who promised that no one who gives a cup of water to a thirsty man for the sake of his name will be deprived of his own reward.* Will he get back the same measure which he gave* or, if he is not content merely to offer water, but pours out his blood, drinking the cup the Saviour offers him, will his recompense be greater? This is no cup of cold water he offers, but a cup as intoxicating as it is excellent,* a cup of undiluted wine, yet well-mixed.* My Lord Jesus Christ alone had undiluted wine; he alone was perfectly pure and is always able to make pure the person conceived of unclean seed.* He alone had unadulterated

Marginal references:
Gal 6:8
Is 40:6-7
Is 40:8
Lk 21:33
2 Co 9:6
Mt 10:41
Mt 10:42
Mt 7:2
Ps 23:5
Ps 75:9
Jb 14:4

wine, who as God is all pervasive wisdom because of his pureness—and nothing defiled gains entrance to him*—and as man 'committed no sin; nor was guile found on his lips.'* He alone tasted death* not as an obligation of his condition, but simply by the good pleasure of his will. He did this not for his own advantage—for he has no need of our goods*—nor even in order to pay us grace for grace,* but he laid down his life for his friends* only so that he might make of his enemies, friends. For while we were yet enemies, we were reconciled to God by the blood of his Son.* Or rather, he did it for those already his friends, for even though they did not yet love him, they were already loved. In this lies grace, not that we loved God, but that he loved us first.* Do you want to know to what extent he was first? The apostle tells us: 'Blessed be the God and Father of Our Lord Jesus Christ who has blessed us in Christ with every spiritual blessing in the heavenly places, even as he chose us in him before the foundation of the world.'* And after that, 'He freely bestowed his grace on us in his beloved Son.'* How then was it possible for us not to be loved already in him, when we were chosen in him? How could we fail to be acceptable to him by whom we had been accepted? So then, in the temporal order Christ died for the ungodly;* but in that of predestination he died for his brothers and friends.

4. In all this, then, he alone has the unadulterated wine.* Let no one ever dare presume to say that this is not so and apply to him this word of the prophet: 'Your wine is mixed with water.'*

Wis 7:24-5
1 P 2:22
Heb 2:9

Ps 16:2
Jn 1:16
Jn 15:13

Rm 5:8-10

Jn 4:10

Eph 1:3-4
Eph 1:6

Rm 5:6

Ps 75:9

Is 1:22

Firstly, because here below, 'No one can bring

Jb 14:4
a clean thing out of an unclean,'* no one can

Pr 20:9
boast that he has a perfectly pure heart.* Then, because the day will come when everyone shall have to pay his debt to death. Thirdly, because

Jn 13:37
those who lay down their lives for Christ,* deserve in return the reward of eternal life; but woe to those who are ashamed to witness to

2 Tm 1:8
him!* Fourthly, because they repay a very tiny and unequal part of so privileged and freely-offered a love. Yet, he who is without mixture does not disdain their mixture, so long as they faithfully do what the apostle says, complete in

Col 1:24
their bodies what is lacking in Christ's passion.* In this way, all those chosen will together re-

Mt 20:1-15
ceive the one same penny* of eternal life. And yet, just as star differs from star in glory, and just as the brightness of the sun is one thing, the brightness of the moon another, and the brightness of the stars yet another, so it will be

1 Co 15:41-2
with the resurrection of the dead.* And although there is one house there are in it many

Jn 14:2
rooms,* so that as regards eternity and sufficiency, he who has gathered little will have no lack, and he who has gathered much will have

2 Co 8:15
nothing over.* But with regard to preeminence and the distinction of merits, each shall receive

1 Co 3:8
according to his labors,* so that nothing whatever which has been sown in Christ may be lost.

5. I have said all this, brothers, that grace may prepare us for that very spiritual answer which we must consider today. BECAUSE YOU, O LORD, ARE MY HOPE. Whatever must be done, whatever must be refused, whatever must be borne, whatever must be chosen, YOU, O LORD, ARE MY

HOPE. This is the only reason for all the promises made to me, this is the whole reason for my
expectation. Someone else may pretend to have
merit, he may pride himself on having borne
the burden and heat of day,* he may say he has
fasted twice a week, and finally he may boast
that he is not like other men.* But 'for me it is
good to cling to my God; to place my hope in
the Lord my God.'* Let others hope in other
things: one may trust in the knowledge of literature, one in the cleverness of the world, and
someone else in some other vanity. Because of
you I have incurred the loss of everything and
counted it as dung,* FOR YOU, O LORD, ARE MY
HOPE. Let anyone who likes hope in uncertain
riches* but as for me, I hope for nothing other
than the bare necessities* from you, for I trust
your word, on which I threw everything else
away: 'Seek first the kingdom of God and his
righteousness, and all these things shall be yours
as well.'* For 'the hapless beggar commits himself to you; you will be the helper of the father-
less.'* If rewards are promised me, it is through
you I hope to obtain them; if a host encamps
against me,* if the world fumes, if the evil one
rages, if the flesh itself lusts against the spirit,*
I will hope in you.

6. Brothers, to savor this is to live by faith.*
No one can pronounce the sentence, BECAUSE
YOU, O LORD, ARE MY HOPE, except the person
who is inwardly persuaded by the Spirit that,
as a prophet admonishes, he casts his burden
upon the Lord, knowing that he will be cared
for by him,* as is in keeping with what the apostle Peter said, 'Cast all your anxieties on him, for

Mt 20:2

Lk 18:11-12

Ps 73:27

Ph 3:8

1 Tm 6:17
Pr 30:8

Mt 6:33

Ps 10:16

Ps 27:3
Gal 5:17

Rm 1:17

Ps 55:23

1 P 5:7

he cares about you.* Why then, if we have savored all this, do we hesitate to throw away all our wretched, vain, useless, seductive hopes, and cling with all the fervor of our spirit, with all the devotion of our mind to this one so solid, so perfect, so blessed hope? If there is something impossible to him, if there is anything difficult, then look for someone else in whom to

Heb 1:3

hope. But he can do all things by his word.* What is easier than to speak? Yet I want you to understand this speaking. If he decides to save

Est 13:9

us,* then we shall at once be set free. If it pleases

Ps 30:5

him to quicken us, life is in his will.* If he wants to bestow eternal rewards, then he can do what he wants. You probably have no doubt about the ease with which he can do all this, but do you perhaps wonder whether it is his will? Surely the testimonies to this will are very cred-

Ps 93:6

itable.* 'Greater love has no man than this, that

Jn 15:13

a man lay down his life for his friends.'* And when did that majesty ever forsake those who

Ps 9:10

hope in him,* those whom he so carefully urges to hope in him? No, he will not abandon those who hope in him. 'He will help them and deliver them and save them, and he will rescue

Ps 37:41

them from sinners.'* Why? By what merits? Listen to what follows: 'Because they hoped in

Ibid.

him.'* This is a sweet reason; yet one that is both effective and indisputable. This surely is justice,

Ph 3:9

but one based on faith, not on law.* He has said,

From the Introit
Saluus populi for
Thursday in the
third week of Lent

'They will call to me in any tribulation whatever, and I will hear them.'* Look at how many tribulations there are. According to the number of them, his consolations are going to cheer

Ps 94:19

your soul,* as long as you do not turn aside to

others, as long as you call out to him,* as long   Ps 4:3
as you hope in him and take your refuge in the
Most High and not in any lowly or earthly
thing. 'Who ever hoped in him and was put to
shame?'* It is easier for heaven and earth to pass   Sir 2:11
away than for his word* to be cancelled out.   Mt 24:35

7. YOU HAVE MADE THE MOST HIGH YOUR
REFUGE, it says. The tempter shall not reach it,
nor the slanderer get up to it, nor the terrible
accuser of the brethren* come near it. For this   Rev 12:10
was said to him — remember the first words of
the Psalm — it was said to him who dwells in the
protection of the Most High, taking refuge
there from indecisiveness of spirit and from the
tempest.* The need for flight is twofold: fight-   Ps 55:8
ing without and fear within.* And we should   2 Co 7:5
have less need to flee if inward strength of soul
were able manfully to support exterior tumult,
or if outward calm nurtured our own faintheartedness. YOU HAVE MADE THE MOST HIGH
YOUR REFUGE. Brothers, let us fly there fre-
quently: it is a fortified place* where no enemy   Ps 71:2
is to be feared. If only we were able to stay
there always! But that is not for the present.
What is now a refuge will one day be a dwelling
place and an eternal dwelling place. Meanwhile, even though we may not tarry there, we
may however frequently have recourse to it. In
every temptation, in every trial, and in any need
of any kind whatever, it is an open city of refuge for us, a mother's open bosom. The clefts
of the rock* are ready, the bowels of the tender   Sg 2:14
mercy of our God* accessible. If anyone should   Lk 1:78
turn away from this refuge, it will be no won-
der if he does not deserve to escape.

8. Now, brothers, if the prophet had said, as we find in another psalm, 'Because I have hoped in you,'* then what we have already said in explaining this verse would be sufficient. But because he said YOU, O LORD, ARE MY HOPE, something different and deeper resounds, because it is not just in him that the soul hopes, but for him. For what has been said about our hope concerns more what we hope than in whom we hope. There are, as it happens, people who yearn to obtain spiritual or physical benefits from the Lord, but perfect love* thirsts after the Most High alone, crying out with all the might of that desire: 'Whom have I in heaven, and what is there upon earth that I desire except you? God is the strength of my heart and my portion for ever.'* Today's reading from Jeremiah the prophet says all this beautifully in a few words, 'You are good, O Lord, to those who wait for you, to the soul that seeks you.'* Notice carefully this distinction of numbers: whereas it says in the plural that many hope in him, this being general to many, it says in the singular that one seeks him, because it is unique to purity, unique to grace, unique to perfection, not only to hope for nothing except from him, but to seek nothing except him. And if the one is good, how much better is the other?

9. Is is right then that the soul seeking him should be answered, YOU HAVE MADE THE MOST HIGH YOUR REFUGE. A soul thirsting for God* like this does not want with Peter to make a shrine on the earthly mountain,* nor wish with Mary to touch him on earth,* but it cries out simply 'Fly, my beloved; be like a gazelle or a

Ps 16:1

1 Jn 4:18

Ps 73:24-5

Lam 3:25

Ps 42:2

Mt 17:4

Jn 20:17

young stag atop the mountains of Bethel.'* For
it has heard him say, 'If you loved me, you
would have rejoiced, because I go to the Father; for the Father is greater than I.'* It has heard
him say, 'Do not touch me, for I have not yet
ascended to my Father.'* And now, not unaware of the heavenly plan, it cries with the apostle, 'Even though we once recognized Christ
according to the flesh, we no longer recognize
him that way.'* 'Atop the mountains of Bethel,'
it says. That is, atop all power and dominion,*
atop the angels and the archangels, even the
cherubim and the seraphim — for the mountains
are the house of God,* which is the meaning of
Bethel*—surely at the right hand of the Father,
where the Father will no longer be greater than
he,† the soul goes, desiring to grasp the right
hand of him who is co-equal with the Most
High. This then, brothers, is eternal life, that
we should know the Father, the true God, and
him whom he has sent, Jesus Christ,* true God
and one with him, God over all and blessed for
ever. Amen.*

Sg 8:14

Jn 14:28

Jn 20:17

2 Co 5:16
Eph 1:21

Is 2:2
*Cf. Jerome,
*Liber interpr.
hebr. nom.*;
ed. de Lagarde, p. 3
†Jn 14:28

Jn 17:3

Rm 9:5

SERMON TEN

On the Tenth Verse:

NO EVIL SHALL BEFALL YOU,
NO SCOURGE COME NEAR YOUR TENT

1. IT IS NOT UNIQUE to me or new to
you, but a very well-known watchword
that in the most important matters of our
faith it is easier to know, and more perilous not
to know, what is not than what is. I see no reason why we should not apply this to hope as
well. The human mind, having some experience
of misfortunes, is far more conscious of the
things it lacks than of those it is going to enjoy.
For faith and hope are such close kin that the
one believes shall be what the other already begins to hope shall be for itself. The apostle quite
rightly then defined faith as the substance of
things hoped for,* because no one can hope for
something without first believing in it, any more
than he can paint on empty space. Faith therefore says: 'God has prepared great and impon-
derable things for his faithful.' Hope says: 'All
these things are being kept for me.' And charity,
the third, affirms, 'I am gaining on them'. But,
as I have just reminded you, it is very difficult,
and even impossible, to analyze the nature of
all those good things — unless, of course, the
Spirit himself reveals to someone* what, as the

apostle says, 'no eye has seen, nor ear heard, nor
the heart of man conceived, what God has prepared for those who love him.'* Even Paul himself, almost perfect while still in mortal flesh,*
was obliged to confess, 'Now I know in part',
and again, 'Now we see in a mirror dimly, but
then face to face,'* because this was, as it were,
only a sort of imperfect perfection; otherwise
the apostle would not have said 'Let those of us
who are perfect be of one mind,'* when he had
said just before, in speaking of himself, 'Not
that I have already obtained this or am already
perfect.'* Whatever man is capable of knowing
here below, therefore, is best commended by
good and foresighted inculcation. For it is characteristic of those who suffer to consider deliverance from pain the pinnacle of happiness and
to think of the absence of misery as perfect bliss.
Therefore the prophet says in the psalm, 'Return, O my soul, to your rest; for the Lord has
dealt kindly with you,'* and, instead of enumer-
ating the various gifts assembled for happiness,
he adds, 'For he has delivered my soul from
death, my eyes from tears, my feet from stumbling.'* These words show clearly that he considers he has received great rest and benefit from
the Lord in being freed from trials and dangers.

2. In the phrase of psalm ninety* which we
must discuss today surely we find the same
thing: NO EVIL SHALL BEFALL YOU, NO SCOURGE
COME NEAR YOUR TENT. This verse, as far as I
can see, is easy to understand, and perhaps some
of you have already thought about it. For you
are not so uncultured or untutored in spiritual
studies that you do not easily distinguish be-

Cf. 1 Co 2:9
2 Co 4:11

1 Co 13:12

Ph 3:15

Ph 3:12

Ps 116:7

Ps 116:8

By Vulgate–
Septaguint
enumeration;
Psalm 91 in the
Hebrew text

tween yourselves and your tent, or between
what is called evil and what a scourge. You have
heard the apostle say that after having fought
the good fight,* he will soon put off† his tent.
But what need is there for me to recall the apostle's words? As if a soldier could be ignorant of
what is meant by his tent or need to be told
about it by an outsider. We do indeed see some
who have changed their tents into dwellings
of the worst possible captivity, and instead of
fighting in them, endure a miserable slavery.
And what is more — and utterly ridiculous —
there are others who have gone so astray and
come to be so forgetful and so spiritually frenzied that they seem to think they are nothing
more than their outward tent. Are they anything but unacquainted not only with God* but
also with themselves, when, like people dead
from the heart,* they spend all their energy in
looking after the body, and take such pains over
the tent as if they thought it was never going
to collapse? Yet collapse it must, and very shortly, too. Do not these people so devoted to flesh
and blood,* as though they imagine that they
are only flesh, appear to have no knowledge of
themselves? Have they not taken their souls so
lightly as to seem not to know they have souls?
'If you separate the precious from the vile, you
will be as my mouth,'* says the Lord; this means,
'if you shrewdly discriminate between outer
and inner substance, so that you have no more
to fear for your tent from a scourge than you
do from evil for yourself.' This is what 'evil'
means, which is why it has been said, 'Turn
away from evil and do good.'* It is evil because

*2 Tm 4:7
†2 P 1:14

1 Co 15:34

Ps 31:14

Gal 1:16

Jer 15:19

Ps 37:27

it deprives the soul of animate life,* because it
separates you from God until, once it reigns in
us, our body is, as it were, soulless; and our soul
is godless, truly dead to herself,* like one of
those whom the apostle represents as being
without God in this world.*

3. I do not want to say that you should hate
your own flesh.* Love it as something given
you as a helper* and a partner prepared to share
in eternal happiness. What is more, the soul
should so love the flesh that she not be thought
to change into it, and thus hear the Lord say,
'My spirit shall not abide in man, for he is flesh.'*
The soul should love the flesh, but should even
more tend her own animate life. Let Adam love
his Eve, but he must not love her so much that
he obeys her voice rather than God's.* Finally,
it is not good for him to love her in such a way
that while you protect her against the scourge
of paternal reproof, you store up the wrath* of
eternal damnation. 'You brood of vipers!' says
John. 'Who warned you to flee from the wrath
to come? Bear fruit befitting repentance.'* As
though he would say more openly, 'Learn discipline, lest the Lord be angry.'* Bear the scold-
ing rod,* lest you feel the shattering hammer.†
Why do carnal men say to us, 'Your life is cruel;
won't you spare your flesh?' 'Right you are!
We will not spare the seed. How could we spare
it more? Is it not better for it to be renewed and
multiplied in the field than to rot in the barn?
Alas, "The beasts have rotted in their dung."'*
Is this how you are going to spare your flesh?
We are cruel now by not sparing it, whereas by
sparing it you are even crueler. Our body even

*anima animam
privat*

Jm 2:17

Eph 2:12

Eph 5:28-9
Gen 2:18

Gen 6:3

Gen 3:17

Rm 2:5

Mt 3:7-8

Ps 2:12
*Pr 29:15
†Jer 22:29

Jl 1:17

Ps 16:10

now, dwells in hope.* But you will see what shame yours suffers here, and what misery awaits it in the future?

NO EVIL WILL BEFALL YOU; NO SCOURGE COME NEAR YOUR TENT. These words signify a double garb and a twofold immortality. For how does death occur if not by the separation of body and soul? This is why a dead body is said to be inanimate.* Yet how does this separation come about if not through present scourges, through some acute pain, through the corruption of the body itself, through the penalty of sin? Rightly does our flesh hate and fear the scourge by which it suffers bitter divorce from its own soul, a beloved and honored companion. Here below, until it is recalled, it must willy nilly suffer this separation. It is to your advantage to put up with it, so that you may soon be delivered, and henceforth no scourge may come near your tent.

exanime

4. But here and now, as we remembered earlier and as we should constantly remember, the true life of the soul is God. And there is one only evil which separates them, but it is an evil of the soul: none other than sin. Alas, brothers, we toy with trifles, we delight in indulging in idle pastimes, when this forked serpent is at hand, ready to deprive us of both our lives, that of the body and that of the soul. How shall we sleep securely, unless this negligence in such grave peril indicates less security than despair? And yet, it is up to us to choose to be delivered from both; but here below, we must guard more against sin than the penalty of sin, and therefore turn aside more assiduously from evil than from

the scourge, because it is far more dangerous, and a far sorrier plight for the soul, to be separated from God than from the body. Doubtless, when all sin has been taken away from our midst, the cause having been removed, then the effect as well will no longer remain; so then no evil will be able to approach you, and no scourge come near your tent, because once fault is far removed from the inner man, penalty will be removed from the outer. Nor did he say, 'There will be no evil in you, no scourge in your tent,' but, 'it shall not befall you, it shall not come near.'

5. But we must consider that there are men in whom sin not only resides, but also reigns.* And it seems hardly able to be closer or more intimate, than when it has got such a hold that it cannot be shaken off at all. But one can find others whom sin, though it yet dwells in them, does not dominate or hold sway over, but is on the way to being plucked out, but is not yet pushed out, cast down, not yet completely cast out. It is evident that it was not like this from the beginning,* for before that initial deceit, sin not only did not reign in our first parents, but it did not even exist. Yet it seems somehow to have been very near them, since it got in so quickly. What else was he warning them about, except that this penalty for sin, though not yet in their bodies, was however already, as it were, on the threshold, when he said: 'In the day that you eat of the tree of the knowledge of good and evil, you shall die the death.'* What happy expectation and blessed hope† indeed is ours, for we await a resurrection which will so surpass in

Rm 5:21

Mt 19:8

*Gen 2:17, as cited by Fautus of Riez, *De gratia* 1.1; PL 58:786B
†Tt 2:13

glory our first condition that no fault whatever, no penalty, no evil, no scourge shall dwell in or reign over, or even at any time be able to dwell in or to reign over, our bodies or our souls.

6. But what are we to do, brothers? I fear I am going to be caught out again. You know, of course, that our and your great abbot general* appointed this time to be spent in not preaching but in manual labor.* But I think he will forgive me easily when he remembers that holy fraud by which once long ago Romanus brought him food during the three years he spent in the cave. As we read, 'This holy man stole out of his father's sight for some hours, and on certain days brought to Benedict some food of which he had deprived himself.'* I, too, have no doubt, brothers, that several of you have a greater abundance of spiritual wealth; but what I share with you, I do not steal from myself. Rather, with you I eat more sweetly and surely what the Lord may give me, and this food is not diminished by being shared around, but multiplied by being served up. Yet if I occasionally address you contrary to the usage of our Order, I do not do so out of my own presumption, but by the will of our venerable brothers and fellow-abbots, who even urge me to do what they would never wish to have permission to do themselves. They know that I have another reason and a special need to act like this. I would not be talking to you if I could work with you.* Perhaps my words then would have more effect; they would at least be more acceptable to my conscience. However, since this is denied me because of my sins and,

St Benedict

RB 49

Gregory the
Great, *Dial.* II, 1

Cf. *Vita prima* I.
23, 24; PL 185:240

as you know, the many weaknesses of my bur-
densome body, as well as by demands on my
time, may I, one of those who preach and do not
practice,* deserve to be one of the least in the
kingdom of God.

Mt 23:3

SERMON ELEVEN

On the Eleventh Verse:

FOR HE HAS GIVEN HIS ANGELS CHARGE OF
YOU TO GUARD YOU IN ALL YOUR WAYS

1. IT IS WRITTEN, and truly written, that it is 'By the mercies of the Lord that we are not consumed,'* that he has not given us over into the hands of our enemies.* The untiring and ever-watchful eye of his extraordinary kindness watches over us:* he who keeps Israel neither slumbers nor sleeps.* This is requisite. He who assails Israel neither slumbers nor sleeps either. And just as the former is anxious about us and concerned for us,* the latter is anxious to slaughter and destroy* us, and this is his only concern, that someone who has turned away might be turned back.* Yet we either are heedless or scarcely pay attention to the deference due our defender, to the watchfulness of our protector, to the benefits from our benefactor. We are ungrateful for the graces received, or rather for the many graces by which he anticipates and helps us. Now he fills our souls with splendors through himself, now he visits us through his angels, he teaches us through men, now he even consoles and instructs us by the Scriptures. 'For whatever was written was written for our instruction, that by patience and the encouragement of the Scrip-

Lam 3:22

Ps 41:2

Jer 31:28
Ps 121:4

1 P 5:7
Jn 10:10

Jer 8:4

tures we might have hope.'* Well said, 'for our instruction', that by patience we might hope; for, as it is said elsewhere, 'A man's teaching is recognized by patience.'* And again, 'patience produces character, and character hope.'* Why are we the only ones to be absent from ourselves? Why are we the only ones to neglect ourselves? Should we disregard ourselves because we are surrounded by help on all sides? Surely we ought on that account to be all the more vigilant. Had God not seen that we had great need, he would not have shown such great solicitude for us on earth as in heaven.* He would not have set so many guardians over us had there not been so many obstacles.

2. Blessed are our brothers who have already been set free from the snare of the hunter, who have passed from the tents of the militant to the courts of the recumbent; once the fear of evil has been allayed they are singularly settled in hope.* To one, or rather to all, of them it is said: NO EVIL SHALL BEFALL YOU, NO SCOURGE COME NEAR YOUR TENT. But consider well: this promise was made not to someone living according to the flesh,* but to someone who, though living in the flesh, walks according to the spirit,* so it is impossible to distinguish between himself and his tent. Everything is confused in him, as in a son of Babylon.* He is still a man of the flesh and the spirit does not abide* in him. And where there is no good spirit,* will evil ever be absent? And where evil is, the scourge will necessarily come near as well. For evil is always accompanied by penitence. NO EVIL SHALL BEFALL YOU, NO SCOURGE COME NEAR

Rm 15:4

Pr 19:11
Rm 5:4

Mt 6:10

Ps 4:9

Rm 8:4, 2

2 Co 10:3

Jer 50:2
Gen 6:3
Ps 143:10

YOUR TENT. A great promise; but what reason
have I to hope for it? How do I escape both
evil and the scourge, how do I fly away,* how
do I go so far away that they shall not come
near me? By what merit, wisdom, or virtue shall
I be able to do this? HE HAS GIVEN HIS ANGELS
CHARGE OF YOU TO KEEP YOU IN ALL YOUR WAYS.
In all what ways? Those by which you turn
away from evil,* by which you flee the wrath to
come.* There are many ways, and many kinds
of ways; there is indeed great danger for a wayfarer. How easy it is to wander along one's own
way* when so many intersect, if one lacks the
ability for discerning ways. Now he has not
given his angels charge to help us in all possible
ways, but in all our own ways. Yet there are
some ways from which, rather than in which,
they ought to guard us.

3. Let us examine our ways, brothers. Let us
also investigate the ways of devils, the ways of
the blessed spirits, and the ways of the Lord.*
I am about to undertake something far beyond
me; but you must help me by your prayers, that
God may open up for me the treasures of his
understanding and make the offerings of my
mouth pleasing to himself.* So then, the ways
of the sons of Adam* are directed to necessity
and greed. By both these things are we led, by
both are we dragged along; the only difference
is that we seem to be pushed by need but dragged
by greed. Necessity seems especially concerned
with the body. It is not straight but very winding and very roundabout: it has very few, if
any, short cuts. What man does not know that
the needs of man are many indeed? Who could

Ps 55:6

Ps 37:27
Mt 3:7

Is 47:15

Ps 18:21

Ps 119:108
Jer 32:19

manage to explain how many there are? Experience itself teaches us, hardship itself bestows understanding. By these are we taught that we need to cry aloud to the Lord,* asking to be delivered, not from necessity, but 'from my necessities.'* Anyone not deaf will lend his ear to the warnings of wisdom and desire to be delivered not only from the ways of necessity but also from those of greed. What did it say? 'Avoid your base desires.'* And again, 'Do not chase after your lusts.'* These two evils it is indeed far better to live in need of than in greed for. We have many necessities, but we have more, far many more, forms of greed. Greed is something rooted in the heart, and therefore it is so much greater because the soul is so much more* than the body. Finally, these are the ways which seem right to men,* but they have no end until they plunge into the depths of hell. If you have discovered the ways of men, consider too that it was said probably of them: 'Sorrow and unhappiness are in their ways'*—sorrow in necessity, unhappiness in greed. How is it that greed causes unhappiness and not happiness, as one would think? Does happiness seem to smile on someone rich in the earthly possessions he yearned for? He is all the more unhappy because he has mistaken unhappiness for happiness, clinging to it, or rather wallowing in it and being swallowed up by it. Woe to the sons of men on account of this false and fickle happiness. Woe to him who says,* 'I am rich and lack nothing,'* although he is poor and naked, wretched and pitiable. Necessity arises, of course, from the weakness of the flesh; greed

Ps 3:4

Ps 25:17

Sir 18:30
Ibid.

Mt 6:25

Pr 16:25

Ps 14:7

Cf. Is 5:20, 45:10
Rev 3:17

proceeds from penury of heart and forgetfulness. And because the soul has forgotten to eat her bread,* she begs for someone else's. She yearns for earthly goods because she meditates as little as possible on heavenly ones.

4. Now let us take a look at the ways of the demons: let us look and beware; look and flee, for in these ways lie presumption and stubbornness. Do you want to know how I know this? Consider who their sovereign is: as he is, so are his servants. Consider the source of his ways: did he not leap straight into the most monstrous presumption, saying, 'I will sit on the mount of the covenant, on the banks of the far north. I will be like the Most High'?* What heedless and what horrible presumption! Are not 'Evildoers falling prostrate, thrust down, unable to rise'?* Presumption was their downfall. His stubbornness brought him low and 'he will not rise now that he lies.'* Because of these he is a passing wind that comes not again.* The demons' presumption is amazing enough, but their stubbornness is no less amazing: their pride mounts continually,* so for them there is no change.* Because they refused to turn aside from presumptuous ways, they fell into the way of stubbornness. How perverted and depraved of heart are those sons of men who follow in the demons' steps, who walk in demonic ways! And this is the whole struggle against us by the spiritual hosts of wickedness,* to seduce us into their ways, to induce us into their ways, to reduce us to the fated end that is prepared for them.* Man, flee presumption lest your enemy gloat over you.* He gloats especially in tripping you

Ps 102:4

Is 14:13-4

Ps 36:12

Ps 41:8
Ps 78:40

Ps 74:24
Ps 55:20

Eph 6:12

Mt 25:41

Ps 41:11, Sir 23:3

into these vices, for he knows by experience how difficult it is for you to catch your breath in such a whirlpool.

5. But I would not have you not know* how we go down, brothers, or rather fall into these ways. The first step of the descent that comes to my mind is shutting one's eyes to his own frailty, iniquity, and uselessness. When a man excuses himself, flatters himself, or persuades himself that he is something, when he is nothing,* he has already seduced himself. The second step is self-ignorance. For when someone at the first step has sewn himself a useless apron out of leaves,* what is left but not to see his covered wounds, especially someone who sewed it chiefly so he would not see them? And so it happens that when someone else points them out to him, he argues that they are not wounds, having turned to evil words to make excuses for sins.* And he is now very near to the third step, already bordering on presumption. Is someone who presumes to defend himself going to blush to do evil? Moreover, it will be difficult for him to stand firm in darkness and slippery places,* especially as the evil angel of the Lord is there hounding and impelling him to evil. And the fourth step, or rather the fourth precipice, is contempt; as Scripture says, 'The wicked man when he comes into the depths of evil, contemns.'* And from here on the sink-hole† engulfs him more and more. Contempt leads his soul to impenitence, impenitence settles him in stubbornness. Now this sin will not be forgiven either in this age or in the age to come,* for the hard and hardened heart* neither fears God nor

Rm 1:13

Gal 6:3

Gen 3:7

Ps 141:4

Ps 35:6

*Pr 18:3
†Ps 69:16

Mt 12:32
Ex 4:21

Lk 18:4

*1 Co 6:17
†Qo 23:28

1 Co 10:13

Augustine,
Sermon 164.14;
PL 38:901-2
Jn 1:18

Jn 1:51

Mt 18:10

Ps 25:8

regards man.* And whoever clings like this to the devil in all his ways is manifestly made one spirit with him.* The ways of men,† with which we dealt further up, are those of which it has been said, 'No temptation overtakes you that is not common to man,'* and it is human to sin. Does anyone not know that the ways of the devil are foreign to man's nature? Unless, of course, habit has some power to change his nature. Anyway, even though it happens to some men, to persevere in evil is not human but diabolic.*

6. And what are ways of the holy angels? Surely those spoken of by the Only-begotten* when he said, 'You will see the angels ascending and descending upon the Son of man.'* So their ways consist in ascent and descent: they ascend because of him, and they descend, or rather they condescend, because of us. Just as those blessed spirits ascend by the contemplation of God, so they descend out of compassion for you, that they may guard you in all your ways. They ascend to his face, and descend at his nod, for he has given his angels charge over you. Yet in their descent they are not deprived of the vision of his glory, because they always behold the face of the Father.*

7. I think you would also like to hear something about the ways of the Lord. I should appear most presumptuous if I were to promise to show them to you. Still, we read that he himself will teach us his ways.* Who else indeed is to be believed? Thus he taught us his ways when he opened the mouth of his prophet to say, "All the ways of the Lord are mercy and

truth.'* To each and every one alike he comes in
his mercy and truth. When we presume upon
his mercy and forget his truth, straightaway
God is absent. Nor is he where great terror follows the recollection of truth yet there is no
consolation from the remembrance of his mercy.* Nor does anyone hold truth who fails to
recognize present mercy; nor can there be real
mercy without truth. Therefore, where mercy
and truth have met, there justice and peace have
kissed each other* and he who has made his
dwelling in peace* cannot not be present, too.
We have heard and known* all these things concerning the blissful union of truth and mercy
because our fathers have told them to us.* The
prophet says, 'Your mercy and your truth have
received me.'* And in another place, 'Your
mercy is before my eyes, and I am well pleased
with your truth.'* And the Lord himself has
said of it, 'My mercy and my truth shall be
with him.'*

8. But consider too the manifest comings of
our Lord,* how in him who is now looked forward to you have a merciful Saviour, but in him
who is promised for the end of time, an uncom-
promising judge. This seems meant by the saying: 'God loves mercy and truth: the Lord will
give grace and glory.'* However mindful he
was in his first coming of his mercy and his truth
to the house of Israel,* in his final coming, although he will have to judge the world with
righteousness and the peoples in truth,* this
future judgement will not be without mercy,*
except perhaps for those who have not been
merciful. These are the pathways of eternity

Ps 25:9

Ps 106:7

Ps 85:10
Ps 76:2
Ps 78:3

Ps 44:1

Ps 40:14

Ps 26:3

Ps 89:25

1 Co 1:18

Ps 84:12

Ps 98:4

Ps 96:13
Jm 2:13

of which you read in the prophet: 'The hills of
the world were bowed down by the pathways

Hab 3:6
of his eternity.'* At hand are ways by which I
can easily prove this, for, 'The mercy of the

Ps 103:17
Lord is from everlasting to everlasting,'* and
Ps 117:2
'the truth of the Lord endures for ever.'* By
these pathways have been bowed down the hills
of the world — the proud devils, the rulers of

*Jn 12:31
†Eph 6:12
this world* and of its darkness† who do not
know the way of truth and mercy, or remember his paths. What can there be between truth

Jn 8:44
and him who 'is a liar and the father of lies'?*
Then too you see it clearly written that 'There

Ibid.
is no truth in him.'* And how far removed he
was from mercy is proved by our wretchedness,
inflicted on us by him. How could he ever have
been merciful when he was a murderer from the
beginning? Finally, 'If a man is cruel to himself,

Sir 14:5
to whom will he be good?'* Surely he is very
cruel to himself, he who never laments his own
iniquity, never feels a twinge over his own damnation. His false presumption has driven him

Wis 5:6
away from the way of truth,* his cruel stubbornness has blocked up the way of mercy. He
can never attain this mercy by himself nor ob-

1 Co 7:25
tain it from the Lord.* In this way then the
swollen hills have been bowed down by the

Hab 3:6
pathways of eternity,* while they have turned
Hos 14:10
aside from the ways of the Lord,* which are
straight, by their roundabout and devious, not
so much pathways, as steep slopes. But how
much more profitably and prudently the other
hills were bowed down and brought low, to
their salvation, from these pathways. For they
did not stoop down as though they were depart-

ing from their own uprightness, but they were bowed down by the pathways of his eternity. Do we not see these hills bowing down when the high and mighty bend low* before our Lord and adore his footsteps? Do they not bow down when they turn away from the pernicious heights of vanity and cruelty toward the humble pathways of mercy and truth?*

9. It is not only the good spirits, but also the elect among men who direct their steps in these ways of the Lord.* And the first step for the wretched man extricating himself from the depths of vice is the mercy* which makes him merciful to the son of his mother,* to be merciful to his soul,* and thereby pleasing to God. In this way he emulates the great work of divine pity, being moved to tears with him who was pierced for him, somehow dying for his own salvation, and sparing himself no longer. This first act of pity sustains the person returning to his heart,* and enables him to enter the secret places of his being. It now remains for him to link up with the royal road* and go forward to truth, and join confession of the lips to contrition of heart, as I have so often urged you to do. 'For man believes with his heart and so is justified, and he confesses with his lips and so is saved.'* Turned back to his heart,† he must become little in his own eyes, as Truth himself has said, 'Unless you turn back and become like little children, you will never enter the kingdom of heaven.'* May he not choose to hide what he knows only too well, that he is reduced to nothing.* May he not be ashamed to bring into the light of truth what he cannot see in secret with-

Is 60:14

Cf. Ps 85:10

Ps 18:21

Lk 1:79
Is 49:15
Sir 30:24

Is 46:8

Num 21:22

*Rm 10:10
†Ps 85:8

Mt 18:3

Ps 73:21

out being moved to pity. In this way man enters the ways of mercy and truth, the ways of
the Lord, the ways of life.* And the fruit of
these ways is the salvation of the wayfarer.

Ps 16:11

10. That the angels also walk these same ways
is obvious. For when they ascend to contemplation, they seek truth, in desiring which they
find satisfaction and in satisfaction they desire.
But when they descend to us, they show us
mercy, that they may guard us in all our ways.
These spirits are our ministers, sent to serve us.*
Clearly they are our ministers and not our masters. And in this they imitate the example given
by the Only-begotten who came not to be
served, but to serve,* who stood among his disciples as one who serves.* The fruit of these
angelic ways for themselves is their happiness
and obedience in love. The fruit for us is that
by them we obtain divine grace and are guarded
in our ways here below. So then, HE HAS GIVEN
HIS ANGELS CHARGE OF YOU TO GUARD YOU IN ALL
YOUR WAYS, in all your needs, in all your desires.
Otherwise you would easily run into the ways
of death,* that is to say, either charge into stubbornness out of necessity, or out of greed into
presumption, which are the ways no longer of
men but of demons. For when are men usually
found to be most obstinate, if not in things
which they pretend or esteem to be necessary?
As someone has said, 'If you warn such a man,
he answers I can do what I can do, and I cannot
do more than that. If you can, then you may
feel differently.'* Yet how do we come to fall
into presumption if not because we tear off on
an impulse from our hotter desires?

Heb 1:14

Mt 20:28
Lk 22:27

Jer 21:8

Terence,
Andria, 310

11. Meanwhile, therefore, God has charged his angels not with turning you from your ways, but with keeping you in them, and directing you as it were by their ways into his ways. How do they do this, you ask? Surely just as an angel acts purely out of charity alone, you too, alerted at least by your own necessity, descend and condescend. That is, you strive to show mercy towards your neighbor,* and then, lifting up your desires with the same angel, you strive to acsend with all the greediness of your soul to sublime and eternal truth. Here we are admonished to lift up our hearts with our hands;* here every day we hear, 'Lift up your hearts;'* here we are reproached in our negligence and told, 'O Sons of men, how long will you be dull of heart? Why do you love vanity and seek after lying?'* An unburdened and a lightened heart is better lifted up to seek and love truth.* Do not be astonished that they who deign to keep watch over us deign to admit us with them into the ways of the Lord, or better, that they do not disdain to direct us into them. How much more happily, how much more securely do they walk in them! And yet as they follow in mercy and truth, they are far inferior to him who is Truth itself, Mercy itself.*

12. How aptly God has set each of the competitors at his own level. He himself is sovereign Being, at the summit; beyond him there is nothing, above him there is nothing. Next he has placed his angels, not at the top, but in safety, that clinging very closely to him who is at the summit, they may be confirmed with strength from on high.* Now men are neither

Lk 10:27

Lm 3:41
Preface to the Eucharistic Canon

Ps 4:2
Ps 84:12

Ps 40:14

Lk 24:29

at the summit nor in safety, but on alert. In fact, they are on something solid, that is to say the earth, and have the bottom but not the basest place, and this is why it is necessary and possible for them to be on their guard. The demons, however, waft suspended on the windy, worthless air. While unworthy to ascend to heaven, they still deign to descend to earth.*

Rom 10:6-7

And that will do for today. May he from whom comes our sufficiency give us grace enough to thank him. For we are not sufficient of ourselves* to think anything by ourselves or of ourselves, unless he grants it, who gives to all generously,* and is above all, God blessed for ever and ever.*

2 Co 3:5

Jm 1:5
Rm 9:5

SERMON TWELVE

On the Twelfth Verse:

ON THEIR HANDS THEY WILL BEAR YOU UP
LEST YOU DASH YOUR FOOT
AGAINST A STONE

1. IN YESTERDAY'S SERMON, if you remember, I spoke to you about the ways of
demons, presumption and stubbornness,
nor did I mince words about why I spoke of
them. I can, however, if you think it necessary,
track down their ways another way. For though
they do their very best to hide them from us,
the Holy Spirit points them out in many ways
and in many ways in the sacred Scriptures ex-
plains the paths of the wicked.*   Pr 4:14
we read that 'the wicked prowl on every side.'*   Ps 12:9
Of their prince we read 'he circles around seeking someone to devour.'* And this is what he   1 P 5:8
himself was forced to confess when he stood in
the presence of the divine majesty among the
sons of God and was asked where he came from:
'I have been circling the earth, and walking up
and down it.'* We say then that his ways are a   Jb 1:7
circuit and a circumvention. The one concerns
us, and the other him. He is always being raised
up, and always being thrown down; he is always
climbing up by pride,* and always being hu-   Ps 74:24
miliated. Is that not a circuit? Anyone who

Ps 12:9
Mt 18:7

prowls around* in circles sets out, but never gets anywhere. Woe to the man* who follows this circuit, who never steps back from his own will. If you try to drag him away, he will seem to follow for a little while, but it will be a ruse. He is in a circuit, he is on the point of returning from somewhere but he cannot be led out of it. He bustles around everywhere, he flies around, but he clings forever to his own will.

2. But yet, if one's own circuit is a bad thing, someone else's circumvention is far worse. This is what the devil mostly does. But how is it, brothers, that he who is so proud condescends to circumvent a wretched man? Even in this, look at the circuit of the godless. His eyes behold everything lofty, yet he pries curiously into the basest things, but only in order to climb higher, to puff harder; and when he has trodden a humble person underfoot, he fancies he is more exalted; as it is written, 'When the god-

Ps 10:2

less shows off, the poor man is burned.'* How depravedly does the bad angel ape the ascend-

Gen 28:12

ing and the descending of the good angels.* He ascends by his eager vanity and he descends by jealous spite. His ascent is counterfeit and his descent is cruel. As we said yesterday, he is devoid of mercy and truth. Yet, if wicked spirits

Ps 40:5

descend to circumvent us,* we have every reason to be grateful to God by whose command good angels also come down to help us, to guard us in all our ways. And not only this, but he said, ON THEIR HANDS THEY WILL BEAR YOU UP, LEST YOU DASH YOUR FOOT AGAINST A STONE.

3. What great instruction, warning, and encouragement there is for us, brothers, in these

words of Scripture. What other psalm so wonderfully encourages the weak-willed, warns the careless, and instructs the ignorant? This is why divine providence desires his faithful have the verses of this psalm constantly on their lips especially during the lenten season. And from their very usurpation by the devil, opportunity was snatched to make that thoroughly wicked and unwilling servant* serve the sons. What could be more vexing for him or happier for us than that even his evil should work for our good?* HE HAS GIVEN HIS ANGELS CHARGE OF YOU TO GUARD YOU IN ALL YOUR WAYS. 'Let them thank the Lord for his mercy, for his wonderful works for the sons of men'.* Let them give thanks and say 'among the nations, "The Lord has done great things for them"'.* O Lord, what is man that you should regard him,* and set your heart upon him?'* You have set your heart upon him, you attend to his needs* and take care of him.* And so you sent your only Son,† you sent out your spirit,* and you even show forth your own countenance.* And so that nothing in heaven should rest from efforts on our behalf, you send those holy spirits to serve us,* you assign them as our guardians, and you order them to be our tutors. And this is not all, you not only made your spirits* angels,† you also made them the guardians of little ones, whose 'angels always behold the face of the Father'.* You make these blessed spirits not only your angels to us, but ours to you.

4. HE HAS GIVEN HIS ANGELS CHARGE OF YOU. What marvelous esteem and what truly great love of charity! For who gives charge, to

Mt 18:32

Rm 8:28

Ps 107:8

Ps 126:3

Ps 144:3

Jb 7:17

1 Mac 16:14

*Lk 10:35/†1 Jn 4:9

Ps 104:29

Ps 89:16

Heb 1:14

*i.e. messengers
†Ps 104:4

Mt 18:10

whom, of whom, and to what end? Let us consider this carefully, brothers, and fix diligently in our memory this very great charge. Who gives the charge? Whose angels are they? With whose charge do they comply? Whose will do they obey? Surely, HE HAS GIVEN HIS ANGELS CHARGE OF YOU, TO GUARD YOU. Nor do they hesitate to bear you in their hands.* Sovereign Majesty has charged, and charged his angels — those sublime, those blessed beings, intimately united, closely cleaving to himself, those true members of the household of God.* He has charged them with you. Who are you?* 'Lord, what is man* that you are mindful of him, or the son of man that you should regard him?'* As if man were not 'a maggot and the son of man a worm.'* Now what do you think he charged them to do for you? Has he assigned them bitter tasks against you?* Have they shown his power to you, as against a leaf that is snatched up by the wind and chased you like dry chaff?* Did he charge them to carry off the wicked so that he should not see the glory of God?* They will be charged with this one day, but this is not his charge. Do not draw away from the aid of the Most High, linger in the protection of the God of heaven, lest someday he give this charge against you. For he whom the God of heaven protects will not have this charged against him; all will be for him. And if this charge is put off till later, it is all for the sake of his elect.* The provident householder says to his servants, ready and willing to go gather scattered weeds, 'Wait until the harvest, lest in gathering the weeds you root up the

Ps 91:12

Eph 2:9
Jn 8:25
Ps 8:4
Ps 144:3

Jb 25:6

Jb 13:26

Jb 13:25

Jn 11:40

Mt 24:33

wheat along with them.'* How then will the
wheat be preserved until then? That clearly is
the present task, the charge of the present time.

5. HE HAS GIVEN HIS ANGELS CHARGE OF YOU
TO GUARD YOU. O wheat among the weeds! O
grain among chaff!* O lily among brambles!† Mt 3:12
Thank him, brothers, thank him. He has en- Sg 2:22
trusted to us a precious deposit, the fruit of his
cross, the price of his blood.* He is not satisfied Mt 27:6
with this guardianship so little sure and so very
useless, so frail, so ineffective. 'Upon your walls,
O Jerusalem, he has set watchmen.'* Even those Is 62:6
who are reputed to be walls, or pillars* in the Gal 2:9
walls, need these watchmen, they most of all.

6. HE HAS GIVEN HIS ANGELS CHARGE OF YOU
TO GUARD YOU IN ALL YOUR WAYS. How this
word ought in you to produce respect to pro-
mote devotion and to provide confidence! Respect because of the presence of angels, devotion because of their friendliness, and confidence because of their guardianship. Walk cautiously;* his angels are everywhere, as he has Eph 5:15
charged them, in all your ways. In every little
nook or cranny, respect your angel. Would you
dare to do in his presence what you would not
dare in my sight? Perhaps you doubt he is present because you do not see him? What if you
heard him? What if you touched him? What
if you smelled him? Notice that things are not
proved present only by sight. Not even all material things are open to sight. So how much
more removed from physical senses are spiritual
things, which need to be sought by spiritual
senses? Your faith, if you refer to it, proves that
the angels are never absent from you. I make

no apology for saying that this is proved by faith, which the apostle defines as being 'the conviction of things not seen.'* They are present then, and present to you; not only with you, but even for you. They are present to protect you and to benefit you. What shall you repay to the Lord for all he has given you?* If anything, honor and glory* to him alone. Why to him alone? Because it is he who has given the charge, and because every perfect gift* comes from him alone.

Heb 11:1

Ps 116:11
1 Tm 1:17

Jm 1:17

7. But even if it is he who has given them this charge, we would do ill to be ungrateful to them as well for the great love with which they obey and come to our help in such necessity. So let us show devotion to our guardians and be grateful to them. Let us love them in return. Let us honor them as much as we can and we should. But our whole love and our whole honor must go to him from whom they as well as we receive everything that enables us to give honor and to love and makes them worthy of being honored and loved. When the apostle says, 'To him alone be honor and glory,'* we should not imagine that he is contradicting the words of the prophet who stated that the friends of God are greatly to be honored.* I think this sentence of the apostle is like another where he says, 'Owe no one anything, except to love one another.'* He did not want to make this an excuse for disclaiming other obligations, especially as he himself said, 'honor to whom honor is due,'* and other things of the sort. In order to understand more fully what he meant and taught in both these sentences, mark how the

1 Tm 1:17

Ps 139:17

Rm 13:8

Rm 13:7

rays of the sun blot out the lesser luminaries. Do we for all that think that the stars have been taken away? Or put out? Of course not. They have been covered up, as it were, by a brighter light and cannot be seen for the moment. Thus love outranks all other obligations then, and it alone should so reign in us that whatever we owe to others love claims to itself, that we may do everything out of love. Thus God's honor must prevail over and somehow prejudge everything else, so that he alone is glorified not only before everything but in everything.* The same thing should be said about love. For what does someone leave behind for others once he has given his whole heart, his whole mind, and his whole strength* to the Lord his God in love? In Him then, brothers, let us love the angels affectionately, as our future fellow heirs,* though here below our guardians and tutors* established by the Father and set over us. For now we are God's children, even though it may not yet appear so,* because we are still children under guardians and tutors, no different meanwhile than servants.*

8. Still, even though we are children having a long, a very long, and dangerous way to go, what have we to fear under such guardians? They who guard us in all our ways cannot be overcome or led astray, or much less lead us astray. They are faithful, they are prudent, they are powerful. What should we fear? Let us simply follow them, stay close to them, and we shall dwell in the protection of the God of heaven. See how necessary their protection is, their guardianship over all your ways. ON THEIR

1 P 4:11

Mk 12:30

Rm 8:17
Gal 4:2

1 Jn 3:2

Gal 4:1-2

HANDS THEY WILL BEAR YOU UP, it says, LEST YOU DASH YOUR FOOT AGAINST A STONE. Does it seem to you a little thing, a stone of offence set in the way?* Consider what follows, YOU WILL WALK ON THE ASP AND THE BASILISK: YOU WILL TRAMPLE UNDERFOOT THE LION AND THE DRAGON. How necessary is a tutor or even a porter, especially for a child clambering among these things. He says, ON THEIR HANDS THEY WILL BEAR YOU UP. They will keep you in your ways, and they will lead the child where a child can walk. Moreover, they will not allow you to be tempted beyond what you can bear,* but they will lift you on their hands, that you may pass over any snag. How easily someone borne on their hands passes over. As a popular saying goes, how blithely someone swims when another is holding up his chin.

9. Each time you feel some great temptation pushing you and strong tribulation pressing in, call on your guardian, your guide, him who is your helper in tribulation and opportunity. Call upon him and say, 'Save us, Lord, we are perishing.'* He does not sleep, nor does he slumber,* even though he may pretend to do so for a time, for fear you might tumble out of these hands into some greater danger simply because you were not aware that you were being borne up by them. These hands are spiritual, and the aids surely spiritual, which are allotted to each of the elect by their judgement according to the various difficulties encountered—like so many heaps of stones, this is done in many and spiritual ways by the angels set over them. I mention those difficulties, which I think the most

Margin notes:
Is 8:14, Rm 9:32
1 Co 10:13
Mt 8:25
Ps 121:4

frequent, and few among you will not have experienced them. Is someone grievously disturbed either by some physical infirmity or by some worldly tribulation or by lukewarmness of spirit and the listlessness of mental fatigue? Already, he would be beginning to be tempted beyond what he can bear,* already he would be stubbing his toe and stumbling over a stone, if someone did not come to help. But what is this stone? I understand it to be the stone of offence and rock of stumbling* which bruises anyone who falls over it, but crushes anyone upon whom it falls;* it is the cornerstone, chosen and precious; it is the Lord Christ.* To murmur against him is to dash our foot against this stone, stumbling from weakness of spirit and the storm.* There is a need for angelic work, for angelic comfort, for angelic hands, when someone is already fainting, already close to stumbling over the stone. And someone who murmurs and blasphemes does stumble against the stone, bruising himself, not the stone he furiously runs into.

10. I think that men are sometimes borne up by angels as if by two hands, so that almost unconsciously they pass over the temptations and dangers which terrify them most. And afterwards they are not a little astonished at how easily they got over what at first seemed so difficult. Do you want to know what I understand these two hands to be? A double indication of the brevity of tribulation here below and the eternity of reward later on, or rather, painting and imprinting it on the heart so that it feels by some intimate disposition how this 'slight mo-

1 Co 10:13

Is 8:14

Mt 21:44
1 P 2:6

Ps 55:8

2 Co 4:17

Ps 78:50

mentary affliction is preparing for us a far sur-
passing and eternal weight of glory.'* Who
could not believe that such good thoughts are
produced in us by the good angels, when it is
certain, on the contrary, that wicked innuen-
dos come from bad angels?* Be familiar with
the angels, brothers, visit with them often by
careful meditation and devout prayer, for they
are always near to comfort and protect you.

SERMON THIRTEEN

On the Thirteenth Verse:

YOU WILL WALK ON THE ASP AND THE BASI-
LISK: YOU WILL TRAMPLE UNDERFOOT
THE LION AND THE DRAGON

1. WE CAN APPLY this verse, 'On their hands they will bear you up,' and so forth, not only to present comfort, but even to that to come. Of course the holy angels guard us in our ways, but once this way is finished, that is, once this life is finished, they carry us in their hands. We have no lack of reliable witnesses.* Only a little while ago you read of our blessed Father Benedict, truly blessed in all things, that 'while the piercing gaze of his eyes seemed to behold the brightness of lightning, he saw the soul of Germanus, bishop of Capua, carried by angels into heaven in a fiery ball.'* But why do we need this kind of witness?† Truth himself said in the Gospel that Lazarus, poor and covered with sores, 'was carried by angels into Abraham's bosom.'‡ We could never walk by ourselves in such new and unknown territory, especially when there is such a great stone in the way. What stone? He who in times past was adored in stones, who offered stones to the Lord, saying, 'Command these stones to become loaves of bread.'* Moreover,

Is 8:2

*Gregory the Great, *Dial.* II.35, used as the *Benedictus* antiphon at Lauds on the feast of St Benedict (21 March)
†Mk 14:63
‡Lk 16:22

Mt 4:3

your foot is your affection, the foot of the soul borne up by angels lest it stub that foot against a stone. How could a soul not be greatly troubled if it had to sally forth alone, if it set out along that way without comfort, clambering on foot among those stones?

2. And now hear even more clearly how necessary it is to be borne up by other hands, those of the angels. YOU WILL WALK ON THE ASP AND THE BASILISK: YOU WILL TRAMPLE UNDER-FOOT THE LION AND THE DRAGON. What can the human foot do amid such things? What human affection could remain unperturbed among such horrible monsters? For they are spiritual abom-

Eph 6:12

inations* and are not inappropriately given such names. Yet I suppose you have not let slip that it was said of them: A THOUSAND MAY FALL AT YOUR SIDE, TEN THOUSAND AT YOUR RIGHT HAND. But who can know whether the works of malice and the ministers of iniquity are divided among these spirits to represent their different crafts, or better craftinesses, by these different names? One may be called the asp, another the basilisk; one the lion, another the dragon, because they do their harm in some unique unseen manner: one by biting, one by glancing, another by roaring, or by pouncing, another by breathing. I have read that one kind of demon can only be cast

Mk 9:28

out by prayer and fasting.* The apostles' re-buke did nothing to it. Could it not have been an asp, that deaf asp in the psalm which stops its

Ps 58:4-5

ears so it does not hear the voice of the charmer?* Do you want not to be afraid of so fearful a monster? Do you want to tread safely on this asp after death? Then take care not to follow it here and now. Take care not to imitate it, and you will have no need to fear it hereafter.

3. There is indeed a vice which I suppose is dominated by this sort of spirit. And if you want to know what, it is the going around in circles we warned you against in yesterday's sermon, the stubbornness we spoke against the day before. I do not tire at every opportunity of warning you against this very grave plague,* so that you can fly from it by every means possible. This is the greatest ruination of all religion and surely, as the Lawgiver testified, it is the 'incurable poison of the asp.'* The asp is said to press one of its ears as hard as it can to the ground, and stop up the other with its tail, so as not to hear. So what can the voice of the charmer, the words of the preacher do about it? I will pray over it, I will humble my soul by fasting.* On behalf of the dead I will baptize myself with a flood of tears, for I see that no wisdom of a human charmer, no effort of warning is of any avail. Let the obstinate man realize that he is not raising his head to heaven, but affixing it to the ground. The wisdom which comes from above is not only pure, but also peaceable,* whereas his is, if I may say so, asp-like and can only be earthy. But this asp would not be so deaf if it did not stop up its hearing with its tail. What is this tail? It is the tail-end of human determination. The hopeless deafness of someone who clings to his own will here, as if stuck to the ground, and, as if bending his tail back, contemplates some end and sets his mind on getting it. Do not do this, brothers, I beg you, do not block your ears this way, do not blunt your heart.*

Ex 9:3

Dt 32:33

Ps 35:13

Jm 3:17

Ps 95:8

It is for this reason that we find such biting and bitter speech in the mouth of an obstinate man, because no well-meaning warning can ever get through to him. It is because he has stopped his ears so zealously against the tongue of the charmer that the venom from the strike of the asp's tongue takes effect.

4. And the basilisk, they say,* has poison in his eyes — the worst and most detestable animal. Are you anxious to know about this poisonous eye, this wicked eye, this hypnotic eye? Think about envy. What is envy if not seeing evil?* If the devil were not a basilisk, death would never have entered our world through his envy.* Woe to the wretched man who has not forestalled envy. Let us combat this vice, too, as long as we live if we do not want to fear this servant of iniquity after our death. Let no one look with envious eyes upon the goods of another. For this is, as best one can, to inject toxin into someone and somehow kill him. Anyone who hates a man, murders him. Truth himself bears witness. What did he say about someone who hates the good in a man? Can he not be called a murderer?* The man he hates is still living, and already he is guilty of his death.* The fire which the Lord Jesus sent into the world is still burning,* and the envious person, like someone who has already extinguished the spirit, is already damned.

5. Woe to us because of the dragon! It is a savage beast. Anything it touches with its fiery breath, it destroys, not only the beasts of the field, but even the birds of the air.* What else is it, I suppose, but the spirit of anger. We grieve

Isidore of Seville, *Origines* XII. 4.6; PL 82:443

invidere/ malum videre

Wis 2:24

1 Jn 3:15
Mt 26:66

Lk 12:49

Ezk 38:20

at how many men who seemed to be important in life have fallen basely into the mouth of this monster and been miserably scorched by its breath. What could be better than to be angry with themselves and yet not sin?* Anger is a natural emotion of man, but those who abuse a good thing of nature will be grievously punished and perish miserably. Let us be prepared for this, brothers, wherever expedient, lest it burst out illicitly and uselessly. As love generally blots out love, so fear usually drives out fear. 'Do not fear those who kill the body', the Lord said, 'and after that have no more that they can do.'* And immediately he adds, 'I will show you whom to fear: fear him who has the power to cast body and soul into hell. Yes, I tell you, fear him'*—as if he would say more openly, fear him and not the others. Let the spirit of the fear of the Lord fill you,* and any other fear will have no place in you. I tell you* yet not I, but Truth; not I,* but the Lord:† Do not be angry with those who take away passing goods, who outrage you, who perhaps cause you to suffer, but after that can do no more. I will warn you whom to fear.* Be angry with that one which alone can harm you, do that alone, so all the others will have no power over you. Do you want to know what this is? It is your own iniquity. So I tell you, be angry against it. For 'no adversity shall harm them if no iniquity dominates them'.* Anyone really angry against this is not moved by others, even more, he embraces them. 'I am ready for scourging', it says.* For condemnation, for insult, for physical injury: I am ready and 'I am not troubled',* for my grief

Ps 4:4

Lk 12:4

Lk 12:5

Is 11:3
Lk 11:9 etc.
*1 Co 15:10
†1 Co 7:10

Lk 12:5

Lk 12:5

Ps 38:18

Ps 119:60

is always before me.* Why should I not make light of all outward affliction when I consider this sorrow? 'The son of my own body persecutes me, shall I worry about a reproachful servant?'* My heart fails me, my strength fails me, and the light of my eyes,'* and should I moan over temporal loss or take any notice of physical discomfort?

6. From this surely comes not only meekness, which the dragon's breath cannot harm, but even magnanimity, which the lion's roar does not terrify. Peter says 'Your adversary is like a roaring lion.'* Thanks to the Lion of the tribe of Judah,* the other can roar but not maul. Let him roar as much as he likes. The sheep of Christ need not flee, no matter how much he menaces, how much he exaggerates, or how much he threatens! But let us not be beasts who let this empty roaring lay us low. Those who study these things curiously say that a beast unable to bear his roaring cannot stand up to the lion to fight boldly back against his pouncing and survive his mauling. Truly it is to be like a beast, devoid of reason, to be so weak-witted as not only to give way to fear alone but, overcome by the mere thought of future effort, to be laid low not by the lance but by the trumpet. 'You have not yet resisted to the point of bloodshed,'* said that very energetic leader who knew how empty the lion's roar is. And someone else has said, 'Resist the devil and he will flee from you.'*

Ps 38:18

2 K 16:1
Ps 38:10

1 P 5:8
Rev 5:5

Heb 12:4

Jm 4:7

SERMON FOURTEEN

On the Thirteenth Verse:

YOU WILL WALK ON THE ASP AND THE BASI-
LISK: YOU WILL TRAMPLE UNDERFOOT
THE LION AND THE DRAGON

1. LET US GIVE THANKS, brothers, to our Maker, our Benefactor, our Redeemer, our Rewarder, to him who is our hope. He is our rewarder; he is our reward, nor should we expect from him anything save himself. In the first place, he preserves us; we are his; for 'it is he who made us, and not we ourselves.'* Does it seem to you a little thing that he made you? Think of what quality he made you. For even with regard to your body he made you a noble creature; and still more so with regard to your soul, inasmuch as you are the extraordinary image of the Creator,* sharing his rationality, capable of eternal happiness. In both body and soul man is the most admirable of all creatures, being integrated with himself by the incomprehensible ingenuity and unsearchable wisdom* of the Creator. Man is then as great as this gift itself. But do you realize how gratuitous this is? It is obvious that man did not deserve it beforehand because he simply did not exist. And once he existed, how could he hope to repay the gift to the bestower? 'I said to the Lord, you are my God, for you have no need of

Ps 100:2

Gen 1:26

Rm 11:33

229

Ps 16:2

my goods.'* So there was no need for man to repay him who is self-sufficient in every way. But there remained the hope of being able to render heartfelt thanks to him who deserved it. Why not give thanks? If someone had helped you in some way to recover the use of your eyes,* your ears, your noses, your hands, if someone had healed a limping foot, if someone had restored your addled reason, would he not be aroused to indignation against you if you were heedless of such great gifts or ungrateful to your benefactor? Surely the Lord your God, the bestower of all these, has made all these things out of nothing.* Not only did he make them, but he also knit them together and formed them, and he showed them their functions. How should he not, by every right, demand yet more gratitude?

Tob 10:4

Dt 32:27

2. Not content merely with this gift — however great — he who granted you being when you were not, once you were, gave you everything necessary to subsist. And he was no less generous in this than he was awesome in the other. He said, 'Let us make man in our image and likeness.'* And then what did he say? 'And let him have dominion over the fish of the sea and the beasts on the land'* and so on. That he had created the elements for your use he had already taught. For, if you remember, he made them to 'be for signs and for seasons and for days and years.'* And for whom, do you think? For no one but you. All the other creatures either had no use for all these things or else were incapable of understanding them. How generous, and how extraordinarily liberal, he showed

Gen 1:26

Ibid.

Gen 1:14

himself in this second gift. How many things he lavished on you for your subsistence, how many for your instruction, how many for your consolation, and how many even then for your correction, and how many too for your delight! Truly indeed these two graces are doubly gratuitous. Why do I say 'doubly gratuitous'? Without deserving on your part, or effort on his. 'For he spoke and it was done.'* Are we to be less devout, less indebted, less thankful because he made them out of nothing and for nothing? But it is characteristic of a perverse heart to seek occasions for ingratitude. Only a man who is ungrateful even for gifts does such a thing. I do not think either of these gifts is any less useful just because it was less difficult to bestow. If you fancy perhaps that a laborious gift would be more useful to you, this is only your own judgement on yourself. You more willingly render your brother service when it does not inconvenience you. Even when you do something for nothing, you nevertheless expect gratitude in return.

Ps 33:9

3. And now mark the third work: your redemption. There is no excuse for ingratitude; great effort went into it. Freely was it accomplished, but free on your part. Clearly it was not without cost to him. You were saved for nothing, but not by nothing. How can affection doze in these circumstances? What is more, it has died out; it is not dozing when it fails to respond to so great a benefit, when it does not pour itself out in thanksgiving and songs of praise.* This third [gift] very clearly gauges the other two and proves that true love under-

Ps 26:7

lay them, and it is easily eminent not because he did not choose to do it some other way, but because no other way was suitable. So then, your God made you, he made many things for your benefit, and he even, as it were, made himself for you: 'The Word was made flesh and dwelt among us'.* What was left after that? He himself became one flesh with you: may he also make you one spirit with him.* Let these four things never fade from your heart, from your memory, from your affection. Think on them always, forever delight in them. Let them be as so many goads spurring your soul on, like torches setting it afire to return love to him who has commended to you his love for you in so many ways. Remember that he said, 'If you love me, keep my commandments'.* Keep the commandments of your Creator therefore. Keep the commandments of your Benefactor, your Redeemer, your Rewarder.

4. But if these gifts are four, how many commandments are there? We all know there are ten. And if you multiply the decalogue of the law by the four gifts, you get forty,* and you have the spiritual lent.* Only, 'Keep yourself in fear and prepare your soul for temptation'.* Beware the craftiness of the serpent, look out for the enemy's ambushes. By four trials will he try to prevent us from making the fourfold thanksgiving which we owe. Christ was tempted by all of them, that the apostle could truthfully write, 'He was tempted in every respect as we are, yet without sin'.* Perhaps there is someone surprised at this, who says that he has never read about the Lord's four temptations? In fact, I

Marginal references:

Jn 1:14

1 Co 6:16-7

Jn 14:15

quadragesima
quadragesima
Sir 2:1

Heb 4:15

think, no one would say this if he remembered
having read that 'the life of man on earth is a
temptation.'* Anyone who bears this in mind   Jb 7:1
will not contend that our Lord's triple tempta-
tion of fasting in the desert, [being carried to]
the pinnacle of the temple, and to the top of the
mountain* was all there was. Of course, in all   Mt 4:3 *ff.*
these he was obviously tempted. But what is
more, from then until his death on the cross*   Ph 2:8
he bore a temptation less obvious, yet stronger.
Nor was he seen to shrink from being like us in
this. The three benefits which are already passing away are evident and perceived with great
certitude. But the one bearing on the hope of
eternal life,* has not yet been shown, has not   Tt 3:7
yet been divulged to us. No wonder then that
the corresponding temptation is less apparent
than the others, when even the cause for this
temptation was hidden. And it was longer-last-
ing and stronger because the enemy brought up
all his reserves of wickedness to combat our hope.

5. Thus he first, in order to make us ungrateful to the author of nature, engenders a height-
ened concern for nature, just as he dared to say
to Christ when he was hungry, 'Command these
stones to become bread,'* as if he who moulded†   *Mt 4:3/†Rm 9:20
us were unaware of our constitution, or as if he
who feeds the birds of the air* took no care of   Mt 6:26
man. How ungrateful to him who made the
whole world for man is anyone who shamelessly falls down to worship the devil in order
to acquire the goods he covets? What did he
say? 'All these I will give you, if you will fall
down and worship me.'* Wretch, did you make   Mt 4:9
those things? How can you give what another

has created? How can we hope to receive from you, how can we seek by worshipping you, things created by him and placed in his keeping?

Now, about the words, 'Throw yourself down.'* Watch out for yourself, any of you who have climbed up to the pinnacle of the temple.* Watch out for yourself, supervisor of the house of the Lord,* watch out, you who hold in the Church of Christ the highest rank. How ungrateful, indeed how harmful, to the great mystery of godliness* you are, if you consider godliness a means to gain.* How unfaithful [you are] to him who consecrated this ministry by his own blood,* if in it you seek your own glory,* which is nothing; if you look after your own interests and not those of Jesus Christ.* How unworthily you respond to his condescension, when he made you sublime by the dispensation of his own humility, when he gave you charge of heavenly mysteries, when he delivered to you a heavenly power even greater than that of the heavenly spirits themselves; [how ungrateful you are] if you throw yourself down, setting your mind not on the things that are above but on those of the earth.* Yet all those who cast themselves down from the heights of virtue to the void of vainglory* and seek their own satisfaction, offend the Lord of hosts instead of thanking him when he bore among us so very much in order to impress on us the likeness of his own holiness.

6. Now, brothers, let us consider more carefully whether that first temptation, which disturbs the mind with physical needs, may not be compared to the asp. This animal injures people

Mt 4:6

Mt 4:5
Ezk 3:17,33:7

1 Tm 3:16
1 Tm 6:5

Heb 9:12
Jn 7:18

Ph 2:21

Col 3:2

Gal 5:26

somehow with its bite, and stops up its ear so as
not to hear the voice of the charmer.* Does not
the tempter try to do something like this, except
that he stops up and hardens the ear of the heart
against the consolation of faith? But against
Christ the enemy made no gains; he did not stop
up his hearing, but replied, 'Man shall not live
by bread alone, but by every word that proceeds from the mouth of God.'* To this he said,
'All these things I will give you, if you will fall
down and worship me.'* Pay attention here to
the persuasive hissing of the insidious dragon.
They say it lies hidden in the sand and attracts
even birds with its poisonous breath. How dead
this breath is: 'All these things I will give you, if
you will fall down and worship me.' But Christ
was no ordinary bird: the dragon's breath could
do nothing to him.

7. What shall we say about the basilisk? It is
said he infects and kills people even more mon-
strously, simply by a glance. Unless I am mistaken, this is vain glory. 'Beware of practising
your piety before men to be seen by them,'* it
says, as if to say, 'Watch out for the eye of the
basilisk.' But whom do they say the basilisk
harms? The person who does not see the basilisk. Otherwise, if you see it first, so they say, it
cannot harm you but itself dies. So it is, brothers. Empty conceit* injures those who do not
see it; the blind and careless, those who show
off, those who expose themselves instead of
being on the lookout; those who do not watch
out and do not dispel it and fail to see how frivolous, perishable, vain, and futile it is. If anyone
looks at it this way, the basilisk dies; then conceit

Ps 58:4-5

Mt 4:4

Mt 4:9

Mt 6:1

Gal 5:26

Ps 72:22 (Vulg.)

Mt 4:6

Mt 4:6

does not kill the person, it is itself put to death, being as it were turned to dust, even brought to nothing.* I do not think it necessary to go into the way in which vain glory is involved when it was said: 'If you are the Son of God, throw yourself down.'* What other reason could there be except that to be praised would be to be spied by the basilisk?

8. And see how this basilisk disguised himself in order not to be seen beforehand. He said, 'It is written, "He has given his angels charge over you, and on their hands they will bear you up"'.* What is written, wicked fellow, what is written? HE HAS GIVEN HIS ANGELS CHARGE OVER YOU. What did he charge? Attend carefully and see that he deceitfully omits what would have destroyed the fabrications of his own deceit. Well, what did he charge? In the psalm it follows, TO KEEP YOU IN ALL YOUR WAYS. Isn't this from precipices? What sort of way is this, to cast oneself down from the pinnacle of the temple? This is no way, it is ruin. And if it is a way, then it is yours, not his. Foolishly do you twist things to tempt the Head with something written to console the body. This [body] had to be guarded for fear it might dash its foot against a stone. There is nothing to guard against when there is nothing to fear. So why do you pass over in silence the words which follow: YOU WILL WALK ON THE ASP AND THE BASILISK: YOU WILL TRAMPLE UNDERFOOT THE LION AND THE DRAGON? For this parable concerns you. By monstrous names is designated monstrous cruelty deserving to be trodden underfoot, not only by the head but also by the whole body. [This merciless enemy] having been confounded

three times, employs snake-like craftiness no
longer but leonine cruelty against the Lord: insults, whippings, blows, death, even the death
of the cross.* But clearly the Lion of the tribe
of Judah* will trample underfoot even you,
lion. As our adversary sees himself frustrated
by all the others, he will with full fury stir up
against us, brothers, persecution such as has not
been from the beginning of the world,* with
the intention of blockading us from the heavenly kingdom by the very violence of these
tribulations. Happy is the soul which treads this
lion underfoot with powerful courage and suc-
ceeds in snatching the kingdom by violence.*

9. From now on then, dearest ones, let us
walk more carefully and cautiously, as if treading on asps and basilisks. Let us be on our guard
against every root of bitterness* that no one of
us may be found biting in his words, no one de-
fiant or seething, no one inflexible or rebellious.
And let us never throw ourselves down, but
rather leap beyond and transcend the lethal
speculation of temporal glory, that as it is written 'In vain is a net spread in the sight of the
bird,'* we may tread upon the lion and the dragon as well, so the one's roaring does not alarm
nor the other's breath destroy us.

These four monsters seem to generate four
vices like themselves. Whom does the dragon
most easily ambush? To my way of thinking,
it is the greedy person because we know greed
is the root of all evil,* and it most perverts the
heart. That was why Satan wheedled, 'all these
I will give you.'* As to the lion, it is obvious that
it lets out its terrifying roars only at the gate of
fear. The asp, moreover, lies in wait at the portal

Ph 2:8
Rev 5:5

Mt 24:21

Mt 11:12

Heb 12:15

Pr 1:17

1 Tm 6:10

Mt 4:9

of dejection, esteeming it the best entryway for his bite. This was why he did not sidle up to the Lord Christ until he noticed he was hungry. On the other hand, elation must watch out for the basilisk, because it is by that access that he usually injects his venomous glance, just as vain glory injures us by elation tinged with vanity.

10. Consider then whether we ought not to set up four virtues against these four dangers. 'The lion roars, who will not fear.'* If anyone, it will be the courageous man. But once the lion has been foiled, the dragon lies hidden in the sand to attract the soul by its stinking breath, inspiring him, somehow, with the lust for earthly things. Who do you think will survive these ambushes? No one at all, except the prudent. And perhaps, as soon as you are on your guard against falling into them, some vexation troubles you, and immediately the asp pops up; he sees that this is just the right moment for him. Who can escape being irritated by the asp? Surely the temperate and modest man who knows how to suffer want and enjoy abundance.* I think the evil hypnotic eye will seize this occasion to fascinate you evilly. Who will turn away his gaze? The just person, of course, who not only refuses to appropriate to himself the glory which is God's, and who refuses to accept it when it is offered by another: if he is just, he justly pursues what is just; he does not practise his justice before men* and, even though he is just, he does not lift up his head. This virtue consists especially in humility. It purifies his intention, and obtains greater and more effective merit in arrogating less to self.

Am 3:8

Ph 4:12

Mt 6:1

SERMON FIFTEEN

On the Fourteenth Verse:

BECAUSE HE HOPED IN ME I WILL DELIVER
HIM, I WILL PROTECT HIM BECAUSE
HE KNOWS MY NAME

1. 'COME TO ME, ALL WHO LABOR and are heavy laden, and I will refresh you,' says the Lord. 'Take my yoke upon you, you will find rest for your souls, for my yoke is easy, and my burden light.'* He invites laborers to refreshment, he summons the heavy laden to rest. Yet he does not here below withdraw either the burden or the labor; rather he changes one burden for another, one labor for another, but for a light burden and an easy yoke in which we find rest and refreshment, even though at first this may not seem so. Iniquity is a heavy burden resting on a leaden weight;* groaning beneath this load was the man who said: 'My iniquities have gone over my head; they weigh like a burden too heavy for me.'* What then is Christ's burden, what is this light burden? As I feel it, it is the burden of his benefits. A sweet burden, but only to him who feels it, who has experience of it. Otherwise, if you do not find it so, if you do not perceive it so, it is exceedingly heavy and dangerous. Man is a beast of burden all his life long. If he still bears his sin,* his burden is heavy. But if he is disburdened from his sin, it is less heavy; but if

Mt 11:28-30

Zech 5:7

Ps 38:4

Lev 30:20

239

he has good sense, he will find disburdenment
from sin no less a burden, as I have said. God
burdens us when he disburdens us: he burdens
us with grace when he disburdens us of sin. The
voice of the burdened man [cries]: 'What shall
I repay to the Lord for all he has given me?'*
The voice of the burdened man [cries]: 'Depart
from me, for I am a sinful man, O Lord.'* The
voice of the burdened man [cries]: 'I have always feared God as waves swelling over me.'*
He says, 'I have always feared', before as well as
after receiving forgiveness of sin. Blessed is the
man who is always this timid* and is no less dis-
tressed at being overwhelmed by benefits than
by sins.

2. Such unremitting and lavish divine liberality is shown toward us to stimulate us to grace
and to invite us to love. HE HAS GIVEN HIS AN-
GELS CHARGE OVER YOU TO GUARD YOU IN ALL
YOUR WAYS. What more can he do for you and
has not done?* I know what you are thinking,
noble creature. You are grateful for the angels
of the Lord, but you aspire to the Lord of angels himself. You pray, you plead that, not content with messengers, he who spoke might be
present, that he might kiss you, not as it were
through an intermediary, but with the very kiss
of his mouth.* You have heard that you will
walk on the asp and the basilisk, and on the lion
and the dragon as well, and you know all about
the victory of Michael and his angels over the
dragon.* Yet your desires cry out not to Michael, but to the Lord. 'Deliver me and set me beside you; and let any man's hand fight against
me.'* This is no longer a seeking after any ordi-

Ps 116:11

Lk 5:8

Jb 31:23

Pr 28:14

Is 5:4

Sg 1:1

Rev 12:7-8

Jb 17:3

nary shelter, but a striving to reach the highest
of all refuges, so that the words, 'Because you,
O Lord, are my hope', may deserve the reply,
'You have made the Most High your refuge'.

3. The kind and merciful Lord does not disdain being the hope of the wretched. He does
not refuse to be both the liberator and the protector of those who hope in him. BECAUSE HE
HOPED IN ME I WILL DELIVER HIM; I WLL PRO-
TECT HIM BECAUSE HE KNOWS MY NAME. For,
'Unless the Lord watches over the city, the
watchman keeps watch in vain',* be he man or
angel. Mountains are round about Jerusalem;
but this would be of little avail, even of no avail
at all, if the Lord were not round about his people.* Rightfully, likewise, is the bride described
in the Canticle as having found the watchmen—
or rather, as having been found by them, since
she was not looking for them; she was not satisfied at being with the watchmen, but, having
inquired briefly of the beloved, she fled after
him more swiftly. For her heart had set all its
trust in the Lord, not in the watchmen, and had
anyone coaxed her otherwise she would have
said, 'In the Lord I trust; how can you say to
me, "Fly like a sparrow to the mountains"?'*
The Corinthians were less watchful about doing
that when, having come up against watchmen
as it were, they fell out among themselves and
progressed very little, 'I belong to Cephas', they
said. 'I belong to Paul, I belong to Apollos'.*
But what did these sober watchmen, these vigilant watchmen do? They could not take the
bride for themselves, these watchmen who envied her in the best sense, who envied her with

Ps 127:1

Ps 125:2

Ps 11:1

1 Co 1:12

God's envy, who had pledged to deliver her a chaste virgin to one husband, Christ.* She says, 'They beat me, they wounded me.'* Why did they do that? Unless I am mistaken, they were urging her to go on her way to find the beloved. Then too 'they took away my mantle,'* she says, doubtlessly so that, unencumbered, she might run more swiftly. Notice how strongly the apostle beats those who seemed to turn aside to amuse themselves with the watchmen, and with what arrows he wounds them: 'Was Paul crucified for you? Or were you baptized in Paul's name?'* And again, 'When someone says, "I belong to Paul," and another, "I belong to Apollos," are you not merely men? What then is Apollos? What is Paul? Servants through whom you believed.'* BECAUSE HE HOPED IN ME I WILL DELIVER HIM. Not in watchmen, not in a man, not in an angel, but in me he hoped, he says, expecting no good thing except from me, not by them. 'Every good endowment and every perfect gift is from above, coming down from the Father of lights.'* It is because of me that men's watches are useful, at any rate those having to do with work open to view; it is I who have deputized men as watchmen. From me comes the wardship of angels observing the more secret movements of the soul, especially careful to turn aside wicked suggestions. On the other hand, the intimate keeping of the most secret places of the heart is accomplished not only because of me but by me, because the eyes of neither men nor angels are able to penetrate them.

4. Let us acknowledge this triple guardianship, brothers, and live in fitting harmony with

2 Co 11:2

Sg 5:7

Ibid.

1 Co 1:13

1 Co 3:4-5

Jm 1:17

each. Let us bring forth good things in the sight
of men,* of angels, and of God. Let us strive to
please all in all things, but most of all him who
is highly exalted above all. In the sight of angels,
let us sing psalms to him, so what is written in
Scripture may be accomplished: 'Those who
fear you shall see me and rejoice, because I have
set all my hope in your word.'* Let us obey
those set over us, who keep watch and shall have
to render account for our souls,* so that they
may do this without grief. But at least — thank
God from whom alone all gifts come — I need
not exhort you much, I need not fear much for
you in this regard. What else is my joy* and my
honor, except your prompt obedience and your
irreproachable way of life?* What if I knew
for certain that not even the angels could find
anything unseemly in you, anything among any
of you connected with the curse laid on Jeri-
cho;* what if I were sure that no one murmurs
or disparages in secret, behaves hypocritically or
negligently, ever mulls over in his mind wicked
thoughts which, alas, sometimes are physically
disquieting? My joy would be greatly increased,
but not yet quite full. For we are not so great
that we can consider it a very small thing to be
judged by men, and even be unaware of anything against ourselves.* Again, if even important people are afraid of the most secret Judge,
how much more does it behoove us to tremble at
the very thought of his examination? Oh, if only
I could be certain that there is nothing in any of
us to offend that eye which alone knows full
well what is in a man,* seeing in each what he
does not even see in himself. Let us especially

2 Co 8:21

Ps 119:74

Heb 13:17, cf. RB2

Ph 4:1

conversatio

Josh 6:18

1 Co 4:3-4

Jn 2:25

ponder this judgement, brothers, and consider
it frequently in fear and trembling, that we may
be able to comprehend the unsearchable depths
of God's judgements and his irrevocable dispensation. Hope gains from fruitful fear.

5. If any one stops to ponder carefully, he
will find that this very fear contains the sound-
est and most effectual grounds for hope. For
this fear is God's greatest gift; from the unwav-
ering perception of things present rises the anticipation of things to come. Lastly, 'The Lord
takes pleasure in those that fear him';* and 'Life
is in his will'* and in his good pleasure life eternal. BECAUSE HE HOPED IN ME I WILL DELIVER
HIM. What wonderful generosity: he never fails
those who hope in him. Man's whole merit consists in placing all his hope in him who has saved
the whole man. 'In you our fathers trusted; they
trusted and you delivered them. They cried to
you and were saved; they trusted in you, and
were not disappointed.'* 'Has anyone hoped in
him and been disappointed?'* 'Hope in him all
you peoples.'* 'Every place on which your foot
treads shall be yours.'* Your foot surely is your
hope. However far it advances, it shall possess,
if only it is firmly fixed in God, so firmly set
that it cannot totter. What has it to fear from
the asp and the basilisk? Why should it shrink
at the lion's roar and the dragon's hiss?

6. BECAUSE HE HOPED IN ME I WILL DELIVER
HIM. And so that the person once freed will not
again be assailed and again need to be set free,
I WILL PROTECT HIM and keep him safe, if only
he has known my name, not attributing to himself his freedom, but giving praise to my name.*

Ps 147:11
Ps 30:5

Ps 22:4-5
Sir 2:11
Ps 62:8
Dt 11:24

Ps 115:1

I WILL PROTECT HIM BECAUSE HE KNOWS MY
NAME. In the presence of God's countenance
glorification is made manifest and protection in
the knowledge of his name. In the name is hope,
the thing hoped for is in his presence. Who
hopes for what he sees?* Faith comes by hear-   Rm 8:24
ing,* and, according to the same apostle, is the   Rm 10:17
assurance of things hoped for.* I WILL PROTECT   Heb 11:1
HIM BECAUSE HE HAS KNOWN MY NAME. No
one knows this name who takes it in vain;* he   Ex 20:7
merely says Lord, Lord, and does not do what
he says.* No one knows his name who neither   Lk 6:46
honors him as Father nor fears him as Lord. No
one knows his name who turns aside to vanities
and false follies. 'Blessed is the man whose hope
is the name of the Lord and who does look back
at vanities and false follies.'* Peter knew this   Ps 40:5
name and he said, 'There is no other name given
among men by which we may be saved.'* We   Ac 4:12
are too, if we know this holy name called down
upon us,* which we should desire always to be   Jer 14:9
sanctified in us, and should pray according to
the teaching of the Saviour, 'Our Father, you
are in heaven, hallowed be your name.'* So   Mt 6:9
listen to what follows in the psalm: 'He has
called upon me and I will hear him.' Calling out
in prayer is the fruit of knowing his name; and
the fruit of calling out is the Saviour's listening.
For how can someone be heard who does not
call out* or invoke the name of the Lord, with-   Rm 10:43
out knowing it? Thanks be to Him who showed
men the Father's name, placing the fruit of salvation* in the invocation of this name, as it is   Sir 1:22
written, 'Whoever calls upon the name of the
Lord shall be saved.'*   Jl 2:32

SERMON SIXTEEN

On the Fifteenth Verse:

HE HAS CALLED TO ME, I WILL ANSWER HIM;

I AM WITH HIM IN TROUBLE, I WILL

RESCUE HIM AND GLORIFY HIM

Sir 45:30

Jer 16:5

*Introit of the
Mass for the first
Sunday in Lent,
cf. Ps 91:15

†Dt 32:4

‡Ps 24:4

Pr 20:9

Ps 130:5

1. 'HE HAS CALLED TO ME AND I WILL HEAR HIM'. This is clearly a covenant of peace,* a treaty of godliness, a pact of compassion and mercy.* 'He has hoped in me, I will deliver him; he has known my name, I will protect him; he has called upon me and I will answer him.* He did not say, 'He has been worthy, just and upright has he been,† innocent of hands and pure of heart;‡ therefore will I deliver him, protect and hear him'. For if he had said this or other like things, who would not despair? 'Who can boast that he has made his heart pure?'* But now, 'With you there is forgiveness, and because of your law I have relied on you, Lord'.* An easy law, indeed which has set the price at being heard in a cry of appeal. 'He has called to me', he says, 'and I will answer him'. No one is heard, deservedly, if he pretends to call, or does not ask at all, or asks lukewarmly and indifferently. To God's ears burning desire is a mighty shout, whereas an indifferent intention is a whimper. How can that ever pierce the clouds? How can that be heard

246

in heaven? Surely man should have realized this
need for clamoring when, right at the beginning
of the Lord's own prayer, he was clearly told to
pray to the Father who is in heaven; this was
to remind him to hurl his prayer up as if by the
force of his spirit. 'God is spirit,'* and anyone   Jn 4:24
who wants his crying out to reach up to him
must cry in spirit. For just as he does not look
at a man's face, as a man would do, but peers instead at the heart,* so his ear attends more the   1 K 16:7
voice of the heart than of the body; of him it has
been rightly said: 'The God of my heart.'* This   Ps 73:25
is how Moses, outwardly silent, was heard in-
wardly, and the Lord said, 'Why do you cry
to me?'*   Ex 14:15

2. HE HAS CALLED TO ME AND I WILL ANSWER
HIM. Not undeservedly. The magnitude of our
need forces out a mighty cry. And what does
the person who cries out seek, if not consolation, liberation, glorification? Otherwise how
will he be answered in these areas, if he cries out
for something else? I WILL ANSWER HIM. How
will you answer, O Lord, and in what circumstances? I AM WITH HIM IN TROUBLE, I WILL
RESCUE HIM AND GIVE HIM GLORY. It seems to me
this threefold help should be related to the great
triduum we are soon to celebrate, inasmuch as it
was for our sakes that he suffered distress and
anguish* when 'for the joy that was set before   Ps 116:4
him he endured the cross, despising the shame.'*   Heb 12:2
And yet the things he had to do, as he foretold
before his death, came to an end, and as he said
at his death: 'They are finished,'* and then he   Jn 19:30
rested. Nor was the glory of his resurrection
long delayed: the third day, at the crack of

Mal 4:2

dawn, the Sun of righteousness* rose from the grave for us. Thus, in the showing forth of his glorification appeared both the fruit of his suffering and the reality of his deliverance. This triduum seems no less to be alloted as well to us. I AM WITH HIM IN TROUBLE. When is this, if not in the day of our tribulation, the day of our cross, when what he said will be fulfilled: 'In the world you will face oppression,'* and what his apostle said, 'All those who choose to live committed to Christ will suffer persecution.'* There can be no complete and perfect deliverance before the day of our burial, for there remains 'a heavy yoke upon the sons of Adam from the day they leave their mother's womb until the day they are buried in the mother of all.'* Even on that day 'I will rescue him,' he says, when the world has nothing more it can do against either his body or his soul. Truly glorification waits for the last day, the day of resurrection, when what is meanwhile sown in dishonor will rise in glory.*

Jn 16:33

2 Tm 3:12

Sir 40:1

1 Co 15:43

3. How do we know that he is with us in tribulation? From being in that tribulation. Who would endure, who would hold out, who persevere without him? We must consider it a great joy when we fall into various tribulations,* my brothers, not only because 'it behooves us through many tribulations to enter the kingdom of God,'* but because 'the Lord is near the brokenhearted.'* As someone said, 'Even though I walk through the valley of the shadow of death, I fear no evil, for you are with me.'* He is indeed with us every single day until the end of the world. But when shall we be with him?

Jm 1:2

Ac 14:21

Ps 34:18

Ps 23:4

When 'we shall be caught up in the clouds to meet Christ in the air, of course, then shall we be always with the Lord.'* When shall we appear with him in glory? Surely when Christ, our life, appears.* Meanwhile he must remain hidden, that tribulation may precede rescue, and rescue glorification. The voice of the freedman [says], 'Return, my soul, to your rest; for the Lord has dealt bountifully with you. He has rescued my soul from death, my eyes from tears, my feet from stumbling.'* I SHALL RESCUE HIM AND I SHALL GLORIFY HIM. Happy are you who have even now someone to comfort and help you, 'a helper in good times [and] in tribulation.'* But how much happier is someone already free from the snare of the hunters, already 'caught up lest malice change his understanding or guile deceive his soul.'* By far the happiest of all will be he whom you have filled with the good things of your house and conformed to your own brightness.*

4. So now, my wee sons, let us call out to heaven, and our God will take pity on us. Let us call out to heaven, because under heaven all is effort and grief, vanity and affliction of spirit.* For the heart of man is perverse and unsearchable,* and his senses incline to evil.† There is in me nothing good, that is in my flesh.* The law of sin dwells in it,* lusting against the spirit.† Finally 'my heart fails me,'* and my body is dead because of sin.* But sufficient unto the day is its own malice,* and the world is set in maliciousness.* How wicked this world is in every way! How wickedly worldly desires are known to war against the soul. Then there are the

1 Th 4:17

Col 3:4

Ps 116:7-8

Ps 9:9

Wis 4:11

Ph 3:21

Cf. Ps 10:7,
Qo 1:14, 9:3
*Jer 17:9
†Jer 8:21
Rm 7:18
*Rm 7:23
†Gal 5:17
Ps 40:15
Rm 8:10
Mt 6:34
1 Jn 5:19

Jn 12:31 princes of this world,* of its darkness, evil spirits of wickedness, powers of the air, and among
them the serpent more coldblooded than any
other living thing. All these then under the sun,
all these under heaven. Where are you going to
find a haven from all this? How do you hope
for any comfort, any help amid all these? If
you look within yourself, your heart will wither
away and you will find that you are forgotten as
one dead from the heart. If you look beneath
yourself, 'the corruptible body weighs down
Wis 9:5 the soul.'* If you look around yourself, 'this
Ibid. earthly habitation burdens the ability to think.'*
Seek above then, but be careful to skirt the in-
flated army. They know that every excellent
Jm 1:17 and every perfect gift comes only from above,*
and robbers are lying in ambush along the way.
Pass by therefore, pass by these ever watchful
wicked creatures who so untiringly besiege and
spy on that city in the hope of being able to turn
someone away from it. If they smite you, if
Sg 5:7 they wound you,* leave them your coat, as Jo-
seph in Egypt once abandoned his to an adul-
Gen 39:12 teress;* leave your shirt to flee naked from them
Mk 14:52 like the young man in the Gospel.* Surely into
the hands of the ungodly was given more than
the coat of the fellow of whom God said: 'Only
Jb 9:24 spare his life.'* Lift up your heart, lift up your
cry, lift up your desires, lift up your way of life,
lift up your determination, and let all your expectation come down from above. Cry out to
heaven that you may be heard, and your Father
who is in heaven 'will send you help from the
Ps 20:2 sanctuary, and watch over you from Zion.'* He
Ps 60:11 will send you help in tribulation,* he will rescue

you from tribulation,* he will glorify you in
the resurrection. These are great expectations,
but you, great Lord, have promised them. We
hope because of your promise, so we dare to
say:

Ps 54:7

> If we cry out with a godly heart
> then surely you must keep your
> promise. Amen.*

*From the hymn *Summi largitor praemii*, sung at Compline
during Lent in Bernard's lifetime. During the seventeenth
century it became the hymn at lenten Vigils.

SERMON SEVENTEEN

On the Sixteenth Verse:

WITH LENGTH OF DAYS SHALL I SATISFY HIM
AND SHOW HIM MY SALVATION

1. **B**ROTHERS, THIS CONCERNS US very much: this verse of the psalm is quite in keeping with the season. We are about to celebrate the Lord's resurrection, and already each one of us is assured of his own. In this way the members celebrate more merrily what was accomplished in their head, and prepare for it to be accomplished one day in them. An appropriate ending to this psalm, where a blissful end is promised the psalm-singers. It ends on a joyful note, as it promises happy fulfilment: WITH LENGTH OF DAYS SHALL I SATISFY HIM AND SHOW HIM MY SALVATION.

I have often warned you, brothers, that in Paul's opinion, godliness contains the promise of the life which now is as well as of the life to come.* For this reason the same apostle says, 'You will have your fruit in holiness now, but at the end, eternal life.'* It is this fulness which is here promised, this length of days. What could be as long as something eternal? What could be as long as something cut off by no end? A good end, eternal life; a good end which has no end. And, of course, anything that has a good end is

1 Tm 4:8

Rm 6:22

252

itself good. So let us embrace holiness because it is good, because its end is life without end. Let us strive for the holiness and the peace without which no one shall see God.* WITH LENGTH OF DAYS SHALL I SATISFY HIM AND SHOW HIM MY SALVATION. This is the promise of God's right hand;* the gift of his right hand which a holy man once longed to have extended to him: 'To the work of your hand', he said, 'shall you extend your right hand.'* In this right hand are delights until the end. This right hand he hoped God would extend to him and he achieved it; as the psalmist says: 'He asked life of you and you gave him length of days in this world and in the world without end.'* And the Sage said the same thing more openly: 'In his left hand are riches and honor; but in his right hand is length of life.'* Who is the man who desires life, and would love to see good days.* This life we are living is more like death: it is not simply life, but mortal life. A man is dying, we say, when actually he is on the point of dying. Yet what do we really do from the very moment we begin living except move closer to death and begin to die?* The days of this life are short and evil,* as the holy Patriarch bears witness. One is truly alive when life is lively and vital; days are good when there is unending length of days. Let us give thanks to him who has disposed all things not only strongly, but also sweetly:* for the day's own trouble is sufficient for the day,* and these few days* will shortly come to an end: but where there is goodness of days, there also is eternity.

2. WITH LENGTH OF DAYS SHALL I SATISFY HIM. What he had earlier said, I WILL GLORIFY

Heb 12:14

Ac 2:33

Jb 14:15

Ps 21:4

Pr 3:16

Ps 34:12

Jn 4:47
Eph 5:16

Wis 8:1
Mt 6:34
Jb 10:20

HIM, he now says more explicitly. Who would not be content at being glorified by him whose works are perfect? Yet such great Immensity could not do otherwise than glorify immensely. The glorification which comes down from such magnificent glory must necessarily be great. Peter said, 'The voice issued down from magnificent glory.'* Magnificent glory indeed, thus magnificently glorifying him, in length and number of days and fullness of light. Glory is deceitful and brightness vain,* the day of a man is short. The Sage did not aspire to this; he spoke rather from the heart to him who gazes into the heart,* 'I have not desired the day of man, you know.'* As for me I do not desire what he did not desire, nor do I wish even to receive it. I know whose voice it is who said, 'I do not receive brightness from men.'* How wretched we are to seek glory from one another and refuse that which comes from God alone.* That glory alone, the only one we neglect, has length of days and that alone fulfilment. The days of man are short,* and his day blooms 'as the flower of the field.'* 'The grass withers, the flower fades, but the word of the Lord endures for ever.'* The true day, of course, knows no dusk: eternal truth, true eternity, and in like wise true and eternal satisfaction. How can a glory which is deceitful and vain* give satisfaction? This is precisely why it is called hollow,* because you know that by it you can never be fulfilled but only drained. Here below therefore abjection is a greater good than elevation. Need is a greater good than cravings, because though both will pass swiftly away, the latter

2 P 1:17

Pr 31:30

1 K 16:7
Jer 17:16

Jn 5:41

Jn 5:44

Jb 14:5
Ps 103:15

Is 40:8

Cf. Pr 31:30
Gal 5:26

brings sorrow in its wake* while the former
will impart a crown.

3. Tribulation which produces endurance* is
useful; it leads to glory. I AM WITH HIM IN
TROUBLE, he says, I WILL RESCUE HIM AND GLO-
RIFY HIM. Let us give thanks to the Father of
mercies who is with us in tribulation and consoles us in all our tribulations.* A necessary
thing, as I have said, is the tribulation which will
be changed into glory, as is the sadness which
will be turned into joy, a long lasting joy indeed,
which no one will take from us,* a manifold joy,
a full joy. This need is a necessary thing: it produces the crown. Let us not be scornful, brothers; the seed is tiny,* but a great fruit will grow
up from it. Perhaps it is a bitter seed, perhaps
a tasteless seed, perhaps a mustard seed. Let us
consider not what we see, but what within it is
not seen, 'for the things that are seen are temporal, but those that are not seen are eternal.'* Let
us have a foretaste of the first-fruits of glory,
let us glory in the hope of the glory of our great
God.* Yet not only this but, as I have expressly
said, let us glory in tribulation, for in it lies the
hope of glory. See whether this is what the
apostle wanted to teach you when he added,
'because tribulation produces endurance,'* and
so forth. Obviously what he intended, since
previously he had urged us to glory in hope, is
not to say something different but merely to explain things more fully by saying: 'Yet not only
this, but we glory also in tribulation.'* He is
not commending a different glory, but adding
instead that where there is hope of glory there
must also be the hope of glorification. The hope

1 Jn 4:18

Rm 5:3-4

2 Co 1:3-4

Jn 16:20-4

Mt 13:32

2 Co 4:18

Rm 5:2-3

Rm 5:3

Ibid.

of glory lies in tribulation, and surely glory itself is contained within that same tribulation,
just as the hope of the fruit lies in the seed, and
as the fruit itself is in the seed. In this way too
Lk 17:21 the kingdom of God is now within us,* a trea-
2 Co 4:7 sure in a clay vessel, in a worthless field.† It is
†Mt 13:44 there, I tell you, but it is hidden. Happy is the
person who shall find it. Who is he? Surely it
is he who gives more thought to the harvest than
to the sowing. The eye of faith discovers this
treasure, not judging according to appearances,
but seeing what is not apparent, discerning
things as yet unseen. How true it is that he
found a treasure which he wanted others to discover as well and therefore said, 'This slight
momentary tribulation produces in us an eternal
2 Co 4:17 weight of glory beyond all comparison.'* He
did not say, will be awarded us, but 'produces
in us an eternal weight of glory.' The glory is
hidden, my brothers, concealed from us in tribulation. In this moment eternity lies hidden, in
this slight thing a sublime and matchless weight.
Let us therefore hasten to buy this field, to buy
Mt 13:44 this treasure lying hidden in the field.* Let us
count it utter joy when we fall into various trib-
Jm 1:2 ulations. Let us say from our soul,† let us say
†*animus* from conviction: 'It is better to go to the house
Qo 7:3 of mourning than to the house of feasting.'*

4. I WILL BE WITH HIM IN TRIBULATON, says
God. Shall I then seek anything here below
apart from tribulation? 'For me to cleave to
Ps 73:27 God is good,* and not that alone, but also 'to
put my hope in the Lord God' because he has
said, I WILL RESCUE HIM AND GLORIFY HIM. I
WILL BE WITH HIM IN TRIBULATION. 'My delight

is in the sons of men,'* he says. Emmanuel, God
with us.* 'Hail, full of grace,' said the angel to
Mary, 'the Lord is with you.'* In the fullness of
grace he is with us; in the fullness of glory shall
we be with him. He came down* to be near
those who are brokenhearted,* so that he might
be near those who are troubled at heart, that he
might be with us in our tribulation. The time
will come, however, when we shall 'be caught
up in the clouds to meet Christ in the air; and so
shall we be forever with the Lord.'* On condition, however, that we be careful here below to
have him with us, so that he may accompany us
on the way, who shall restore the homeland to
us in the future, who in fact will be the way
and is now the homeland.

It is good for me to be troubled, Lord, as long
as you are with me, better than reigning without
you, of feasting without you, of being glorified
without you. It is good for me to embrace you
in tribulation, to have you with me in the furnace, better than being without you even in
heaven. 'For whom have I in heaven but you?
And there is nothing on earth that I desire beside you.'* The furnace tests gold, and the trial
of tribulation just men.'* There, yes, there you
are present with them, Lord. You are there in
the midst of those gathered in your name,* as
you once deigned to appear [in the fiery fur-
nace] with the three young men even to a
heathen, so that he might say 'the appearance of
the fourth is like the son of God.'* Why should
we tremble, why should we hesitate, why flee
this furnace? The fire rages, but the Lord is
with us in tribulation. 'If God is with us who

Pr 8:31
Mt 1:23
Lk 1:28

1 Th 4:16
Ps 34:18

1 Th 4:16

Ps 73:24
Sir 27:6

Mt 18:20

Dan 3:92

Rm 8:31

Jn 10:28

can be against us?'* If he snatches us out of their hands, who can grab us out of his? Is there anyone who can pluck us out of his hand?* Lastly, if he glorifies us, who will humiliate us?

5. Then hear about the glory with which God glorifies us: WITH LENGTH OF DAYS WILL I SATISFY HIM. First of all, in using the word days in the plural, he wished to emphasize not so much their alternation as their great number. You might suppose he meant alternation, did you not know that one day in the courts of the Lord is better than a thousand.* And we read

Ps 84:10

that holy and perfect men leave our lifespan full of days, by which we understand that they were filled with virtues and graces. Surely until they attain this fullness, they are being transformed day by day, from brightness to brightness,* not by their own spirit but by the Spirit

2 Co 3:18

of the Lord. So if day signifies grace and if, as we recalled above, man's day signifies the brightness which comes from man and glistens with a fell glory which we seek from one another, how much more is the fullness of true glory to be likened to true day and full midday? And if we call the many days diverse graces, how can we not understand by number of days manifold grace? Finally, listen to this very clear explanation of the unchanging length of days: 'The light of the moon will be as the light of the sun,' says the Prophet, 'and the light of the sun will be sevenfold, as the light of seven days.'*

Is 30:26

Unless I am mistaken, it was during all these days of [eternal] life that the Lord's faithful king hoped to sing psalms in the house of the

Ps 27:4

Lord.* Being grateful to God for the gifts

of such abundant glory, and giving unending
thanks for them will be like singing psalms to
his name all the days of our life.

6. WITH LENGTH OF DAYS WILL I SATISFY HIM.
This is as if he said openly, 'I know what he
would like. I know what he thirsts for, what
his tastes are. He has no taste for silver or gold,
for pleasure or curiosity, for any worldly digni-
ties. He has considered them all as loss, he has
despised them all, reckoning them dung.* He   Ph 3:8
has utterly emptied himself,* nor has he allowed   Ph 2:7
himself to get involved with these things which
he knows can never satisfy him. He is not unaware in whose image he has been made,* of   Gen 1:27
whose greatness he is capable, and he will not
put up with increasing the little and thereby de-
creasing the greatest. So WITH LENGTH OF DAYS
WILL I SATISFY HIM, who can be refreshed only
by true light,* and satisfied with eternal things; Jn 1:9
its duration has no ending, its daylight no wan-
ing, and its satisfaction no surfeit. For assurance
will be founded on eternity, glorying on truth,
exultation on satisfaction. AND I WILL SHOW
HIM MY SALVATION.

This means that he will deserve to see what
he desired when the King of glory* presents to   Ps 24:7
himself his bride, the glorious church without
spot or wrinkle* against the brightness of the   Eph 5:27
day and his own all-encompassing fullness. To
the radiance of his light will soar the soul which,
as it is not impure, is also neither anxious nor
agitated. That is why, as I remarked above, we
are advised to strive for peace and virtuousness
alike, for without these no one shall see God.*   Heb 12:14
When he has satisfied you with the good things

Ps 103:5

you desire,* therefore, until there is nothing
left for you to hanker for, your mind having
become entirely serene by this very fullness,
then, having been made like to God, you will be
able to see the serenity and the fullness of maj-

1 Jn 3:2

esty, for you will see him as he is.* Or perhaps
once he is filled with all that glory himself, the
completely delighted dweller of a completely
delightful world shall spy outside the salvation
God has wrought and see all about him the
whole earth filled with his majesty. And we
might also take this to be what is referred to by
what follows: I WILL SHOW HIM MY SALVATION.

7. Or, if you prefer, let us take it this way:
that to those whom he has promised he shows
the days of salvation by this very revelation.
WITH LENGTH OF DAYS WILL I SATISFY HIM, he
says. And you may wonder how these days
can exist in a city where we read that the sun

Rev 21:23

will not shine by day,* and in it there will be no
night. I WILL SHOW HIM MY SALVATION, he says.
Just as it says in the same [passage] of Scrip-

Ibid.

tures, 'Its lamp is the lamb.'*

'I will show him my salvation.' I shall no
longer instruct him by faith, or drill him by

in specie

hope, but I shall fill him with sight.* I WILL
SHOW HIM MY SALVATION: I will show him my
Jesus, so that for all eternity he may see him in
whom he has believed, whom he has loved,
whom he has longed for. 'Show us your mercy,

Ps 85:7

O Lord, and grant us your salvation.'* Show us
your salvation, O Lord, and we shall be satis-

Jn 14:8-11

fied.* Anyone who sees him, sees you too, because he is in you and you are in him. ' For this
is life eternal, that we know you the one true

God, and Jesus Christ whom you have sent.'* Jn 17:3
And then you will let your servant depart in
peace, O Lord, according to your word, for my
eyes shall have seen your salvation,* your Jesus, Lk 2:29-30
our Lord, who is God over all, blessed for ever
and ever.* Rm 9:5

TABLE OF ABBREVIATIONS

CCh	Corpus Christianorum series. Turnhout, Belgium: Brepols, 1953–.
CF	Cistercian Fathers series. Spencer; Washington; Kalamazoo, 1970–.
Consol. Phil.	Boethius, *Philosophiae Consolatio (The Consolation of Philosophy)*.
Conv	Bernard of Clairvaux, *Sermo de conversione ad clericos* (On Conversion: A Sermon to Clerics).
CSEL	Corpus scriptorum ecclesiasticorum latinorum series. Vienna, 1866–.
Dial.	Gregory the Great, *Dialogorum libri IV* (The Dialogues).
En. in Ps.	Augustine of Hippo, *Enarrationes in Psalmos* (Commentaries on the Psalms).
Ep.	*Epistola* (Letter)
Ep aur	William of St Thierry, *Epistola aurea ad fratres de Monte Dei* (The Golden Epistle).
Liber interpr. hebr. nom.	Jerome, *Liber interpretationis Hebraicorum nominum* (The Interpretation of Hebrew Names).
LXX	The Septaguint
PL	J. P. Migne, *Patrologia cursus completus, series latina.* 221 volumes. Paris, 1857–66.
QH	Bernard of Clairvaux, *Sermones super psalmum Qui habitat* (Sermons on the Psalm 'He Who Dwells').
SBOp	Jean Leclercq, H. M. Rochais, C. H. Talbot, *Sancti Bernardi Opera.* 8 volumes. Rome: Editiones Cistercienses, 1957–1979.
SC	Bernard of Clairvaux, *Sermones super Cantica canticorum* (Sermons on the Song of Songs).
SCh	Sources chrétiennes series. Paris: Editions du Cerf, 1941–.
Vita prima	William of St Thierry, Arnold of Bonnevaux, Geoffrey of Clairvaux, *Vita prima Bernardi* (The First Life of Saint Bernard).

Scriptural citations have been made according to the enumeration and nomenclature of The Jerusalem Bible.

262

SELECTED BIBLIOGRAPHY

THE BIBLIOGRAPHY of studies on Saint Bernard and his works is so extensive that three successive volumes have been required to keep it up to date. These should be consulted by anyone interested in pursuing Bernard studies.

L. Janauschek, *Bibliographia Bernardia*. Vienna, 1891, rpt. Georg Olms, Hildesheim, n.d.

Jean de la Croix Bouton. *Bibliographie Bernardine, 1891-1957*. Commission d'histoire de l'ordre de Cîteaux, No. v. Paris: P. Lethielleux, 1958.

Eugène Manning. *Bibliographie Bernardine (1957-1970)*. *Documentation cistercienne 6 (1972)*.

WORKS CONCERNING THE WRITINGS OF SAINT BERNARD

Jean Leclercq. *Etudes sur S. Bernard et la texte de ses écrits, Analecta* S.O.C., fasc. 1-2. Rome, 1953.

———. *Recueil d'études sur S. Bernard et ses écrits*, 3 volumes. Rome: Edizioni di Storia et Letteratura, 1962, 1966, 1969.

———. 'Saint Bernard écrivain d'après les sermons sur le psaume Qui Habitat', *Revue bénédictine*, 77 (1967) 364-374.

———. *Introduction* to *Les Sermons sur le psaume Qui Habitat*, in *Sancti Bernardi Opera*, IV, pp. 119-128. Rome: Editiones Cistercienses, 1966.

WORKS CONCERNING MEDIEVAL CULTURE

Henri de Lubac. *Exégèse médiévale*, volume 2. Paris, 1959.

Jean Leclercq. *The Love of Learning and the Desire for God*. Translated by Catherine Misrahi. New York: Fordham University Press, 1961, 1976.

R. W. Southern. *The Making of the Middle Ages*. New Haven-London: Yale University Press, 1953.

INDEX

On Conversion, A Sermon to Clerics, is indicated by Conv and is cited by paragraph number in *italic* type, without reference to the roman numerals appearing in the text.

Lenten Sermons on the Psalm 'He Who Dwells' is indicated by QH and is cited by sermon number in roman numerals and paragraph number in arabic numerals, both in *italic* type.

Abstinence, *QH III.4, IX.3*
  false, *QH IX.5*
  humbling the soul by fasting, *QH III.3*
Affection, human, *QH XIII.2, XIV.3*
Ambition
  and charity, *Conv 38*
  impeding spiritual insight, *Conv 30*
  rebuke to the ambitious, *Conv 32*
  results of, *Conv 40*
Angels
  hierarchy of, *QH XI.12*
  ways of, *QH XI.6, 10-11, XII.2-10, XIII.1,2, XIV.8, XV.2*
Anger
  spirit of, as dragon, *QH XIII.5*
Anima, animus
  contrasted, *Conv 2*
Apostasy, *QH III.5*
Arrow (of vain glory), *QH VI.3,7*
  See also Glory, vain
Asp, *QH XIII.4, XIV.1,6,9*

Babylon, *QH VII.5*
Balaam, *QH VII.5*
Basilisk, *QH XIII.4, XIV.1,7-9*
Beasts
  men as, *QH III.1*
  of burden, *QH VII.3*
Benedict, St, *QH XIII.1*
Boasting and self-praise, *Conv 10*
Body, *See also* Flesh, Resurrection
  bearing Christ in, *QH VII.3,8*
  burdening soul, *QH XVI.4*
  dwelling in hope, *QH X.3*
  enslaved to curiosity, servants of vanity, *Conv 10*

Body — *continued*
  man as carnal being, *Conv 7*
  reason for taking up b., *Conv 6*
  rebels, *Conv 11*
  resurrection, *QH VIII.2*
  temple of Holy Spirit, *QH VIII.5,6*
  whole b. becoming eye, *Conv 10*
  vexations of, *QH VI.1*
Bride, *QH XV.3*
Bridegroom, *Conv 21*

Celibacy
  assuming title of, *Conv 36*
Charity
  angels act from c., *QH XI.11*
Children
  entering heaven, *Conv 1*
  of wrath, *Conv 32*
  sacred plan revealed to, *Conv 26*
Chosen, the, *QH IX.4*
Christ, Jesus, *See also* Good Shepherd
  reason for death, *QH IX.3*
Church, *QH VI.7, VII.10*
  body of, injured, *Conv 35*
  growth of, *Conv 34*
Circuit
  man in, *QH XII.1,2, XIII.3*
Commandments, *QH XIV.3,4*
Conscience
  torment of guilty c., *Conv 7*
  worms of, *Conv 7*
Consolation
  from hearing of blessedness of heaven, *Conv 12*
  fleeting c. from curiosity, *Conv 14*
  from tribulation, *QH Pref.1*
  grace of, *Conv 37*
  in God's word, *QH Pref.2*

Contemplation, heavenly
desire for, *Conv 24*
in c. lies rest, *Conv 25*
Contempt, *QH XI.5*
Conversion, *Conv 1,2,7, QH 1.1, VI.1*
Curiosity
impeding spiritual insight, *Conv 30*
leads to emptiness and brings fleeting consolation, *Conv 14*
vanity of, *Conv 13*

Death
certainty of, *Conv 16*
defined, *QH X.3*
opening eyes, *QH VIII.6*
uncertainty of hour of, *Conv 15-6*
ways of, *QH XI.10*
Demons
in hierarchy, *QH XI.12*
ways of, *QH XI.4, XII.1*
Determination, human, *QH XIII.3*
Discipline
shackles of, *QH IX.1*
Distress
enlightens reason, *Conv 11*

Elijah, *QH IV.1*
Enemy
deserves wrath, *Conv 32*
Envy, *QH XIII.4*
Eucharist, *QH III.3*
Evil, *See also* Pleasure, evil
compared with neglecting to do
good, *Conv 20*
distinguishing e. from good,
QH III.1
distinguished from scourge, *QH X.2*
doing e. by presumption, *QH XI.5*
in absence of good spirit, *QH XI.2*
persevering in e. as diabolic,
QH XI.5
turning from e., *Conv 23, QH X.4*
who loves evil hates soul and flesh,
Conv 5
Evildoers, *See* Sinners
Eye
human, *QH VIII.2,4,6*
of resurrection, *QH VIII.3*

Ezekiel, *Conv 34*

Faith
by hearing, *QH VIII.3, XV.6*
defined, *QH X.1*
proves angels' presence, *QH XII.6*
through hope in the Lord,
QH IX.5-6
Fast, *See also* Abstinence
as spiritual combat, *Conv 8-9*
Fear, *QH VII.9*
as temptation, *QH VI.2-3*
of God, *Conv 22, QH 1.1, II.2,*
XIII.5-6
of men's opinions before God's,
Conv 19
Flesh, *QH VIII.2,8*
See also Body
a body of death, *Conv 30*
eternal suffering of, *Conv 6*
God becoming f., *QH XIV.3*
freedom of celibacy as opportunity
for, *Conv 36*
lacking good, *Conv 23*
living in f. distinguished from living according to f., *QH XI.2*
man as carnal being, *Conv 7*
not hating one's f., *QH X.3*
rebellion of f. to abstinence,
Conv 9-10
rebuking lures of f., *Conv 13*
resists doing good, *Conv 22,*
QH V.1
ruled by sin, *Conv 12*
sowing in and reaping of the f.,
QH IX.2-3
temptation of, *QH VIII.5*
weakness of, *QH VIII.5*
who loves evil hates f., *Conv 5*
Forbearance, *See* God's forbearance
Fortune(s), *See* Money

Gift
four gifts, *QH XIV.3-4*
of ingenuity and wisdom,
QH XIV.1-2
Glory, *QH XVI.2, XVII.1,3-5*
See also God's glory
Glory, vain, *QH VI.3-4*
as basilisk, *QH XIV.7*

God
  as examiner, *QH II.3*
  as sovereign, *QH XI.12*
  is spirit, *QH XVI.1*
  observes sinners, *Conv 18-9*
  owing gratitude to, *QH XIV.1*
  terrible and merciful, *Conv 21*
God, fear of, *See* Fear
God, shelter of, *QH I.2-4, II.1-2,VII.7*
  See also Shelter, divine
God, word of, *QH IV.2, IX.2*
Godliness, *QH VII.5, VIII.5, XIV.5*
God's forbearance, *Conv 28*
God's glory, *Conv 21*
God's image, *QH XIV.4*
God's kindness, *QH IV.4, V.2-3,*
  VII.15, XI.1
God's kiss, *Conv 29, QH XV.2*
God's mercy, *QH VII.7, VIII.7,*
  XI.1,7-8
God's right hand, *QH XVII.1*
God's truth, *QH XI.7-8*
  as shield, *QH V.1,3*
God's voice, *Conv 2,3,8,26*
Good Shepherd, *Conv 40*
  See also Christ, Jesus
Grace
  as burden, *QH XV.1*
  of consolation, *Conv 37*
  of divine protection, *QH V.2*
  of gift, *QH XIV.4*
  power of, *QH VII.1*
  preparing for spiritual answer,
    QH IX.5
  reason for, *QH IX.3*
  rejected, *QH I.2*
  stimulated by divine liberality,
    QH XV.2
  ungrateful, *QH XI.1*
Greed
  leading, *QH XI.3*

Happiness
  false, *QH XI.3*
Heart
  as perverse, *QH XVI.4*
  need for purification, *Conv 30,32*
  observed by God, *Conv 18*

Heart—*continued*
  place where salvation is shown,
    Conv 7
  reason for being on left side,
    QH VII.15
Heart, unrepentant, *See also* Flesh;
  Pleasure, evil
  compared with madman, numbing
    soul, *Conv 5*
Heaven, kingdom of, *QH VII.7*
  blessedness of, *Conv 11*
  conversion necessary for entrance
    to, *Conv 1*
  impure grab sign of, *Conv 34*
  unattainable if sin rules flesh,
    Conv 12
Hiding
  in cloisters, *QH V.3*
Hireling
  distinguished from shepherd,
    Conv 39
Hope, *QH II.3*
  in mercy, *QH I.2*
  in the Lord, *QH XV.3,5,6*
  of glory, in tribulation, *QH XVII.3*
  through the Lord, *QH IX.5,8*

Ignatius of Antioch, *QH VII.3*
Image, God's, *See* God's image
Impure (people)
  not ashamed to defile orders,
    Conv 34,36
Iniquity, *QH XV.1*
Inner judge, *See also* Soul, substance
  of
  no fraud or fault may be hidden
    from, *Conv 4*
Insight, spiritual
  impeded by lust, *Conv 30*
John (the apostle), *Conv 30-1*
Kindness, *See* God's kindness
Kiss, *See* God's kiss

Laborers
  invited to refreshment, *QH XV.1*
Lazarus, *Conv 21*
Lord
  as hope of the wretched, *QH XV.3*
  name of the L., *QH XV.6, XVI.1*
  ways of the L., *QH XI.7-9*

Lord's word, *See also* Word of God;
 God's voice
 and Simon's fishing, *Conv 2*
 led the way to conversion, *Conv 3*
Lust, *See also* Sin
 impeding spiritual insight, *Conv 30*
 l.ing against spirit, *QH VI.1*
 l.'s appetites, *Conv 13*
 rebellious will may obey her l.s,
  Conv 22
 spirit lusting, *QH I.3*

Malice
 human, *QH VII.16, XVI.4*
 obdurate, *QH VI.13*
Mankind
 dual substance of, *QH I.1*
Manna, hidden, *Conv 25*
Marriage
 abstaining from, *Conv 36*
Martin of Tours, *QH VII.2*
Mary
 as Christophora, *QH VII.3*
Members (physical)
 by sin, *QH VIII.4-6*
 governance of, *Conv 9,10,12,*
  QH I.4
 unsatisfied, *Conv 10*
Memory
 cleansed through mercy, *Conv 29*
 component of soul, *Conv 11*
 foul and fetid, *Conv 11*
 need for purification, *Conv 28*
Mercy, *See also* God's mercy
 for merciful, *Conv 29*
 for neighbor, *QH XI.11*
 for repentant, *Conv 29*
 man devoid of, *QH XII.2*
 natural home of, *Conv 12*
 usurpers of dignity separated from,
  Conv 33
Misery, *See also* Pain
 source of man's happiness, *Conv 12*
Money
 love of, *Conv 13,14,26*
 lucre, *QH VII.14*
 misfortune of amassed fortunes,
  Conv 15

Mourn
 who turns from evil must m.,
  Conv 23

Nature
 concern for, *QH XIV.5*
Necessity
 leading, *QH XI.3*
Neglecting
 n. to do good, compared with evil,
  Conv 20
 to cleanse eye, *Conv 30*

Obligation
 and honor, *QH XII.7*
Order, divine, *QH VII.10*

Pacified (person), *See also* Peacemaker
 repaying good for good, *Conv 31*
Pacifying (person), *See also* Peacemaker, *Conv 31*
Pain
 from restraint, *Conv. 9*
 of body, *Conv 6, QH VI.1*
 of soul, *Conv 5-6*
 sufferings of present time, *Conv 37*
Paradise
 at gate of p., voice heard, *Conv 26*
 of inner pleasure, *Conv 25*
Peacemaker(s)
 blessing, *Conv 31-2,39*
 returning good for evil, *Conv 31*
 status of, *Conv 38*
 usurped dignity of, *Conv 33*
Penance
 balm of suffering, *Conv 6*
 exhortation to, *Conv 37*
 for men of the world, *QH III.3*
 impossible without body, *Conv 6*
 wrongness of reducing p.,
  QH Pref.1
Persecution
 according to beatitude, *Conv 39*
 human, *QH VII.13*
Peter, *See* Simon (Peter)
Pleasure, evil, *Conv 4*
Poverty, *See also* Abstinence
 QH III.4

Prayer, *QH XV.6, XVI.1-2,4*

Predestination, *QH VII.6*

Presumption, presumptiousness,
QH XII.1
exhortation to flee from, *QH XI.4-5*

Promise, *QH IV.3*

Protection, under the
distinguished from 'in the presence', *QH I.4*

Providence, divine
desires for the faithful, *QH XII.3*

Prudence, *QH XIV.10*
as mercy's first step, *Conv 29*
need for, *Conv 21*

Punishment, eternal, *QH VI.2*

Reason
component of soul, *Conv 11*
enlightened through mercy,
Conv 29
grasps sacred plan, *Conv 26*

Redemption, *QH XIV.3*

Resurrection
awaiting a r., *QH X.5*
glory of r. not delayed, *QH XVI.2*
of body, *QH VII.2,6*

Riches, *See* Money

Righteousness, *QH II.1, III.3, VII.5,16*
hunger and thirst for, *Conv 26-7*
persecution for r.'s sake, *Conv 39*
Sun of r., *QH XVI.2*

Sainthood
disadvantage of early reward,
QH IV.3

Salvation (personal), *QH XVII.1, 6-7*
shown in heart, *Conv 7*

Scourge, *QH XI.2*
distinguished from evil, *QH X.2*

Sermons
Bernard comments on his own,
QH VIII.1

Shield of the Lord, *QH V.3, VI.1,3,
VII.1-2,16*

Shelter, divine
See also God, shelter of
recognizing those within, *QH I.1*

Shepherd
distinguished from hireling, *Conv 9*

Shepherd, Good, *See* Good Shepherd;
Christ, Jesus

Shoulders, Lord's, *QH IV.1,3-4*

Sickness
utility of, *Conv 12*

Simon (Peter) *QH VIII.10-13, XV.6*
addressed by Jesus, *Conv 32*
appointed a fisher of men, *Conv 2*

Sin
as burden, *QH XV.1*
causing death of body, *QH XVI.4*
consciousness of, *Conv 37*
conspicuous before judgement,
QH VII.12
contempt as s., *QH XI.5*
dims and blurs eyes, *Conv 30*
forgiving, *Conv 28*
guarding against, *QH X.4*
men in whom s. reigns, *QH X.5*
punished and forgiven, *Conv. 27*
ruling flesh, *Conv 12*
thinking upon, *QH VI.2*

Sinner
cast down, *QH VIII.12*
consideration of s.s, *QH VIII.7-9,11*
fate of evildoer, *Conv 20*
forgiving s.s, *Conv 29*
impossibility of lying hidden,
Conv 18-9
s.s flock to do penance, *Conv 38*

Sinning
compared with drain overflowing,
Conv 8
reason why s. not given up, *Conv 33*

Son of God, *See also* Christ, Jesus
is Word of Father and brightness
of his glory, *Conv 3*
standing arrogated, *Conv 33*

Soul
after death, *Conv 6*
contaminated from within, *Conv 12*
immortality, *QH VIII.2*
loving flesh, *QH X.3*
place of, *QH I.1*
reasoning power of, *Conv 11*
seeking the Lord, *QH IX.8-9*

Soul, substance of
  components of, *Conv 11*
  memory and reason, *Conv 3-4*
  spiritual and simple, *Conv 3*
Spiritual being, *Conv 5*
Stewards
  trustworthiness, *Conv 32*
Suffering, *See also* Pain
  sharing s., *QH Pref.1, III.3*
Sun, brightness of, *QH XII.7*
Sun of justice, *QH IV.4*

Temperance
  need for, *Conv 21*
Temptation, *QH IV.1, V.1,3, VI.1-2,
  5-7, VII.2,5, XII.9, XIV.6*
  fleeing from, *QH II.1*
  Lord's t.s, *QH XIV.4*
  opposed by truth, *QH VI.4*
  overcoming t., *QH Pref.1, IV.2*
  t. of the elect, *QH II.2*
Tent, *QH XI.2*
  one's t. distinguished from one's
    self, *QH X.2*
Timidity, *QH XV.1*
Tribulation
  as temptation, *QH XII.9-10*
  God's presence with us in t.,
    QH XVI.3-4
  useful, *QH XVII.3-4*
Truth, *See* God's truth

Vanity
  v. of vanities, *Conv 14,16*
  search for v., as sigh of degenerate
    soul, *Conv 15*
Vice, *See also* Evil
  servitude to, *Conv 15*
Voice, *See* God's voice

Watchmen, *QH XV.3*

Wealth, *See* Money
Weep, *See also* Mourn
  exhortation to, *Conv 29*
  tears wash darkness from eyes,
    Conv 23
Will
  and heavenly contemplation,
    Conv 24-5
  as crazy hag, *Conv 10*
  compared with dry fountain,
    Conv 28
  component of soul, *Conv 11*
  giving way to reason, *Conv 22*
  mortifying, *QH IX.1*
  provoked and enraged, *Conv 9*
  spreading suppuration, *Conv 11*
  taming of, *Conv 12*
Wisdom
  laughing at ruination, *QH VIII.10*
  of scorning the world, *Conv 25*
  of serpent, *QH VII.12*
  power of, *Conv 7*
  pure and peaceful, *QH XIII.3*
  warnings of, *QH XI.3*
Wise Men
  compared with those who mourn,
    Conv 24
Word of God, *See also* God's voice
  finding consolation in W.,
    QH Pref. 2
  hearing and observing, *Conv 1*
  living and active, incomparable
    with human discourse, *Conv 2*
  power of, *QH Pref.1*
Works, temporal
  as seeds of eternal reward, *Conv 16*
  confounded by the light, *Conv 19*
  good w. compared with trees bear-
    ing fruit, *Conv 20*
  need of justice to do good w.s,
    Conv 21

SCRIPTURAL INDEX

First column indicates the scriptural book and its abbreviation. Second column indicates paragraph number in *Conv*, and sermon number and paragraph in *QH*.

GENESIS (Gen)

1:3	Conv 2
1:9	QH I.3
1:14	QH XIV.2
1:26	QH XIV.1, 2
1:27	QH XVII.6
2:8	Conv 24,25
2:9	Conv 25
2:10	Conv 25
2:17	QH X.5
2:18	QH X.3
3:1	QH VIII.8
3:5	QH VI.7
3:7	QH XI.5
3:9-10	Conv 33
3:17	QH X.3
3:24	Conv 26
4:7 (LXX)	Conv 21
6:3	QH X.3, XI.2
8:21	QH VII.15
19:1-29	Conv 35
24:7	QH I.3
27:1	Conv 30
27:8	QH III.1
27:28	QH VII.11
27:29	Conv 25
27:45	Conv 24
28:12	QH XII.2
28:17	Conv 24
37:9	Conv 9
39:12	QH XVI.4
49:10	QH VII.6

EXODUS (Ex)

1:8-10	QH VIII.5
1:14	Conv 22
2:15	Conv 22
2:22	QH IV.3
4:21	QH XI.5
9:3	QH XIII.3
14:15	QH XVI.1
14:25-31	QH VII.16

EXODUS (Ex) — *continued*

14:29	QH V.3
15:3	QH VII.16
20:7	QH XV.6
23:3	QH VIII.11
28:43	Conv 36

LEVITICUS (Lev)

19:8	Conv 36
30:20	QH XV.1

NUMBERS (Num)

12:1	Conv 4
21:22	QH XI.9
22:5	QH VII.5
23:10	QH VII.5

DEUTERONOMY (Dt)

5:26	Conv 36
11:24	QH XV.5
32:4	QH XVI.1
32:11	QH IV.4
32:27	QH VIII.5, XIV.1
32:33	QH XIII.3
32:42	Conv 19

JOSHUA (Josh)

6:18	QH XV.4
21:36	Conv 37

FIRST SAMUEL (1 S)

21:11	QH VII.10

SECOND SAMUEL (2 S)

4:41	Conv 37

FIRST KINGS (1 K)

16:7	QH XVI.1, XVII.2
19:5-8	QH IV.1

SECOND KINGS (2 K)

4:41	QH Pref.1
16:1	QH XIII.5

Tobit (Tob)
1:10   QH I.1
4:7   Conv 29
10:4   QH XIV. 1

Esther (Est)
13:9   QH IX.6
16:6   QH III.1

First Maccabees (1 Mac)
8:20   QH III.2
13:27 QH V. 3
16:14 QH XII.3

Second Maccabees (2 Mac)
9:9   Conv 11

Job (Jb)
1:7   QH XII.1
2:6   QH VII.12
2:8   Conv 4
3:25   Conv 19
7:1   QH V.1, XIV.4
7:17   QH XII.3
7:20   Conv 29
9:24   QH IV.3, XVI.4
10:20 Conv. 23; QH XVII.1
12:9   QH VIII.5
13:14 Conv 5
13:25 QH XII.4
13:26 QH XII.4
14:4   QH IX.3, 4
14:5   QH XVII.2
14:15 QH XVII.1
16:17 Conv 23
17:3   QH XV.2
19:23 Conv 4
19:26 QH VIII.3
19:27 QH II.3, VIII.2
23:2   QH VII.14
25:6   QH XII.4
28:12-13 Conv 25
28:24 QH I.3
29:21 QH VIII.12
31:23 QH XV.1
38:41 QH IV.4
40:18 QH VII.10
41:25 Conv 33; QH VI.2

Psalms (Ps)
2:11   QH III.4
2:12   QH X.3
3:4   QH XI.3
3:5   QH II.1
4:2   QH XI.11
4:3   QH IX.6
4:3, 5 Conv 24
4:4   QH XIII.5
4:9   QH XI.2
6:6   Conv 29
7:1   QH VII.9
7:9   Conv 19
8:4   QH XII.4
9:9   QH XVI.3
9:10   QH IX.6
9:18   Conv 40
10:2   QH XII.2
10:7   QH XVI.4
10:13 Conv 36
10:16 QH IX.5
11:1   QH XV.3
11:6   Conv 5, 35
12:4   QH VI.7
12:6   Conv 30; QH VII.7
12:9   QH XII.1
14:7   QH XI.3
15:4   QH VII.9
16:1   QH IX.8
16:2   QH IX.3, XIV.1
16:9   QH VII.12, 14
16:10 QH X.3
16:11 QH XI.9
17:8   QH VII.14
18:21 QH XI.3, 9
18:29 QH VIII.1
18:35 QH II.1
19:14 QH VI.2
19:15 QH II.2
20:2   QH XVI.4
21:4   QH XVII.1
22:4-5 QH XV.5
22:9   QH I.1
23:4   QH Pref.1, VII.9, XVI.3
23:5   QH IX.3
23:6   QH VII.7
24:4   QH XVI.1
24:7   QH VII.1, XVII.6
24:9   QH VII.7
24:8   QH VII.2, XI.7
25:9   QH XI.7

PSALMS (Ps) — *continued*

25:17	QH XI.3
26:3	QH XI.7
26:4	Conv 17
26:7	QH XIV.3
27:1	QH Pref.1
27:3	QH IX.5
27:4	QH XVII.5
27:5	QH 4.3
27:15	QH VIII.3
29:4	Conv 2
29:8	Conv 2
30:5	Conv 1; QH IX.6, XV.5
31:4	QH IV.4
31:14	QH X.2
32:10	QH VII.3
33:1	Conv 1
33:6	QH Pref.1
34:8	Conv 25
33:9	QH XIV.2
34:12	QH XVII.1
34:18	QH XVI.3
34:14	Conv 21
35:6	QH XI.5
35:13	QH XIII.3
35:16	Conv 10
36:12	QH XI.4
37:1	QH I.1
37:24	QH II.1
37:27	QH X.2, XI.2
37:41	QH IX.6
38:3	Conv 23
38:4	QH XV.1
38:10	QH XIII.5
38:18	QH VI.2, XIII.5
39	QH III.4
40:5	Conv 34; QH XII.2, XV.6
40:14	QH XI.7, 11
40:15	QH XVI.4
41:2	QH XI.1
41:3	QH III.1
41:8	QH II.2, XI.4
41:11	QH XI.4
42:1	QH III.1
42:2	QH IX.9
42:4	Conv 24
42:6	Conv 3
44:1	QH XI.7
45:8	QH VI.6
45:11	QH VIII.3
49:6	QH I.1

PSALMS (Ps) — *continued*

49:12	Conv 26; QH III.1, VII.3
50:10	Conv 25
50:21	Conv 3
50:23	Conv 7
51:1	Conv 29
52:8	QH I.1
54:6	QH IX.1
54:7	QH XVI.4
55:6	QH III.5, VII.5, XI.2
55:8	QH I.2, IX.7, XII.9
55:13-14	Conv 32
55:20	QH XI.4
55:23	QH IX.6
57:5	QH III.2
58:1	Conv 2
58:4-5	QH XIII.2, XIV.6
58:9	QH VIII.9
59:10	QH VII.7
60:11	QH XVI.4
62	QH III.4
62:2	QH I.1
62:6	QH I.1
62:8	QH XV.5
62:10	QH VII.14
63:12	QH IV.1
64:10	QH III.1
66:5	Conv 21
66:12	Conv 30
68:2	QH VII.9
68:9	Conv 12
68:33	Conv 2, 3
69:3	QH VIII.2
69:16	QH XI.5
69:26	Conv 10
71:2	QH IV.4, IX.7
71:14	QH VIII.11
72:9	QH VII.9
72:22	QH XIV.7
73:3	QH I.1
73:21	QH VII.3, XI.9
73:21-2	QH VII.3
73:17	Conv 36
73:22	QH VII.12
73:24	QH XVII.4
73:24-5	QH IX.8
73:25	QH XVI.1
73:27	QH VIII.11, IX.5, XVII.4
74:13	QH VIII.10
74:14	QH Pref.2
74:24	QH XI.4, XII.1

Psalms (Ps) – *continued*

75:9	QH IX.3, 4
76:2	QH XI.7
77	QH III.4
77:2-3	QH Pref.1, IV.2
78:3	QH XI.7
78:40	QH XI.4
78:25	Conv 24
78:50	QH XII.10
79:13	Conv 33
84:10	QH XVII.5
84:12	QH VII.1, XI.8, 11
85:7	QH XVII.7
85:8	Conv 3; QH V.3, VI.1, XI.9
85:10	QH XI.7, 8
88:9	QH VIII.2
89:5	QH VI.7
89:16	QH XII.3
89:25	QH XI.7
90:3	Conv 2
90:10	QH III.5
91	QH *passim*
91:1-2	QH II.1
91:5	QH V.1, VII.16
91:6	Conv 17
91:9	QH VIII.12
91:12	QH XII.4
91:15	QH XVI.1
93:3	QH VIII.12
93:6	QH IX.6
94:9	Conv 18
94:19	QH IX.6
95:8	QH XIII.3
95:10	Conv 3
96:13	QH XI.8
98:4	QH XI.8
100:2	QH XIV.1
100:3	QH III.2
102:4	QH XI.3
103:5	QH XVII.6
103:14	QH IV.4
103:15	QH XVII.2
103:17	QH XI.8
103:18	Conv 1
104:4	QH XII.3
104:29	QH XII.3
106:7	QH XI.7
106:24	QH VII.6
107:8	QH II.1, XII.3
107:42	QH VIII.7
112:7	QH III.3

Psalms (Ps) – *continued*

112:10	QH VII.7, VIII.7
112:13	QH II.2
115:1	Conv 21; QH XV.6
116:4	QH XVI.2
116:7	QH X.1
116:7-8	QH XVI.3
116:8	QH X.1
116:11	QH XII.6, XV.1
117:2	QH XI.8
118:16	QH VIII.5
119:25	QH VII.15
119:36	Conv 8
119:37	Conv 8; QH VIII.6
119:68	QH XIII.5
119:74	QH XV.4
119:108	QH XI.3
119:136	Conv 23
121:4	QH XI.1, XII.9
121:5	QH VII.12
121:8	QH VII.2, 7
124:6	QH III.5
125:2	QH XV.3
126:3	QH XII.3
127:1	Conv 14; QH XV.3
127:2	Conv 8
127:6	QH VII.2
130:5	QH XVI.1
131:1	Conv 38
137:1-3	QH VII.5
137:5	QH VII.14
139:17	QH XII.7
140:5	QH VII.9
140:7	QH IV.4
141:4	QH XI.5
141:5	Conv 10
141:7	QH VIII.11
143:4	Conv 9
143:10	QH XI.2
144:3	QH XII.3, 4
144:12	QH III.1, VI.7
147:1	Conv 25
147:11	QH I.2, XV.5
147:12	Conv 1
147:17	Conv 7
148:5	Conv 2
148:14	QH VIII.5

PROVERBS (Pr)

1:17	QH XIV.9
1:20-21	Conv 3
1:26	QH VIII.10
1:26-7	QH VIII.10
2:14	Conv 33
3:16	QH VII.11, XVII.1
3:18	Conv 37
4:14	QH XII.1
4:23	QH VII.12
6:4	Conv 23
8:31	QH XVII.4
10:28	QH IV.3
16:20	QH I.1
16:25	QH XI.3
18:3	Conv 23; QH XI.5
19:11	QH XI.1
20:9	QH IX.4, XVI.1
23:1	QH I.4
24:16	QH II.1
25:27	QH VI.3
26:11	QH III.5
28:14	QH XV.1
29:15	Conv 4; QH X.3
30:8	QH IX.5
31:30	QH XVII.2

ECCLESIASTES (Qo)

1:2	Conv 13, 16
1:8	Conv 10
1:14	Conv 23; QH III.5, XVI.4
5:10	Conv 14
7:3	QH XVII.3
7:17	QH IV.4
8:11	Conv 20
9:3	QH XVI.4
12:12	Conv 6
23:28	QH XI.5
43:9	QH VIII.9

SONG OF SONGS (Sg)

1:1	Conv 29; QH XV.2
1:2	Conv 25
1:6	QH VI.6
1:11	Conv 25
2:3	Conv 25
2:4	QH VIII.11
2:9	Conv 24
2:12	Conv 25, 26
2:14	Conv 25; QH VII.15, IX.7
2:22	QH XII.5

SONG OF SONGS (Sg) — *continued*

4:6	QH VII.9
4:16	Conv 25
5:3	Conv 4
5:4	Conv 24
5:7	QH XV.3, XVI.4
6:9	QH VII.9
8:14	QH IX.9

WISDOM (Wis)

1:3	QH VII.10
2:12	Conv 39
2:24	QH XIII.4
4:11	QH XVI.3
4:15	QH VII.12
5:6	QH XI.8
5:20	QH VI.3
6:7	QH VI.4
6:25	QH VIII.7
7:24-5	QH IX.3
8:1	QH XVII.1
9:5	QH XVI.4
9:15	Conv 30
10:12	Conv 7
10:17	QH IX.1
16:20	QH IV.2
18:15	Conv 26

ECCLESIASTICUS (Sir)

1:20	QH I.1
1:22	QH XV.6
2:1	QH XIV.4
2:11	QH IX.6, XV.5
4:25	QH II.2
10:9	QH III.1, VI.3
14:5	QH XI.8
15:6	QH VIII.3
18:6	QH I.3
18:30	QH VIII.5, XI.3
22:1-2	QH II.1
23:3	QH XI.4
23:25	Conv 18
24:29	Conv 27; QH I.1
27:6	QH XVII.4
30:24	QH III.1, XI.9
34:1	QH I.2
36:1	QH II.2
40:1	QH XVI.2
45:30	QH XVI.1
50:31	QH VII.1

ISAIAH (Is)
1:18	Conv 29
1:20	Conv 1
1:22	QH IX.4
2:2	QH IX.9
2:6	Conv 10
3:9	QH II.2
3:12	Conv 14
3:14	QH VIII.11
5:4	QH XV.2
5:7	Conv 33
5:20	QH XI.3
6:10	QH VI.4
8:2	QH XIII.1
8:14	QH XII.8, 9
9:3	Conv 34; QH VI.7
9:6	Conv 1
10:17	Conv 25
11:3	QH XIII.5
14:13-4	QH XI.4
14:19	Conv 15
14:29	Conv 33
17:10	Conv 25
26:10	QH III.2
30:26	QH XVII.5
33:15	Conv 3, 8
40:6-7	QH IX.2
40:8	QH IX.2, XVII.2
40:12	QH Pref.1
42:8	Conv 21
45:10	QH XI.3
46:8	Conv 3, 7; QH XI.9
47:15	QH XI.2
49:15	QH XI.9
50:5	QH VIII.3
51:3	QH VIII.7
52:11	Conv 33
55:6	QH I.1
58:1	Conv 3
58:3	Conv 8
58:4	Conv 8
58:6	Conv 8
60:14	QH XI.8
62:6	QH XII.5
64:4	QH IV.3, VIII.3
64:6	QH VI.3
66:24	Conv 7

JEREMIAH (Jer)
3:3	QH II.2
4:19	Conv 4

JEREMIAH (Jer) — *continued*
6:14	QH VI.7
8:4	QH XI.1
8:21	QH XVI.4
9:21	Conv 7, 11; QH VIII.4, 6
14:9	QH XV.6
15:16	QH VII.5
15:19	QH X.2
16:5	QH XVI.1
17:9	QH XVI.4
17:16	QH XVII.2
17:18	QH VIII.1
21:8	QH XI.10
22:29	QH X.3
31:28	QH XI.1
32:19	QH XI.3
48:6	Conv 37
50:2	QH XI.2
50:40	Conv 34
51:6	Conv 37

LAMENTATIONS (Lam)
3:1	Conv 33
3:22	QH XI.1
3:25	Conv 24; QH IX.8
3:41	Conv 6; QH VII.15, XI.11
3:51	QH III.5

BARUCH (Bar)
3:36-8	Conv 28

EZEKIEL (Ezk)
2:5	QH III.2
3:17	QH XIV.5
8:8-10	Conv 34
13:10	QH VI.7
18:20	Conv 21
18:23	Conv 1
33:7	QH XIV.5
38:20	QH XIII.5

DANIEL (Dan)
3:92	QH XVII.4
9:24	QH VII.4
13:17	Conv 6

HOSEA (Hos)
1:2	Conv 3
2:7	Conv 15
7:9	QH VII.14
7:11	Conv 33
8:4	Conv 32
14:10	QH XI.8

JOEL (Jl)
1:17　QH X.3
2:32　QH XV.6

AMOS (Am)
3:8　QH XIV.10
6:5　QH VII.5

JONAH (Jo)
1:4　QH VII.5

NAHUM (Nah)
1:9　QH VIII.12

HABAKKUK (Hab)
1:16　QH VII.10
3:6　QH XI.8

ZEPHANIAH (Zeph)
1:2　Conv 19
3:11　Conv 29

ZECHARIAH (Zech)
5:7　QH XV.1

MALACHI (Mal)
4:2　QH XVI.2

MATTHEW (Mt)
1:23　QH XVII.4
2:1　Conv 24
3:2　QH III.3, VII.7
3:7　Conv 32; QH XI.2
3:7-8　QH X.3
3:10　Conv 20
3:12　QH XII.5
4:2-3　QH VI.5
4:3　QH XIII.1, XIV.4, 5
4:3-4　QH IV.2
4:4　QH IV.2, VI.5, XIV.6
4:5　QH VII.4, XIV.5
4:5-7　QH VI.5
4:6　QH XIV.5, 7, 8
4:8-10　QH VI.5
4:9　QH XIV.5, 6, 9
4:10-11　QH Pref.2
4:11　QH IV.1, 2
4:19　Conv 2
5:3　Conv 12
5:5　Conv 12, 23
5:6　Conv 26, 27

MATTHEW (Mt) — *continued*
5:7　Conv 29
5:8　Conv 30, 32
5:9　Conv 31, 32, 39
5:10　Conv 39
5:15　Conv 20
5:48　Conv 32
6:1　QH XIV.7, 10
6:1-2　QH IV.3
6:2　Conv 39
6:5　QH IV.3
6:9　QH I.4, XV.6
6:10　QH IV.3, XI.1
6:12　Conv 29
6:13　QH I.4, V.1
6:19　Conv 40; QH VI.4
6:21　Conv 5; QH VII.5
6:24　Conv 15
6:25　QH XI.3
6:25-31　QH V.2
6:26　QH V.2, XIV.5
6:33　QH V.2, IX.5
6:34　QH VIII.1, XVI.4, XVII.1
7:2　QH IX.3
7:6　Conv 25
8:6　Conv 9
8:20　Conv 12; QH III.2
8:25　QH XII.9
8:26　Conv 40
9:36　QH III.1
10:16　QH VII.12
10:39　QH IX.1
10:41　QH IX.3
10:42　QH IX.3
11:12　QH VII.7, XIV.8
11:14　Conv 1
11:25　Conv 26
11:28-30　QH XV.1
11:29　Conv 24
11:30　QH III.3
12:32　QH XI.5
12:45　QH III.5
13:27-30　QH XII.5
13:32　QH XVII.3
13:42　QH VIII.7
13:43　QH VIII.6
13:44　QH XVII.3
13:47-8　QH VIII.11
13:47　Conv 20
13:48　Conv 20
14:25-6　QH VI.6

MATTHEW (Mt) — *continued*
15:19   Conv 4
15:32   QH IV.1, VII.4
16:26   QH VI.4
17:4   Conv 24; QH IX.9
17:16   Conv 22
18:3   Conv 1; QH XI.9
18:7   QH XII.1
18:10   QH XI.6, XII.3
18:20   QH XVII.4
18:32   QH XII.3
19:8   QH X.5
19:11   Conv 36
19:27   QH VIII.11, 12
19:27-8   QH III.2
19:28   QH VIII.11
19:29   Conv 25
20:1-15   QH IX.4
20:2   QH IX.5
20:12   QH VI.1
20:16   QH VI.7
20:28   QH XI.10
21:7   QH VII.3
21:8   QH VII.4
21:44   QH XII.9
22:11   QH VI.4
22:13   QH VI.4
22:14   QH VI.7
23:3   Conv 39; QH X.5
24:12   QH IV.4
24:21   QH XIV.8
24:28   Conv 6
24:33   QH XII.4
24:35   QH IX.6
24:45-7   QH VIII.5
25:1-13   Conv 20
25:4   Conv 21
25:12   Conv 21
25:21   QH IV.1
25:30   Conv 13
25:32   QH II.1, VIII.7
25:32   Conv 39
25:33   QH VII.15
25:34   QH VIII.7
25:41   Conv 20, 37; QH III.3, XI.4
25:41-2   QH III.4, VIII.7
25:46   QH VI.2
26:23   Conv 32
26:28   Conv 37
26:41   QH V.1
26:66   QH XIII.4

MATTHEW (Mt) — *continued*
27:6   QH XII.5
28:6   Conv 24
29:22   QH VI.7

MARK (Mk)
2:5   Conv 28
2:7   Conv 28
3:5   Conv 14
4:8   QH VII.14
4:11   QH III.3
9:17   Conv 10
9:28   QH XIII.2
9:41   Conv 31
9:43   QH VIII.7
10:30   QH IV.1
12:30   QH III.2, XII.7
14:52   QH XVI.4
14:63   QH XIII.1

LUKE (Lk)
1:28   QH XVII.4
1:29-30   QH VI.6
1:30   QH VII.7
1:35   QH IV.3
1:78   Conv 33; QH IX.7
1:79   QH XI.9
2:14   Conv 21
2:29-30   QH XVII.7
5:5-6   Conv 2
5:8   QH XV.1
5:11   QH II.2
6:22   Conv 40
6:25   Conv 33
6:46   QH XV.6
6:49   QH I.3
8:26-33   QH VII.9
9:25   QH VI.4
10:27   QH XI.11
10:35   QH XII.3
11:9   QH XIII.5
11:21-2   Conv 27
11:22   QH VII.14
11:24   Conv 12, 23
11:28   Conv 1
11:41   Conv 29
11:52   Conv 32
12:2   Conv 19
12:4   QH VII.13, XIII.5
12:5   QH III.3, XIII.5
12:16   Conv 16

LUKE (Lk) — *continued*

12:19-20	Conv 16
12:35	Conv 20
12:49	QH XIII.4
14:4	Conv 19
14:8-10	Conv 38
14:11	Conv 38
14:28	Conv 36
14:30	QH I.3
14:31	QH VI.3
15:12-3	QH VIII.4
15:13	Conv 5
15:14	Conv 26
15:15-6	Conv 15
15:15-24	Conv 15
15:16	Conv 15, 26, 27
15:17	Conv 5
16:22	QH XIII.1
16:26	QH VIII.8
16:24-5	Conv 20
16:25	Conv 21
17:10	QH IV.3, VI.2
17:21	QH VII.14, XVII.3
18:4	Conv 19; QH II.2, XI.5
18:11-12	QH IX.5
18:13	QH VIII.2
18:22	Conv 29
19:8	Conv 29
19:22	Conv 13
21:18	QH VIII.2
21:19	Conv 31
21:33	QH IX.2
22:27	QH XI.10
22:31-2	QH V.1
22:48	Conv 32
23:34	Conv 32
24:29	QH XI.12
32:37	QH VIII.11

JOHN (Jn)

1:9	QH XVII.6
1:14	QH XIV.3
1:16	QH IX.3
1:18	QH XI.6
1:51	QH XI.6
3:20	Conv 19
3:31	QH VIII.10
4:7	QH VII.16
4:10	QH I.1, IX.3
4:24	QH XVI.1
4:35	QH VIII.3

JOHN (Jn) — *continued*

4:47	QH XVII.1
5:25	Conv 1
5:41	QH XVII.2
5:44	QH XVII.2
6:31	QH I.3
6:54	QH III.3
6:61	QH III.3
6:64	QH Pref.1
6:67	QH III.3
6:69	Conv 1
7:18	QH XIV.5
8:25	QH XII.4
8:32	QH VI.7, VII.5
8:37	Conv 22
8:44	Conv 2; QH XI.8
8:50	Conv 2
· 10:10	QH XI.1
10:12	Conv 39
10:17	Conv 24
10:25	QH IX.1
10:28	QH XVII.4
10:38	Conv 38
11:11	Conv 4
11:12	Conv 5
11:40	QH XII.4
12:25	Conv 4
12:26	Conv 31
12:31	QH XI.8, XVI.4
12:50	Conv 30
13:37	QH IX.4
14:2	QH IX.4
14:8-11	QH XVII.7
14:15	QH XIV.3
14:23	Conv 24
14:28	QH VII.13, IX.9
14:30	QH VII.2
15:2	Conv 21
15:13	QH IX.3, 6
16:2	QH VI.7
16:20-4	QH XVII.3
16:33	QH XVI.2
17:3	Conv 30; QH IX.9, XVII.7
17:12	QH VIII.10
19:15	QH III.2
19:26	QH VII.4
19:30	QH XVI.2
19:34	QH VII.15
20:17	QH IX.9
21:15	Conv 2
21:16-7	Conv 32

ACTS (Ac)
1:1	Conv 25
1:4	QH IX.1
1:18	QH VIII.10
1:25	QH VIII.10
2:28	QH III.4
2:33	QH XVII.1
4:12	QH XV.6
7:59	QH VI.7, VIII.12
13:44	Conv 1
14:21	QH XVI.3
16:17	QH VI.7
17:19	Conv 9
19:10	Conv 1
20:7	Conv 31
22:11	Conv 23
23:1	Conv 25
26:24	Conv 24

ROMANS (Rm)
1:11	QH V.2
1:13	QH Pref. 2, XI.5
1:17	QH IX.6
1:18	QH Pref.2
1:26	Conv 34
2:1	QH IV.1
2:5	Conv 5; QH X.3
2:13	Conv 39
5:1	Conv 29
5:2-3	QH XVII.3
5:3	QH XVII.3
5:3-4	QH XVII.3
5:4	QH XI.1
5:5	QH IV.4
5:6	QH IV.4, IX.3
5:8-10	QH IX.3
5:10	Conv 29
5:17	QH IV.4
5:20	Conv 37
5:21	QH X.5
6:6	Conv 30
6:12-3	QH VIII.5
6:12	Conv 9, 27
6:19	Conv 27; QH VIII.5
6:21	Conv 29
6:22	QH XVII.1
6:23	Conv 17
7:18	QH XVI.4
7:23	Conv 30, QH VIII.4, XVI.4
7:24	Conv 30; QH V.3
8:2	QH XI.2

ROMANS (Rm) — *continued*
8:3	Conv 5
8:4	QH XI.2
8:8	Conv 32
8:10	QH VIII.6, XVI.4
8:17	Conv 31; QH XII.7
8:18	Conv 37; QH VI.2
8:19	QH IX.1
8:24	QH VIII.2, XV.6
8:28	Conv 28; QH II.2, XII.3
8:29	QH VII.6
8:30	QH VII.6
8:31	QH XVII.4
8:36	QH Pref.1, VI.1
9:5	QH IX.9, XI.12, XVII.7
9:20	QH XIV.5
9:22	Conv 32
9:29	Conv 34
9:32	QH XII.8
10:6-7	QH XI.12
10:10	QH XI.9
10:16	Conv 12
10:17	QH VIII.3, XV.6
10:43	QH XV.6
11:4	Conv 34
11:20	QH VI.3
11:33	QH XIV.1
12:15	QH VIII.11
12:17	Conv 31; QH VII.16
12:19	QH VII.16
13:7	QH XII.7
13:8	QH XII.7
13:9	QH III.1
13:12	QH VI.3
13:13	QH VI.3
13:14	Conv 15
14:5	QH III.1
14:10	Conv 18
14:17	QH III.4
15:4	QH XI.1
26:20	QH VIII.4

FIRST CORINTHIANS (1 Co)
1:12	QH XV.3
1:13	QH XV.3
1:18	QH XI.8
1:21	QH III.1
1:30	QH III.3
2:6	QH XI.14
2:9	Conv 14; QH VIII.3, X.1
2:10	Conv 25; QH X.1

FIRST CORINTHIANS (1 Co) — *continued*

2:11	Conv 4
2:14	Conv 7
3:4-5	QH XV.3
3:8	QH IX.4
4:1	Conv 38
4:2	Conv 32
4:3-4	Conv 18; QH XV.4
4:5	Conv 3
4:7	QH VI.3
4:21	Conv 24, 33
5:7	Conv 8
5:12	QH I.1
6:2	QH VIII.11
6:9	Conv 34
6:11	Conv 25
6:13	QH VIII.5
6:16-7	QH XIV.3
6:17	QH VIII.11, XI.5
6:19	QH VIII.5
6:20	QH VII.3
7:9	Conv 36
7:10	QH XIII.5
7:25	QH XI.8
7:31	Conv 6
7:32	Conv 12
9:7	Conv 25
9:16	QH IV.3
9:18	Conv 39
9:19	Conv 31
9:27	Conv 28; QH III.5, VI.1
10:12	QH VI.3
10:13	QH VII.10, XI.5, XII.8
10:13	Conv 7; QH V.1, XII.9
10:33	Conv 32
11:16	QH VII.10
12:17	Conv 10
13:12	Conv 30; QH X.1
14:3	QH VIII.1
15:10	QH XIII.5
15:26	QH VIII.6
15:31	QH VI.1
15:34	QH X.2
15:41-2	QH IX.4
15:43	QH VIII.5, XVI.2

SECOND CORINTHIANS (2 Co)

1:3-4	QH XVII.3
1:5	QH Pref.1, IX.1
2:8	QH III.1
2:11	QH III.1, 2, VI.6

SECOND CORINTHIANS (2 Co) — *cont.*

3:5	QH XI.12
3:18	QH XVII.5
4:7	QH VII.4, 14, XVII.3
4:11	QH X.1
4:15	QH II.1
4:17	QH III.3, XII.10, XVII.3
4:18	QH XVII.3
5:1	Conv 12
5:6	Conv 30; QH II.1
5:7	QH VII.9, VIII.3
5:16	QH IX.9
5:18	Conv 31
6:5	QH I.1
6:7	QH VII.16
7:1	QH I.1
7:5	QH IX.7
8:15	QH IX.4
8:21	QH XV.4
9:6	QH VII.14, IX.3
10:3	QH XI.2
11:2	Conv 31; QH XV.3
11:14	QH VI.6, 7
11:23	QH Pref.1
11:27-8	QH Pref.1
13:11	QH IV.3

GALATIANS (Gal)

1:4	Conv 23, 31, 37; QH I.3
1:16	QH VII.14, X.2
2:9	QH XII.5
3:1	QH III.4
4:1-2	QH XII.7
4:2	QH XII.7
5:13	Conv 36; QH VI.1
5:16	Conv 30
5:17	QH I.3, IX.5, XVI.4
5:26	QH VI.7, XIV.5, 7, XVII.2
6:1	Conv 33
6:3	QH XI.5
6:8	Conv 17; QH VII.14, IX.2
6:10	Conv 20, 21

EPHESIANS (Eph)

1:3-4	QH IX.3
1:6	QH IX.3
1:18	Conv 25
1:21	QH IX.9
2:2	QH IV.3, VIII.10
2:3	Conv 32
2:9	QH XII.4

EPHESIANS (Eph) — *continued*
2:12   QH X.2
3:13   QH VII.1
3:17   QH III.3
4:27   QH VII.16
4:28   Conv 8
5:5   Conv 15
5:8   QH VI.3
5:15   QH XII.6
5:16   QH IV.3, VIII.1, 5, XVII.1
5:27   Conv 30; QH XVII.6
5:28-9 QH X.3
5:29   Conv 4
6:12   QH III.1, VII.7, 8, 9, XI.4, 8, XIII.2

PHILIPPIANS (Ph)
2:7   QH XVII.6
2:8   QH XIV.4, 8
2:13   QH IX.1
2:21   Conv 32; QH VI.7, XIV.5
3:3   QH V.2
3:8   QH IX.5, XVII.6
3:9   QH IX.6
3:12   QH X.1
3:13   QH IV.3
3:15   QH X.1
3:21   QH XVI.4
4:1   QH XV.4
4:12   QH XIV.10

COLOSSIANS (Col)
1:18   Conv 35; QH VII.10
1:24   QH IX.4
3:1   Conv 23
3:2   QH XIV.5
3:4   QH XVI.3

FIRST THESSALONIANS (1 Th)
2:7   QH IV.4
4:3   QH VII.16
4:16   QH XVII.4
4:17   QH XVI.3

SECOND THESSALONIANS (2 Th)
2:3   QH VI.7
2:7   Conv 17
2:8   QH VI.7

FIRST TIMOTHY (1 Tm)
1:4   Conv 9
1:15   Conv 26
1:17   QH XII.6, 7
3:13   Conv 31
3:16   QH XIV.5
4:8   QH VII.1, 5, XVII.1
5:25   QH VIII.12
6:5   Conv 33; QH XIV.5
6:8   QH V.2
6:9   QH III.2
6:10   QH VI.4, XIV.9
6:17   QH III.4, IX.5
6:19   Conv 1

SECOND TIMOTHY (2 Tm)
1:8   QH IX.4
1:12   QH VII.12
2:3   QH V.2
2:4   QH VII.14, 15
2:5   QH VII.10
3:5   Conv 37
3:12   QH XVI.2
4:2   QH IV.3
4:3   Conv 7
4:7   QH X.2

TITUS (Tt)
2:12   QH IV.3, VIII.12
2:13   Conv 15; QH X.5
3:7   QH XIV.4

HEBREWS (Heb)
1:3   Conv 3; QH Pref.1, IX.6
1:14   QH XI.10, XII.3
2:9   QH IX.3
4:12   Conv 2, 18, 28; QH II.3, IX.2
4:15   QH XIV.4
5:14   Conv 7; QH III.1
6:8   Conv 23
6:19   QM VII.6
9:11   QH VIII.10
9:12   QH XIV.5
10:31   Conv 18; QH VIII.12
11:1   QH VIII.3, X.1, XII.6, XV.6
12:2   QH XVI.2
12:4   QH XIII.6
12:14   QH XVII.1, 6
12:15   QH XIV.9
13:17   QH XV.4

JAMES (Jm)
1:2   QH XVI.3, XVII.3
1:5   QH XI.12
1:17   QH XII.6, XV.3, XVI.4
2:13   QH XI.8
2:17   QH X.2, XIII.3
4:7   QH IV.2, XIII.6
4:15   Conv 16

FIRST PETER (1 P)
2:6   QH XII.9
2:9   Conv 35
2:13   QH IX.2
2:15   QH VII.16
2:22   QH IX.3
4:6   Conv 1
4:11   QH XII.7
4:13   QH III.3
5:6   QH III.1
5:7   QH IX.6, XI.1
5:8   QH XII.1, XIII.6
5:8-9   Conv 21

SECOND PETER (2 P)
1:14   QH X.2
1:17   QH XVII.2
2:22   Conv 25; QH III.5
3:18   Conv 40

FIRST JOHN (1 Jn)
2:16   Conv 22
2:17   QH IX.2
2:25   QH XV.4
2:27   Conv 25
3:2   Conv 30; QH XII.7, XVII.6
3:15   QH XIII.4
3:17   QH III.4, VII.13
3:20   Conv 19
4:9   QH XII.3
4:16   QH III.3
4:18   QH VI.3, IX.8, XVII.2
5:19   Conv 15; QH XVI.4

REVELATION (Rev)
2:17   Conv 25
3:16   QH III.5
3:17   Conv 33; QH XI.3
3:20   Conv 3
5:5   QH XIII.6, XIV.8
7:14   QH Pref.1
10:4   Conv 23
10:9-10 Conv 4
12:7-8   QH XV.2
12:10   QH IX.7
12:12   QH VII.2
21:23   QH XVII.7
22:20   QH VI.7, VIII.12

This volume was Linotype-set by
Edgecombe/Printer, Galesburg, Michigan, U.S.A.

The face used is Linotype Janson. Body is 11 pt on 13 slug,
notes in 8 pt on 9 slug; other sizes used as appropriate.

CISTERCIAN PUBLICATIONS INC.

TITLES LISTING

THE CISTERCIAN FATHERS SERIES

THE WORKS OF
BERNARD OF CLAIRVAUX

Treatises I: Apologia to Abbot William,
On Precept and Dispensation . . . . CF 1

On the Song of Songs I–IV . . CF 4, 7, 31, 40

The Life and Death of Saint Malachy
the Irishman . . . . CF 10

Treatises II: The Steps of Humility,
On Loving God . . . . CF 13

Magnificat: Homilies in Praise of the
Blessed Virgin Mary [with Amadeus
of Lausanne] . . . . CF 18

Treatises III: On Grace and Free Choice,
In Praise of the New Knighthood CF 19

Sermons on Conversion: A Sermon to
Clerics, Lenten Sermons on
Psalm 91 . . . . CF 25

Five Books on Consideration:
Advice to A Pope . . . . CF 37

THE WORKS OF WILLIAM OF
SAINT THIERRY

On Contemplating God, Prayer,
and Meditations . . . . CF 3

Exposition on the Song of Songs . . . CF 6

The Enigma of Faith . . . . CF 9

The Golden Epistle . . . . CF 12

The Mirror of Faith . . . . CF 15

Exposition on the Epistle to the
Romans . . . . CF 27

The Nature and Dignity of Love . . CF 30

THE WORKS OF AELRED OF RIEVAULX

Treatises I: On Jesus at the Age of
Twelve, Rule for a Recluse,
The Pastoral Prayer . . . . CF 2*

Spiritual Friendship . . . . CF 5*

The Mirror of Charity . . . . CF 17†

Dialogue on the Soul . . . . CF 22

THE WORKS OF GILBERT OF
HOYLAND

Sermons on the Song of Songs
I–III . . . . CF 14, 20, 26

Treatises, Sermons, and Epistles . . CF 34

OTHER EARLY CISTERCIAN WRITERS

The Letters of Adam of Perseigne, I . CF 21

Alan of Lille: The Art of Preaching . CF 23

John of Ford. Sermons on the Final
Verses of the Song of Songs,
I–IV . . . . CF 29, 39, 43, 44

Idung of Prüfening. Cistercians and
Cluniacs: The Case for Cîteaux . . CF 33

The Way of Love . . . . CF 16

Guerric of Igny. Liturgical Sermons
I–II . . . . CF 8, 32

Three Treatises on Man: A Cistercian
Anthropology . . . . CF 24

Isaac of Stella. Sermons on the
Christian Year, I . . . . CF 11

Stephen of Lexington. Letters from
Ireland . . . . CF 28†

THE CISTERCIAN STUDIES SERIES

MONASTIC TEXTS

Evagrius Ponticus. Praktikos and
Chapters on Prayer . . . . CS 4

The Rule of the Master . . . . CS 6

The Lives of the Desert Fathers . . . CS 34

Dorotheos of Gaza. Discourses and
Sayings . . . . CS 33

Pachomian Koinona I–III:
The Lives . . . . CS 45

The Chronicles and Rules . . . . . CS 46

The Instructions, Letters and Other
Writings of St Pachomius and
His Disciples . . . . CS 47

* *Temporarily out of print*   † *Forthcoming*

Symeon the New Theologian. Theological and Practical Treatises and Three Theological Discourses... CS 41†

Guigo II the Carthusian. The Ladder of Monks and Twelve Meditations. CS48

The Monastic Rule of Iosif Volotsky .... CS 36

CHRISTIAN SPIRITUALITY

The Spirituality of Western Christendom .... CS 30

Russian Mystics (Sergius Bolshakoff) CS 26

In Quest of the Absolute: The Life and Works of Jules Monchanin (J. G. Weber) .... CS 51

The Name of Jesus (Irenée Hausherr) .... CS 44

Entirely for God: A Life of Cyprian Tansi (Elizabeth Isichei) ...... CS 43

Abba: Guides to Wholeness and Holiness East and West .... CS 38

MONASTIC STUDIES

The Abbot in Monastic Tradition (Pierre Salmon) .... CS 14

Why Monks? (François Vandenbroucke) .... CS 17

Silence in the Rule of St Benedict (Ambrose Wathen) .... CS 22

One Yet Two: Monastic Tradition East and West .... CS 29

Community and Abbot in the Rule of St Benedict I (Adalbert de Vogüé). CS 5/1

Consider Your Call: A Theology of the Monastic Life (Daniel Rees et al). CS 20

Households of God (David Parry). . CS 39

CISTERCIAN STUDIES

The Cistercian Spirit (M. Basil Pennington, ed.) ...... CS 3

The Eleventh-Century Background of Cîteaux (Bede K. Lackner) ...... CS 8

Contemplative Community .... CS 21

Cistercian Sign Language (Robert Barakat) .... CS 11

The Cistercians in Denmark (Brian P. McGuire) .... CS 35

Saint Bernard of Clairvaux: Essays Commemorating the Eighth Centenary of His Canonization. . CS 28

Bernard of Clairvaux: Studies Presented to Dom Jean Leclercq .... CS 23

Bernard of Clairvaux and the Cistercian Spirit (Jean Leclercq) .... CS 16

William of St Thierry: The Man and His Work (J. M. Déchanet) .... CS 10

Aelred of Rievaulx: A Study (Aelred Squire) .... CS 50

Christ the Way: The Christology of Guerric of Igny (John Morson). . CS 25

The Golden Chain: The Theological Anthropology of Isaac of Stella (Bernard McGinn) .... CS 15

Studies in Cistercian Art and Architecture, I (Meredith Lillich, ed). . CS 66

Studies in Medieval Cistercian History sub-series

Studies I .... CS 13

Studies II .... CS 24

Cistercian Ideals and Reality (Studies III) .... CS 60

Simplicity and Ordinariness (Studies IV) .... CS 61

The Chimera of His Age: Studies on St Bernard (Studies V) .... CS 63

Cistercians in the Late Middle Ages (Studies VI) .... CS 64

Noble Piety and Reformed Monasticism (Studies VII) .... CS 65

Benedictus: Studies in Honor of St Benedict of Nursia (Studies VIII). CS 67

Heaven on Earth (Studies IX) .... CS 68†

THOMAS MERTON

The Climate of Monastic Prayer .... CS 1

Thomas Merton on St Bernard ..... CS 9

Thomas Merton's Shared Contemplation: A Protestant Perspective (Daniel J. Adams) .... CS 62

Solitude in the Writings of Thomas Merton (Richard Anthony Cashen)..... CS 40

The Message of Thomas Merton (Brother Patrick Hart, ed.) ..... CS 42

FAIRACRES PRESS, OXFORD

The Wisdom of the Desert Fathers

The Letters of St Antony the Great

The Letters of Ammonas, Successor of St Antony

A Study of Wisdom. Three Tracts by the author of *The Cloud of Unknowing*

The Power of the Name. The Jesus Prayer in Orthodox Spirituality (Kallistos Ware)

Solitude and Communion

Contemporary Monasticism

A Pilgrim's Book of Prayers (Gilbert Shaw)

Theology and Spirituality (Andrew Louth)

* *Temporarily out of print*   † *Forthcoming*